PEER

<u>TEACHING</u>

Recent Titles in
Contributions to the Study of Education

Black Students in Higher Education:
Conditions and Experiences in the 1970s
Edited by Gail E. Thomas

The Scope of Faculty Collective Bargaining:
An Analysis of Faculty Union Agreements at Four-Year Institutions of
Higher Education
Ronald L. Johnstone

Brainpower for the Cold War:
The Sputnik Crisis and National Defense Education Act of 1958
Barbara Barksdale Clowse

In Opposition to Core Curriculum:
Alternative Models for Undergraduate Education
Edited by James W. Hall with Barbara L. Kevles

PEER
TEACHING
HISTORICAL
PERSPECTIVES

LILYA WAGNER

Contributions to the Study of Education, Number 5

Greenwood Press
Westport, Connecticut•London, England

Library of Congress Cataloging in Publication Data

Wagner, Lilya.
  Peer teaching.

  (Contributions to the study of education, ISSN
0196-707X; no. 5)
  Bibliography: p.
  Includes index.
  1. Peer-group tutoring of students. I. Title.
II. Series.
LC41.W33   371.3'94   82-939
ISBN 0-313-23230-X (Lib. bdg.)   AACR2

Library of Congress Catalog Card Number: 82-939
ISBN: 0-313-23230-X
ISSN: 0196-707X

First published in 1982

Greenwood Press
A division of Congressional Information Service, Inc.
88 Post Road West, Westport, Connecticut 06881

Printed in the United States of America

10 9 8 7 6 5 4 3 2 1

CONTENTS

ACKNOWLEDGMENTS

It is a privilege to express gratitude and give recognition to those who, in some way, contributed to the writing of this volume:

Dr. William B. Hedges, whose encouragement and careful scrutiny of this work, good humor, and example of fine scholarship have been deeply appreciated; Richard and Anna Vinglas, who from the time I was small showed me the wonderful world of books and their infinite possibilities and who assisted in the preparation of the book in many tangible and intangible ways; Dr. John Wagner, whose support, aid, intelligent counsel, and constant love made this a worthwhile project.

PEER
TEACHING

INTRODUCTION

Helping relationships between students in formal and planned school settings have been utilized by teachers for centuries. This concept can be traced to the first century A.D.; since that time, peer teaching has alternately lapsed into obscurity or seen a resurgence of interest. During the last two decades, many educators in the United States have again promoted the use of peer teaching, and considerable literature and research on this topic have resulted.

There is a need for a history of peer teaching as it has evolved and developed throughout past centuries. While the ideas of prominent men such as Joseph Lancaster and Andrew Bell have been studied, a broad view of peer teaching has not yet been made available. Peer teaching can become more understandable and usable when examined in a historical perspective because history can recreate within a prescribed period of time and place a tangible, referential past. A broad view as is developed in this study puts into perspective the developmental stages of peer teaching in the Western Hemisphere.

A historical survey of peer teaching can serve as a reference tool for the practitioner. Knight said:

Much light may be shed upon the purpose of educational institutions by a study and examination of their origins and development. A knowledge of the history of schools and other agencies of education is therefore an important part of the professional training of teachers, school administrators, or other educational specialists, who could profitably approach their problems as the physician or the psychologist approaches his.[1]

Given the social and economic conditions as well as the theoretical bases for a concept, a practitioner becomes increasingly capable of judging possible merits and outcomes of current undertakings. One can understand the influences from the past that set boundaries and limits for the present and the future. Becker, as cited in Sherman and Kirschner, believes that "the more the past is included in the present, the more one can develop a patterned, hypothetical view of the future plans for action."[2]

This study reports the development of peer teaching in Western civilization. Because it is intended for the use of United States educators, the broad view is terminated at the point when peer teaching was established on the North American continent. The latter portion of the study considers peer teaching as it evolved in the United States.

The purposes of this study are:

1.   to trace the development of peer teaching throughout Western civilizations, beginning with the first century,
2.   to identify contributions of individuals or societies to peer teaching,
3.   to compare and contrast the use of peer teaching in various Western countries and at specific times,
4.   to describe how social and economic conditions influenced the idea and use of peer teaching,
5.   to identify what long-lasting effects, if any, are discernible,
6.   to determine how methodology changed during the historical development of peer teaching,
7.   to summarize developments in the United States,
8.   to review the research base for peer teaching.

The writer hopes that at the conclusion of this study the practitioner will be able to place the usefulness of peer teaching into perspective, and subsequently evaluate its usefulness in his own setting. Knight states that

a knowledge of the history of education is important for educational reform and improvement. It should lead educational workers to a willingness to evaluate and to revaluate and perhaps even to change their theories and practices in the light of the past, to take broad and liberal views of educational questions when new needs are to be met and progressive educational policies are to be shaped. Also, it should help to give perspective to education and to make for open-mindedness in teaching.[3]

Peer teaching refers to the concept of students teaching other students in formal and/or informal school learning situations that are delegated, planned, and directed by the teacher. Informal learning from peers—that which is not specifically planned and directed by the teacher—is not included in this definition.

During the nineteenth century, the term "monitorial system" was popular in England, in countries on the European continent, and subsequently, in the Americas as well. Monitorial system meant the use of a student to teach a group of students.

At various times, the term "mutual instruction" also became popular. As defined by most writers, it simply means students teaching students. An additional term currently in use is "cross-age teaching/tutoring," that is, an older student teaching a younger student.

This study uses the terminology that was most popular at the time under discussion. "Peer teaching" is used at all times when other designations are not specified in the source.

Only those events that are directly related to the development of peer teaching are included in this survey. In addition, the study is limited to countries in the Western Hemisphere that experienced movements in peer teaching and, from the mid-nineteenth century on, to developments in the North American continent only.

It is not within the realm of this survey to include an extended study of major figures such as Joseph Lancaster. C.A. Eggertsen analyzed Lancaster's contributions to American education.[4] Ray C. Rost studied the impact of the Lancasterian system on selected North American schools.[5] For the purposes of this survey, Lancaster is included as part of a broader view, one that includes the period of time during which he was influential. He and other prominent persons like him are segments of a broad perspective.

NOTES

1. Edgar W. Knight, *Twenty Centuries of Education* (Boston: Ginn and Co., 1940), p. 8.

6   Introduction

2. Robert R. Sherman and Joseph Kirschner, *Understanding History of Education* (Cambridge, Mass.: Schenkman Publishing Co., Inc., 1976), p. 70.

3. Knight, *Twenty Centuries of Education*, p. 9.

4. C. A. Eggertsen, "The Monitorial System of Instruction in the United States" (Doctoral diss., University of Minnesota, 1939).

5. Ray Charles Rost, "The Influence of Joseph Lancaster and the Monitorial System on Selected Educational Institutions" (Doctoral diss., Rutgers University, 1968).

CHAPTER 1

Peer Teaching from Greek and Roman Times to the Close of the Renaissance

INTRODUCTION

A survey of peer teaching should encompass the first century until the present because the mention of this technique dates from ancient times and continues intermittently into the twentieth century. Accounts of this practice are scarce in ancient and medieval times, which can be partially attributed to the comparatively small number of written records relative to education in those centuries. Another reason for the scarcity becomes clear when the economic and political influences on education during those times are considered. It is the purpose of this chapter to present those instances that are recorded during the centuries until the close of the Renaissance, and to present them in the context in which each occurred.

Efforts to designate exact historical periods of time are generally not effective. Knight stated that "exact chronology in educational and social history is every difficult to establish."[1] However, for purposes of division of time related to a study, Knight attempted to periodize the past in such a way that the ancient period begins with the invention of writing and continues until the beginning of the scholastic period, or medieval period. The medieval period commences with the triumph of the Christian church over pagan Rome and continues throughout the centuries in which the educational and intellectual interests were almost exclusively the concern of the church. The Renaissance has its roots in the late Middle Ages, with the rise of medieval universities in the twelfth and thirteenth centuries, and continues with the increased interest in the ancient classics. Knight included the Renaissance in the modern period. These are the divisions of time utilized in this study. In addition, the modern period is further divided as movements and changes in educational conditions make such divisions logical.

In relation to this chapter, it is particularly useful to note that very little has been previously attempted in the way of a historical survey of peer teaching. Among the few attempts are an eleven-page paper by Charles Hoffman presented at the Annual International Convention for the Council for Exceptional Children, and a much-quoted article by Benjamin Wright that begins with a brief survey of the history of peer teaching.[2,3] More often, accounts of peer teaching tend to begin with the nineteenth century and the practice of Lancaster and Bell. Nevertheless, previous attempts are on record, and though these perhaps did not achieve the widespread use and notoriety as did the monitorial movement of Lancaster and Bell, they are of importance when a historial view is attempted.

GREEK AND ROMAN EDUCATION

The city-states of Greece were the first known political communities to plan deliberately for schooling that would train those who eventually were to become state leaders. Athens had a plan that provided for the development of the individual who would eventually work in behalf of the government. The education was for the small ruling class only, but it is the first evidence of a developing interest in education for the young.[4]

Aristotle is reported to have used peer teaching. The "university" of Athens consisted of an informal group of young men gathered around an eminent philosopher or rhetorician. Wise stated that Aristotle is said to have used archons or student leaders who took care of many details for him.[5] It can be surmised that because of the popularity of a teacher such as Aristotle and the lack of widespread or numerous educational centers or institutions, the use of students as helpers may have been a reality.

Although the above information comes from the centuries before Christ, it is important to consider because of the great influence of Greek education during Roman times. Greek influence was prominent during the latter days of the Republic, and particularly under the Roman Empire. Greece became a Roman province in 146 B.C., and Greek slaves were frequently employed as "litteratores" or teachers. The schools that were opened under the Roman Empire copied Greek curricula and methods. Most freeborn children in Rome were sent at the age of seven to a primary school where they learned to read, write, and count. The grammar school was the second level of education, where Greek and Latin grammar were taught as well as the science of speaking correctly, and where eminent writers were read. Roman culture at that time was bilingual, and both Greek and Latin were utilized in the grammar schools. A significant percentage of the Roman citizens achieved this level of education.[6]

It is of this setting that Bonner wrote:

Some of the boys test each other's ability at taking down and reading back a dictation. . . . Whilst all this is going on, the master has arranged for the very young boys to be taught and tested. They stand in two groups, one, in charge of an older boy, repeating to him their letters and syllables, the other, in charge of the undermaster repeating word-lists, after which its members sit and copy out lines of verse.[7]

While discussing formal schooling during the early days of the Roman Empire, Wise also mentioned that "there were probably some student teachers, older pupils who helped the younger with letters and syllables."[8]

The most advanced type of education was the one frequently mentioned in Roman literature, and was conducted either in the schools of the philosophers or in those of the rhetors, which offered education for public speaking. This was considered of vast importance in Roman life.

Oratory covered practically everything in Roman life except agriculture, which was honorable, and small business, which was sordid. It was the route leading to the practice of law; to public office; to the Senate; to the Forum; to demagoguery, haranguing the multitude . . . ; even to promotion in the army. The Roman orator performed the combined functions of the modern preacher and newspaper editor.[9]

Congruent with a discussion of education during the Roman Empire, it should be noted that there was an absence of a middle class, slavery was common, and corruption existed in which a senate controlled the population by bribes. The schools of rhetoric were primarily for boys of senatorial or equestrian class and were not intended for the majority of Roman citizens.[10]

Treatises on education appeared, of which the one by Quintilian is notable. Quintilian was born about A.D. 40 in Spain and in A.D. 68 was brought to Rome by the Emperor Galba. Here he distinguished himself as a teacher and orator. Quintilian was honored by the Emperor Vespasian, who created for him a chair of rhetoric and conferred on him the title "Professor of Oratory." "This is the first instance in history of State endowment of a chair for teaching a specific subject."[11]

For twenty years, A.D. 69 to 88, Quintilian was the head of a leading school of oratory in Rome. He then retired from public employment and devoted his time to the composition of the *Institutio Oratoria,* "a work which he was the rather induced to undertake by the circumstance that two books on rhetoric had been published in his name by some of his pupils, who had taken notes of his lectures, and had sent them into the world with more zeal than discretion."[12]

The *Institutio Oratoria* appeared in A.D. 93. Quintilian accepted the general educational structure of his time, but he made a number of suggestions to parents and teachers. "His influence was on the side of making it more humane, more moral, more practical, somewhat more profound, slighly broader."[13] Quintilian did not attempt reform, nor did he theorize about education. Kennedy wrote that the *Institutio Oratoria* was "reasonable judgment, unprejudiced by special pleading, and a coherent overall view of how the separate parts of education can fit together to produce an educated man."[14] Books one and two deal with elementary education. The other volumes contain a detailed description of how a school of rhetoric should be conducted.

Quintilian is often credited with suggesting the use of peer teaching. Dillner said, "As early as the first century, the Roman teacher, Quintilian, pointed out in *Institutio Oratoria* how much the younger children could learn from the older children in the same class."[15] Gill stated that "the germ of the monitorial system, or of that part of it which concerns teaching, is found in Quintilian, who maintains that one who has just acquired a subject is best fitted to teach it."[16] While discussing Comenius, Gill also said that "acting on the hint of Quintilian, that the new learner is the best teacher, he [Comenius] employed pupils to instruct less advanced pupils, thus anticipating . . . the monitorial plan of mutual instruction."[17]

Quintilian did point out that emulation is an important educational factor in a school. He said, "Further while emulation promotes progress in the more advanced pupils, beginners who are still of tender years derive greater pleasure from imitating their comrades than their masters, just because it is easier."[18] Whether this does in fact indicate peer teaching is debatable. Certainly, when the methods of the early schools are considered, in which students' education consisted largely of exercises in rhetoric before their fellows, perhaps this could be considered an early form of peer teaching.

EDUCATION IN THE MIDDLE AGES

With the decline of Roman power and influence and the rising predominant influence of Christianity, the idea of education as a preparation for service in a state declined. During the period of AD. 500–1100, the church became the educator of western Europe.[19] Classical learning was not to make its reappearance until the twelfth century. Education during that era could not be considered to be intellectual. "For centuries the aim was almost entirely a preparation for life in the world to come. Throughout all the early Middle Ages this attitude continued, supplemented only by the meager education of a few to carry on the work of the church here below."[20] Education was not to prepare a man for this world, but for the next; not for success in this life, but to be successful as a good Christian and attain the world to come.

Education took place mostly in institutions and was centered around them. Little general learning existed, and even the clergy were, by subsequent standards, considered woefully ignorant. There was little organized learning for the common people. General education was attained only by the highest classes.

For the purposes of this study, it is not necessary to detail the chaotic political and social conditions of the Middle Ages that brought about a neglect of education. Knight pointed out that "the unique function of the Church during these centuries was to prevent the collapse of civilization entirely. Blind theological faith, and not reason or knowledge, was the guide of education."[21]

It might be concluded, then, that because of the concentration of education around the institution of the church, and its highly limited sphere, which excluded common man, no peer teaching, as defined for the purposes of this study, would have been used.

RENAISSANCE AND THE REFORMATION

By the fourteenth century, a new era began in Europe. A knowledge of the classical world was being sought, particularly in Italy. The intellectual freedom of the individual from the stultifying effect of the Middle Ages began to appear. Religious reforms attempted to place restrictions on the authority of the church. The Renaissance movement had the support of secular leaders rather than the support of the church.

Cubberley listed several factors that contributed to a revival of learning.

The recovery of the ancient manuscripts, the revival of the study of Greek in the West, the founding of libraries, the invention of paper and printing, and the revival of trade and commerce—all were new forces tending to give a new direction to scholarly study, and as a result a new race of scholars, more or less independent of the Church, now arose in western Europe.[22]

New aims and methods of education developed. Knight listed these as interest in the real life of the past, especially of the Greeks and Romans; interest in the world of emotions, including the satisfaction of life in this world rather than another world; and interest in the beautiful and aesthetic as well as the world of nature.[23] Graves stated that "the purpose of education was gradually coming to be no longer an attempt to adapt the individual to a fixed system, but to produce a differentiation of social activities and to encourage a realization of the individual in society. The days of mere absorption and assimilation were passing."[24]

The Renaissance in northern Europe is closely tied in with the Reformation. It had little of the nationalistic feeling akin to classical learning so prevalent in Italy. By contrast, the Renaissance in Italy did virtually nothing for the reformation of the church. The new educational aims in Germany and other northern European countries, as well as in large parts of France, were directed to spiritual and moral improvement and reformation. The religious basis of education was strongly emphasized in the schools of Protestant Germany, which were based on the principles of Philipp Melanchthon, a German scholar.

Educational theory was progressive. Schooling in the countries that participated in the Reformation was designed as a preparation for life and study in the religious sense, and was to include all aspects of the population: wealthy or poor, commoners or nobility, boys and girls. Because of the close relation between the Protestant church and the state, it was expedient that the individual learn to read the Scriptures, not only to follow church services more intelligently, but to be of increased service to his State.

In summary, the Renaissance movement in northern Europe (sometimes referred to synonymously with the Reformation) was more religious in purpose and character and attempted to awaken a religious interest in the masses. The aim of education was social reform and improvement of the status of common man. By contrast, the Renaissance movement in southern Europe tended to promote individual and personal satisfaction and happiness and was intellectual in form.[25]

Various forms of institutions grew out of the Renaissance movement. There seems to be no evidence that peer teaching was used in the court schools or municipal colleges of Italy and France or in the schools of the American colonies. However, of more interest are the methods utilized by Protestant reformers such as Sturm, in the grammar schools of England, and in the schools of the Jesuits.

STURM AND TROTZENDORF, EDUCATORS OF THE REFORMATION

The development of the German classical school, the gymnasium, came about through the educational influence and recommendations of Melanchthon to the Elector of Saxony in 1528. It consisted of three classes: the first, of children who were learning to read; the second, of those who were ready for grammar; and the third, of those who were taught etymology, syntax, and other aspects of Latin works as well as the Scriptures. These institutions were intended to prepare students for the university, and they concentrated on the study of Latin to the exclusion of the vernacular, mathematics, science, or history.[26]

The most successful of the gymnasia, and one on which future schools would be based, was the gymnasium at Strasbourg. The rector of this remarkable institution was Johann Sturm, born in 1507. After a career as a student of medicine, logic, Greek and Latin classics, and as a teacher in Louvain and Paris, he was called to Strasbourg to head its gymnasium at the age of thirty. At Strasbourg "he labored for forty-five years as a teacher, and, by this example, correspondence and publications, was greatly influential in introducing a better organization and methods of instruction into the schools of Europe."[27]

Sturm's fame, particularly in the later centuries, came because of his skills in organization and administration. He formulated a definite aim, or set of ideals, for his school.

A wise and persuasive piety should be the aim of our studies. But were all pious, then the student should be distinguished from him who is unlettered by scientific culture and the art of speaking. Hence, knowledge and purity and eloquence of diction should become the aim of scholarship, and toward its attainment both teachers and pupils should sedulously bend every effort.[28]

In short, Sturm's aim was to train pious, learned, and eloquent men for service in church and state.[29]

Sturm's genius for organization is evident in his plan for instruction, which was the earliest systematic, well-articulated scheme for a course of studies. Of primary importance was that the instruction be suited to the age and level of achievement of his pupils. There were other important factors in his plan: all teaching was to be clear and definite; not too much should be demanded at a time, but that which was should be thoroughly mastered and frequently reviewed; and religion was to be taught by interpretation of the New Testament and memorization of passages.[30,31]

Sturm's organizational plan included ten classes, and students entered at the age of six or seven. These classes were followed by a university course of five more years. His educational opinions and plans were published in 1538 under the title *De litteratum ludis recte apriendis* (*The Right Mode of Instituting Schools*).[32] Sturm's organization of his school included the use of decurions, students who became assistant teachers. He used one student for every ten to perform certain duties in the work of the schoolroom.[33,34]

Sturm's gymnasium at Strasbourg achieved immense popularity. In 1578, there were, among the many thousand scholars, two hundred noblemen, twenty-four counts and barons, and three princes. These came not only from Germany but also from Portugal, Poland, Denmark, France, and England. Perhaps Sturm utilized the practice of peer teaching because of this vast number of students; his reasons are not recorded.

"Sturm was the greatest and most successful schoolman of his day. In clearly defined aim, thorough organization, carefully graded instruction, good teaching, and sound scholarship, his school surpassed all others."[35]

Valentine Trotzendorf was born in 1490. Although his family name was Friedland, he assumed the surname Trotzendorf in memory of his birthplace. In 1531, he became rector of the Latin school of Goldberg in Silesia. He filled this office with renown and dignity for twenty-five years, and his school soon became widely known and respected.

Latin, Greek, and religion were the only subjects of instruction, as in other schools of his time, but Trotzendorf's method differed from those of his contemporaries by a unique organization. He taught the older scholars, and these, in turn, instructed the lower classes "that they too, might learn by teaching. . . . He found the need of scholars to aid him, both in oversight and instruction, as the resources of the school were too slender to admit of his hiring an adequate body of sub-teachers."[36] The instruction of the upper classes he took upon himself, but the lower classes he put in charge of older pupils.

Trotzendorf also instituted a system of student government, modeled after the plan of a Roman republic, in which scholars shared in the government and were partly responsible for law and order.[37] "He had his monitors of order, attendance, and recitations, selected from his first class, which he taught himself—and to whom . . . he delegated a portion of his authority and duty."[38] The scheme of organization was successful under Trotzendorf's administration, and "it taught self-government, and inculcated the spirit of freedom as well as an intelligent submission to law."[39]

Because he used his best pupils to instruct the lower classes and supervised them in this process, he was, in essence, preparing them as teachers. Eventually, these "teachers" were sought by schools from all parts of Europe.[40]

ENGLISH SCHOOLS OF LATE MEDIEVAL TIMES AND THE REFORMATION

"The effect of the Renaissance upon English education was to give the schools a new content; the effect of the Reformation was to give them a new master."[41] During the Middle Ages, the English grammar schools, though modeled on the schools of the Roman Empire, taught grammar without the study of literature. During the Renaissance, the subject matter again became important, with grammar becoming a means to an end. Also, in the Middle Ages, the Catholic church had dominated education in England, as it had on the Continent. During the Reformation, the Anglican church assumed this dominant position, and the reading of the Bible in the vernacular was introduced. "The school boy was to be educated as a Christian, God-fearing Englishman rather than as a spiritual citizen of the world, as had been the case earlier."[42]

Winchester College, founded by William of Wykeham in 1382, was a typical grammar school of its time and was linked with the college in Oxford. Winchester was to supply Oxford with scholars prepared for higher education. Because Winchester was a "collegiate" foundation, it became known as Winchester College— " 'collegially,' that is, in community under a routine strictly prescribed by statutes."[43]

In the foundation deed of 1382, Wykeham referred to having "lately erected and founded a perpetual college of seventy poor scholars, clerks, to study theology, canon, and civil law, and arts at the University of Oxford."[44] Students entered school between eight and twelve years of age and left at about eighteen or nineteen. It is probably that the term "poor" did not actually mean those from the ranks of poverty, but the younger sons of poor nobility and gentry.[45] When the Reformation came to England, and shifts in control and emphasis resulted, Winchester was found to amply meet the requirements of an Anglican grammar school, and it was not disbanded, as were many other schools.

Regarding the organization of Winchester, a passage in the revised statutes stated:

In each of the lower [that is, scholars] chambers let there be at least three scholars of good repute more advanced then the rest in age, sense and learning to superintend the studies of their chamber-fellows and diligently oversee them, and when called upon truly to certify and inform the Warden, Sub-Warden and Master Teacher of their morals, behavior and advancement in learning from time to time as often as may be necessary.[46]

Eton College was founded in 1440, and closely modeled Winchester.

The young king, Henry VI, who created Eton and the sister foundation of King's College, Cambridge, was surrounded by those who knew the works of Wykeham. . . . Thus it was, perhaps, that the king adopted Wykeham's idea at the university from a great grammar school established with that end in view.[47]

Peer teaching was also found at Eton. A record dating from 1520 stated: "The Vth. forme learn the versyfycall rules of Sulpicius gevyn in ye mornyng of some of the VIth. forme, and this Vth. forme gevyth rulys to the fowrth."[48]

In St. Paul's school in London, the ancient cathedral school was replaced by a new school directed by John Colet. Colet was a leading exponent of the humanist ideas of the Renaissance, and his school included many new features such as in the organization and arrangement of scholars. The statutes of 1518 indicated that children of all nations and countries should be taught, the total number coming to exactly 153 (in reference to the miraculous catch of fish recorded in John 21:11).[49]

The internal arrangement of the school was described as follows:

He [that is, Colet] divided the school into four apartments. The first, namely the porch and entrance, is for catechumens, or the children to be instructed in the principles of religion, where no child is to be admitted but what can read and write. The second apartment is for the lower boys to be taught by the second master or usher. The third is for the upper forms under the head master: which two parts of the school are divided by a curtain to be drawn at pleasure. . . . The fourth or last apartment is a little chapel for divine service. The school has no corners or hiding places; nothing like a cell or closet. The boys have their distinct forms or benches, one above the other. Every form holds sixteen, and he that is head or captain of each form has a little kind of desk by way of pre-eminence.[50]

Colet was probably following the precedent of Winchester and Eton, where the head boy or captain had "some authority over his fellows ancillary to that of the masters."[51]

Another reference to pupils as teachers is found in the ordinances of Manchester Grammar School, written in 1524.

The high master . . . shall always appoint one of his scholars, as he thinketh best, to instruct and teach in the one end of the school all infants that shall come there to learn their ABC, primer and sorts till they begin in grammar; and every month to choose another new scholar so to teach infants. And if any scholar refuse so to teach infants at the commandment of the high master . . . the same scholar so refusing to be banished the same school for ever.[52]

Westminster School apparently also used peer teaching, although to what extend is not certain. The statutes of 1560 include reference to "two of the highest form who have been appointed by the schoolmaster to teach the rest of the forms."[53] Another reference to peer teaching at Westminster was quoted by Cole. "The best scholars in the 7th form were appointed as Tutors to read and expound places of Homer, Virgil, Horace, Euripides, or other Greek and Latin authors, at those times . . . wherein the scholars were in the school in expectation of the Mr."[54] This passage was from a contemporary account of the curriculum and daily activities at Westminister.

THE COUNTER-REFORMATION AND EDUCATION

The Protestant Reformation made little headway in Italy, Spain, Portugal, much of France, or southern Belgium. These parts of the Western world remained largely loyal to the Roman church. "After the Church Council of Trent (1545–63), where definite church reform measures were carried through, the Catholics inaugurated what has since been called a counter-reformation, in an effort to hold lands which were still loyal and to win back lands which had been lost."[55]

An effective instrument for carrying out the purposes of the Council of Trent was the religious organization known as the Jesuits, recognized by Pope Paul III in 1540.

The work of the Jesuits is often called the Counter Reformation. It sought to repress heresy, to train priests, to teach, and to help to reform within the Church the abuses against which Luther and the Protestants had complained and protested. The growth of the Society was very rapid and its success was remarkable.[56]

The Jesuits carried on their work both by missionary efforts to win back Protestant territory to its former Catholic allegiance and to counteract Protestant education by equally good Catholic education. "Their educational ideal, therefore, had been to equip all youth, whether intending to enter the order or not, with principles and habits of life in harmony with morality, religion, and the teachings of the Catholic Church."[57]

The founder, Ignatius Loyola, and his followers utilized the best educational ideas and methods of their time and incorporated them into a plan of their own.

They accepted the best and used it much as others had worked it out. . . . Knowing why they were at work and what ends they should achieve, intolerant of opposition, intensely practical in all their work, and possesed of an indefatigable zeal in the accomplishment of their purpose, they gave Europe in general and northern continental Europe in particular a system of secondary schools and universities possessed of a high degree of effectiveness.[58]

Jesuit education was free. Elementary instruction was not provided, and boys usually intended for the Jesuit Order or boys from a good family attended the schools.[59]

A manual, which had been prepared with great care and over a long period of time, outlined the educational work of the Jesuits. This manual, the *Ratio Studiorum*, was not published until 1599, and it was based on the educational experience of the Jesuits for the previous sixty years. It also showed that Jesuits were extremely practical.

The *Ratio Studiorum* hardly contains a single principle; but what it does is this—it points out a perfectly attainable goal, and carefully defines the road by which that goal is to be approached. For each class was prescribed not only the work to be done, but also the end to be kept in view.[60]

The use of peer teaching in Jesuit education, and its eventual inclusion in the *Ratio Studiorum*, dates to 1553, when classes were opened in Lisbon, Portugal. "Classes were divided into groups of ten (decuriae), each group having a captain (decurio) in control."[61] Father Cyprian Soarez, in a letter dated April 25, 1553, explained the system.

Each of these classes is divided into certain order, which we call *decuriae* because they contain ten pupils in each. In the class itself one of the students has control of all the decuriae, though the single groups of ten also have their leader, called the *decurio* or captain of the body of ten. Thus without difficulty account can be kept of any who are absent or inattentive to the lessons or negligent of the memory assignments. This arrangement, in my opinion, is most apt for controlling large classes of students. For places in the groups of ten are assigned according to each pupil's progress in studies.[62]

The same system was used at Cologne, except that groups of eight (octuriae) were chosen instead of ten. "Each group of eight had a captain chosen for his ability in studies and for his good deportment, whose duty it was to hear the memory lessons."[63] These captains also took note of absenteeism and reported those whose conduct was questionable or who used the vernacular instead of Latin.

The Jesuit schools were highly regarded in their day. They were well organized and "administered by a set of splendidly trained teachers through the best methods that were known in that day. The schools were interesting and pleasant, and were open without money and without price to all who had the ability and desire for that type of education."[64]

Jesuit education continued after the Renaissance and into succeeding centuries. Finally, by 1764, its influence had declined, the result of reasons that included corruption within its ranks, and the order was expelled from France.

NOTES

1. Edgar W. Knight, *Twenty Centuries of Education* (Boston: Ginn and Co., 1940), p. 6.

2. Charles Hoffman, *Peer Tutoring: Introduction and Historical Perspective* (Atlanta, Ga.: Council for Exceptional Children, 1977, ERIC Document Reproduction Service No. ED 140 593).

3. Benjamin Wright, "Should Children Teach?" *The Elementary School Journal* 60 (April 1960): 353–69.

4. Ellwood P. Cubberley, *The History of Education* (Boston: Houghton Mifflin Co., 1920), p. 428.

5. John E. Wise, *The History of Education* (New York: Sheed and Ward, 1964), p. 14.

6. George Kennedy, *Quintilian* (New York: Twayne Publishers, Inc., 1969), p. 40.

7. Stanley F. Bonner, *Education in Ancient Rome* (London: Methuen and Co., Ltd., 1977), p. 180.

8. Wise, *The History of Education*, p. 39.

9. Catherine Ruth Smith, trans., *Quintilian on Education: Selections from the Institutes of Oratory* (New York: New York University, n.d.), pp. 18–19.

10. Kennedy, *Quintilian*, p. 40.

11. Levi Seeley, *History of Education* (New York: American Book Company, 1899), p. 86.

12. John Selby Watson, trans., *Quintilian's Institutes of Oratory* (London: G. Bell & Sons, Ltd., 1913), p. vi.

13. Kennedy, *Quintilian*, p. 40.

14. Ibid., p. 41.

15. Martha Dillner, *Tutoring by Students: Who Benefits?* (Gainesville, Fla.: Florida Educational Research and Development Council, 1971), p. 3.

16. John Gill, *Systems of Education* (Boston: D.C. Heath and Co., 1889), p. 162.

17. Ibid., p. 14.

18. H. E. Butler, trans., *The Institutio Oratorio of Quintilian*, vol. 1 (New York: G. P. Putnam's Sons, 1920), p. 51.

19. H. G. Good, *A History of Western Education* (New York: The Macmillan Co., 1947).

20. Cubberley, *The History of Education*, p. 429.

21. Knight, *Twenty Centuries of Education*, p. 95.

22. Cubberley, *The History of Education*, p. 429.

23. Knight, *Twenty Centuries of Education*, pp. 153–54.

24. Frank Pierrepont Graves, *A History of Education* (New York: The Macmillan Co., 1910), p. 107.

25. Knight, *Twenty Centuries of Education*.

26. Graves, *A History of Education*, p. 158.

27. "Life and Educational System of John Sturm," *American Journal of Education* 4 (September 1857): 168.

28. Graves, *A History of Education*, p. 159.

29. Cubberley, *The History of Education*, p. 273.

30. Samuel G. Williams, *The History of Modern Education* (Syracuse, N.Y.: C. W. Bardeen, Publishers, 1892), p. 91.

31. A more detailed explanation of Sturm's plan of organization is available in the articles "Life and Educational System of John Sturm," *American Journal of Education* 4 (September and December 1857): 167–82, 400–15.

32. Graves, *A History of Education.*

33. "Monitorial System," *American Journal of Education* 10 (June 1861): 461–66.

34. "The Jesuits and Their Schools," *American Journal of Education* 5 (June 1858): 213–28.

35. Cubberley, *The History of Education*, p. 273.

36. "Valentine Friedland Trotzendorf," *American Journal of Education* 5 (June 1858): 111.

37. Graves, *A History of Education.*

38. "Monitorial System," p. 461.

39. Seeley, *History of Education*, p. 179.

40. Ibid.

41. Luella Cole, *A History of Education, Socrates to Montessori* (New York: Holt, Rinehart and Winston, 1964), p. 276.

42. Ibid., p. 277.

43. John William Adamson, *A Short History of Education* (London: Cambridge University Press, 1919), p. 60.

44. T. L. Jarman, *Landmarks in the History of Education* (New York: Philosophical Library, 1952), pp. 112–13.

45. Ibid., p. 114.

46. Malcolm Seaborne, *The English School: Its Architecture and Organization, 1370–1870* (Toronto: University of Toronto Press, 1971), p. 4.

47. Jarman, *Landmarks*, p. 116.

48. H. C. Barnard, *A Short History of English Education from 1760–1944* (London: University of London Press, Ltd., 1949), p. 63.

49. Seaborne, *The English School*, p. 12.

50. Ibid.

51. Nicholas Orme, *English Schools in the Middle Ages* (London: Methuen & Co., Ltd., 1973), p. 123.

52. David Cressy, *Education in Tudor and Stuart England* (New York: St. Martin's Press, 1974), pp. 72–73.

53. Seaborne, *The English School*, p. 59.

54. Cole, *A History of Education*, p. 282.

55. Cubberley, *The History of Education*, p. 336.

56. Knight, *Twenty Centuries of Education*, p. 176.

57. Graves, *A History of Education*, p. 210.

58. Cubberley, *The History of Education*, p. 339.

59. Jarman, *Landmarks*, p. 158.

60. Robert Herbert Quick, *Essays on Educational Reformers* (New York: D. Appleton and Company, 1896), p. 49.

61. Allan P. Farrell, *The Jesuit Code of Liberal Education: Development and Scope of the Ratio Studiorum* (Milwaukee: The Bruce Publishing Co., 1938), p. 110.

62. Ibid., p. 120.
63. Ibid.
64. Graves, *A History of Education*, p. 219.

CHAPTER 2

The Seventeenth-Century Use of Peer Teaching

INTRODUCTION

In the seventeenth century, practical education, which included mathematics and sciences, began to be stressed in new schools called academies. Modern languages were favored rather than the classical languages, and the great writers began to use their mother tongues. The advances in education and natural science were paralleled by new ideas of religious and political liberty. The need for improved and modernized curricula and methods was stressed by writers such as Comenius and John Locke. Universal education became a popular idea. There were attempts to bring education within closer reach of society, and schools that began to teach trades appeared.[1]

Realism in education took precedence. Its stress was on "concrete knowledge, practical and vocational skills, the learning of languages for commercial or diplomatic rather than for literary use, and the study of history, politics, law, and the sciences. It is, negatively, a reaction against the literary and artistic purposes of the Renaissance and against the classics."[2] Realism promoted a broad curriculum, which, in turn, brought about the introduction of new methods.

Partly as a result of the Reformation and the Counter-Reformation, the use of the vernacular in education as well as education for common people became concepts that were increasingly stressed. In spite of these changes, classical schools remained the dominant institutions during the seventeenth century.

But the hard fact was in the seventeenth century that the average man—the peasant or the domestic craftsman—did not require a book education for his livelihood, and that the economic system could scarcely have borne the expense of providing adequate buildings and teachers for the education of all. Little was in fact done for the people.[3]

It seems, then, that the writers who originated and popularized the idea of realism were not teachers and had little connection with or influence over schools. The force of their ideas was not felt until decades later.

For a great part of the seventeenth century, schools remained largely similar to those that had evolved from the Renaissance, the Reformation, and the Counter-Reformation. In Catholic countries, the common elementary school was the parish school. There were also parish schools in Protestant countries such as England and Germany. In German states, as in France, the vernacular schools flourished. In addition, there was the village school, supported by the citizenry rather than by a church. Later in the century, charity schools and vocational schools appeared, showing the influence of the realists.

To a large extent, the traditional Latin school, the commonest type of elementary school, remained unchanged and did not participate in the educational progress eventually shown by elementary schools.

The conditions in the majority of the seventeenth-century schools were later to become major issues in reform. The discipline was extremely harsh; the dullness and monotony, plus the meaninglessness of the education, caused much unrest in the schoolroom. In addition, inefficient teaching prevailed in most schools. The individual method of instruction was most commonly used, and because of this, the following accounts of peer teaching are exceptional and of much interest.

BRINSLEY AND HOOLE

The English grammar schools had degenerated into a formalistic education that neglected the vernacular, mathematics, and other practical subjects. Students memorized grammar with little understanding of the meaning. The seventeenth-century Puritan, John

Brinsley, had great interest in improving the methods of instruction in the "ordinarie" grammar schools. He said, "I have travelled [travailed] chiefly for our meaner and ruder schools."[4] He also stated:

Amongst others, my selfe having first had long experience of the manifold evils which grow from the ignorance of a right order of teaching, and afterwards some gracious tast of the sweetnesse that is to be found in the better courses truly knowne and practised. I have betaken me almost wholly, for manie yeares, unto this weighty worke, and that not without much comfort, through the goodnesses of our blessed God.[5]

Brinsley, born in 1587, urged the teaching and use of English as well as Latin. He felt that the use of English was vital because the majority of the students did not continue with further study. He further urged the principle that students should understand whatever they learn. In addition, he opposed excessive punishment of children, which resulted in their dislike of school and learning. These and other principles were presented in his two books, *Ludus Literarius (Grammar Schoole)*, published in 1612, and *A Consolation for Our Grammar Schooles*, which appeared in 1622. The latter book assumed the existence of the former and continued to emphasize the right principles of instruction. The standpoint of the *Ludus Literarius* "is frankly empirical, with little or no reference to general principles, and its aim is expressly practical."[6] *A Consolation* describes a course of study for a grammar school and contains an annotated bibliography.

The reform that is of most concern to this study is Brinsley's grouping of children into larger classes than was commonly done. During his time, it was still customary to have only a few boys in each class, and the individual method of instruction was used. As a result of this new method of grouping, Brinsley began to employ monitors. He stated in *Ludus Literarius*, "In every fourme this maybe a notable helpe, that the two or foure seniors in each fourme, be as Ushers in that fourme, for overseeing, directing, examining, and fitting the rest every way before they come to say, and so for overseeing the exercises." He also said that these should "stand forth before the rest and heare them."[7] These monitors were to be elected by the boys, to avoid the problem of favoritism.[8]

Seaborne noted that Brinsley greatly stressed the idea of boys help-ing each other.[9]

Brinsley's other book, *A Consolation for our Grammar Schooles*, was important, not only as an analysis of educational methods in English grammar schools and suggestions for improvement, but it is also connected with the beginnings of education in colonial Vir-ginia. The Virginia Company published the book as one that pre-sented a course of study suitable for the East India School (so named because the East India Company contributed funds for the establishment of the school).

Another eminent English educator of the seventeenth century was Charles Hoole, 1610–1667. In 1660, he published a treatise similar in spirit and character to that of Brinsley, entitled *A New Discovery of the Old Art of Teaching Schools; in Four Small Treatises*. In the first treatise, *A Petty-Schoole*, he said:

Let their lessons be the same to each boy in every forme, and let the Master proportion them to the meanest capacities, thus those that are abler may profit themselves by helping their weaker fellowes, and those that are weaker be encouraged to see that they can keep company with the stronger. And let the two highest . . . give notice to the master when they come to say, of those that were most negligent in geting the lesson.[10]

Another citation from his treatise would indicate the increasing number of students attending the English grammar school. He was, as Brinsley had been, faced with larger classes, and he said forty students should be the limit for one master. He also indicated a slight dissatisfaction with the monitorial system of his time, saying that forty students should be the limit in a classroom so that the master can hear each student "without making use of any of his Scholars to teach the rest, which however it may be permitted, and is practised in some Schooles, yet it occasioneth too much noyse and disorder, and is no whit so acceptable to Parents, or pleasing to the children, be the work never so well done."[11]

Quick, in his book on educational reformers, stated that "our English practice [of children teaching children] received no encour-agement from the early English writers, Mulcaster, Brinsley, and Hoole."[12] While no evidence was found of the use of peer teaching in Mulcaster's works, what is known about Brinsley and Hoole cer-tainly negates Quick's assumption.

COMENIUS AND THE DIDACTICA MAGNA

Jan Amos Komensky, better known by his Latinized name of Comenius, was born in a small village of Moravia in 1592. As a member of the Moravian Brethren, he fell victim to much persecution. Cubberley summed up his life sequence as follows:

As a member, pastor and later bishop of the Moravian church, and as a follower of John Huss, he suffered greatly in the Catholic-Protestant warfare which raged over his native land during the period of the Thirty Years' War. His home twice plundered, his books and manuscripts twice burned, his wife and children murdered, and himself at times a fugitive and later an exile, Comenius gave his long life to the advancement of the interests of mankind through religion and learning. Driven from his home and country, he became a scholar of the world.[13]

Because of the scarce attention paid to his schooling during his youth, Comenius did not have the opportunity to study Latin until the age of sixteen, at which time he was mature enough to perceive the emptiness and absurdity of studying grammar in the manner of his time. This experience was instrumental in his later efforts to improve methods. During his career as a student and a teacher, he formulated in his mind a complete system of the principles of education, including what he wished to see as subject matter and methods. The culmination of his practical experience and thought came while he was an exile in the Polish town of Leszna (Lissa, in German), where he wrote the renowned volume *Didactica Magna (Great Didactic)* between 1628 and 1632. The work was published in 1657.

In this work Comenius formulated and explained his two fundamental ideas, namely, that all instruction must be carefully graded and arranged to follow the order of nature, and that, in imparting knowledge to children, the teacher must make constant appeal through sense-perception to the understanding of the child.[14]

The aims presented by Comenius in the *Didactica Magna* were revolutionary, and were intended "for the schoolmaster whose interest in his work was not confined to the schoolroom, and for nobles, statesmen, and philosophers who wished to reform the schools of their country, but found no scheme ready to hand that was both practical and comprehensive."[15]

The most prevalent phase of his work, both in method and in organization, was one common to realism, that of pansophia, or universal knowledge. "This was most manifest in his desire to teach at least the rudiments of all things to every one."[16] Comenius was a sincere Christian and hoped to regenerate mankind through the religious aim in education of knowledge, morality, and piety. "Education should enable one to become pious through the establishment of moral habits, which are in turn to be formed and guided through adequate knowledge."[17]

Comenius believed education should be a well-rounded training that was a natural one, not artificial and traditional, and should be available to all, without regard to sex, social position, or wealth. Further, he believed in educating human beings because they were human beings, not just for their salvation.

Latin was subordinated to the vernacular, and in conjunction with the aims of realism, he enriched the curriculum with geography, history, the arts, and science. He believed that education should begin with the easy and proceed to the difficult, and from the general to the specific. The teacher should impart knowledge and should guide. Education was not merely a matter of storing material in the memory.

He organized schools into four periods: the mother school, from infancy to the age of six; the vernacular school, from six to twelve years of age; the Latin school, covering the years between twelve and eighteen; and finally, the university, which should be completed by age twenty-four.

Comenius advocated the use of peer teaching. He wrote that "teaching takes place when knowledge that has been acquired is communicated to fellow-pupils or other companions."[18] He explained this idea further:

The saying, "He who teaches others, teaches himself," is very true, not only because constant repetition impresses a fact indelibly on the mind, but because the process of teaching in itself gives a deeper insight into the subject taught. Thus it was that the gifted Joachim Fortius[*] used to say

*Joachim Fortius was born in Antwerp, raised in the court of Maximilian I, and died in 1536. He was a prolific author, a mathematician, a philologist, a painter, and an etcher.

that, if he had heard or read anything once, it slipped out of his memory within a month; but that if he taught it to others it became as much a part of himself as his fingers, and that he did not believe that anything short of death could deprive him of it. His advice, therefore, was that, if a student wished to make progress, he should arrange to give lessons daily in the subjects which he was studying, even if he had to hire his pupils. "It is worth your while," he says, "to sacrifice your bodily comfort to a certain extent for the sake of having some one who will listen while you teach, or in other words, while you make intellectual progress."[19]

Comenius, contrary to the common idea of his time, maintained that one teacher could teach a large number of boys in one class, and placed no limit on the number.

Comenius admits that the teacher of one hundred boys could not personally ascertain whether all did and understood their work, but by arranging them in tens, and putting one of the boys . . . over each troop of ten, he might check their exercises and report to the master. The troops of ten he calls Decuriae, and their captains Decuriones.[20]

Although some of Comenius's contemporaries were cognizant of the value of *Didactica Magna*, it was not fully appreciated until nearly two centuries later. There are various reasons for this: the book required considerable editing, which Comenius did not undertake; also, his reputation was tarnished because of his firm, although innocent, belief in a spurious prophet, Drabik, also a Bohemian. In addition. the seventeenth century was not a time when far-reaching reforms were considered seriously. "Christian Europe was too filled with an atmosphere of suspicion and distrust and hatred to be in any mood to consider reforms for the improvement of the education of mankind."[21] As a result, his reforms were not worked out until the nineteenth century. Since then, however, the *Didactica Magna* has been considered among the greatest writings on education.[22]

THE ORATORIANS

The Jesuits, as was noted earlier, carried on their work during the Counter-Reformation in an attempt to counteract the beneficent effect of Protestant education. Ironically, they, in turn, were somewhat opposed by a new teaching order originally organized as a monastic order within the Catholic church in Italy during the late sixteenth century and introduced in 1611 in France, where it assumed the character of a teaching order.

At first, the education conducted by the Oratorians was for candidates for the priesthood, but soon its function extended to secondary education for all classes of students. "The Oratorians promoted a thorough study of the mother tongue and taught all subjects in it up to the fourth year of school, after which Latin was required save in history which was always taught in French."[23]

The Oratorian system was opposed to the Jesuit emphasis on memorization, which the Oratorians thought was somewhat mechanical and pretentious. Oratorian schools, Wise indicated, were modern in their outlook. "This is shown in the curriculum emphasis of the vernacular, history, mathematics, and science. There was a great deal of freedom in the individual schools. Progress reports were made to parents, in which manners, morals, and piety received mention, as well as school work."[24]

In spite of the silent antagonism between the Oratorians and the Jesuits, and the distinct differences in their methods of education, the Oratorians did use peer teaching, as did the Jesuits. There is no indication whether this was their own invention, or whether they were influenced by its use in Jesuit schools. Barnard said that "each form had its own monitor or decurion whose duty it was to collect the work and within limits to hear the repetition of his fellows."[25]

While the Oratorians did incur the antagonism of Jesuits and others who adhered to a more traditional and rigid curriculum, they were vastly successful. When the Jesuits were disbanded in 1773 in France, the Oratorians were given charge of secondary education. Finally, they, too, fell victim to French rulers and ideas, and were disbanded in 1792. Only in the middle of the nineteenth century were they once again recognized as an order.

LA SALLE AND THE CHRISTIAN BROTHERS

A major movement on behalf of popular education in seventeenth-century France, particularly in the cities, was undertaken by Jean-Baptiste de la Salle. Born in 1651, a member of a wealthy family, he spent his first thirty years of his life within privileged surroundings. By his own confession, he showed little interest in educational efforts, but when asked to assist in the opening of a free

school at Rheims, he consented. The success of that school led to the
opening of similiar institutions, until there were five teachers in the
town. La Salle found that he must act as adviser to these men, and
before long, he resigned both his canonry and his worldly posses-
sions and lived among them, thus establishing the Intitute of Christian Brothers in 1681.[26] From then on, he "turned his attention to
the instruction of the poor with unabated zeal."[27] The Christian
Brothers did a great work in behalf of elementary education in
France and in other Catholic countries, comparable to that performed by the Jesuits for secondary education.

The education of the Brothers of the Christian Schools had a
clearly defined purpose. "It was essentially toward making good
Catholics—good Christians—of the children of the poorer
classes."[28] La Salle "planned his work upon a broad scale and
adapted his methods to the varied conditions of time and place.
Thus he devised a system complete in all its details from the elementary grades to the collegiate curriculum."[29]

From the beginning of their educational ventures, the Christian
Brothers utilized the simultaneous method, dividing a school into
classes rather than instructing each student individually.

De La Salle's Brothers had to cope with classes of anything up to a hundred
boys, and therefore a radically different system was required. In making
use of the Simultaneous Method, by which is meant teaching a large group
together, De La Salle was the slave of necessity, but in so doing he popularized a method which has since become universal.[30]

There is a curious difference of opinion from this point on. Good
acknowledged the fact that the Christian Brothers utilized the class
system of teaching and classified students according to their level of
achievement, but he also stated that they "used monitors to teach
the younger pupils."[31]

A translator of La Salle's treatise on education said in his introduction that La Salle utilized the simultaneous method, with students reciting one after another, while those not reciting at the time
were to listen carefully. He pointed out that this was quite an innovation at the time. He then added, "The more advanced students
were required to aid the others in preparing their tasks."[32]

Adamson explained the actual teaching methods as follows:

Each class was in the charge of a Brother and was divided into three sections, comprising the most advanced, the mediocre, and the most backward: when the Brother was engaged with one section only, the remaining sections were set to do work under the surveillance of monitors, who kept order, heard lessons, and helped the Brother in similar ways; but they did not teach.[33]

Dempsey stated that La Salle compromised "on a method which, preserving something of the 'Mutual system,' still left to the teaching of the master all its educative strength."[34] Apparently, in the first half of the nineteenth century, the Lancasterian system, which was introduced in the French schools, was urged on the Christian Brothers. Dempsey said that the Brothers "were extremely badgered while it was being tried out,"[35] yet they adhered to the rules and traditions that had been part of their system since their foundation.

Lancaster, according to the account by Brother Constantius, was astonished that the French preferred his method to the one espoused by the Christian Brothers. Battersby also stated that the Brothers' use of the simultaneous method was frowned upon during this time, and the hostility of the governing party lasted until the middle 1830s. "After this, however, the popularity of the Mutual System gradually declined, and the Brothers had the satisfaction of seeing the methods of their own Founder universally adopted."[36]

La Salle's principal pedagogical work was the *Conduite des Écoles* (Conduct of the Schools), which was first published in 1720, the year after his death. In the translations available, the exact thoughts of La Salle on peer teaching were not readily apparent.

La Salle's contribution is summed up thus: "On French education La Salle and his Institute exercised the greatest influence in introducing a better class of teachers and a better conception of schools and instruction."[37]

ROLLIN, THE FRENCH EDUCATOR

In a discussion of French education, Barnard wrote that the history of university reform is "a record of mediocre achievement."[38] Yet, toward the end of the seventeenth century, new efforts at reform were made, and the important leader in this cause was Charles Rollin. He was born in Paris in 1661 and was renowned as a

French historian and educator. As rector of the University of Paris three times and head of the College of de Beauvais, he was able to institute major reforms, particularly in the curriculum and in the effort to replace Latin with the vernacular.[39]

Rollin is included in this study because he is thought to have used peer teaching. Hager stated that "the French historian and educator Charles Rollin was familiar with the technique [that is, monitorial teaching]."[40]

Salmon said that "Rollin mentions it as a useful expedient,"[41] and an article in the *American Journal of Education* quoted Baron de Gérando as saying, "The mutual system was practiced long ago among the ancients, was recommended in France by the sage Rollin. . . ."[42]

These citations seem to indicate that mention of it might be found in his *Traite des Études (The Method of Teaching and Studying the Belles Lettres)*, a four-volume work written in the latter years of his life, 1726–1728. The *Traite des Études* is one of the most important of the French works on education, and "is a handbook for the use of the regent who is entering upon his profession, and Rollin also expresses a hope that his work may be of use and interest to parents."[43]

However, the only mention of peer teaching that may even remotely be indicated is in the section entitled "Of the Government of Colleges." "Another advantage to be found in schools is, that a young man meets with such models among his companions as are within his reach, such as he flatters himself he may be able to come up to, and does not despair of surpassing one day."[44] No direct evidence of the use of peer teaching was found in this valued work for educators by Rollin.

SEVENTEENTH-CENTURY EDUCATION IN AMERICA

The colonies of North America had almost no systematic plan of schooling, and the establishment of schools was more or less random. Only New England legislatures showed any interest in educational ventures. Teaching methods were generally of the drill and memorization type. "Methods of instruction were usually individual and often very wasteful, school equipment was meager, unhygienic, and insanitary, and the materials of instruction were for the most part religious."[45] Educational aims, for the most part, were indoctrination in religious principles and church doctrines and the development of rudimentary skills in the three Rs.

There is a single mention of peer teaching during this time. In his autobiography, the Rev. John Barnard, born in 1681 in Marblehead, Massachusetts, mentioned an incident that occurred during his early education.

By that time I had a little passed by sixth year, I had left my reading-school, in the latter part of which my mistress made me sort of usher, appointing me to teach some children that were older than myself, as well as smaller ones.[46]

The autobiography was published when he was eighty-five, in 1766, and is found in the Collections of the Massachusetts Historical Society.

Barnard commented on that isolated incident: "It appears from this statement that this unnamed school-mistress adopted the monitorial system a century and more before Bell, or Lancaster, or their respective adherents convulsed the educational world of England by their claims to its authorship."[47]

NOTES

1. H. G. Good, *A History of Western Education* (New York: The Macmillan Co., 1947).
2. Ibid., p. 171.
3. T. L. Jarman, *Landmarks in the History of Education* (New York: Philosophical Library, 1952, p. 196.
4. John Brinsley, *A Consolation for our Grammar Schooles* (New York: Scholar's Facsimiles and Reprints, 1943), p. iv.
5. Ibid., p. 14.
6. John William Adamson, *Pioneers of Modern Education, 1600–1700* (London: Cambridge University Press, 1905), p. 21.
7. John Brinsley, *Ludus Literarius* (London: Thomas Man, 1612), p. 272.
8. Adamson, *Pioneers of Modern Education*, p. 25.
9. Malcolm Seaborne, *The English School: Its Architecture and Organization, 1370–1870* (Toronto: University of Toronto Press, 1971), p. 64.
10. Charles Hoole, *A New Discovery of the Old Art of Teaching Schools; in Four Small Treatises* (Liverpool: The University Press, 1913), p. 35.
11. Ibid., p. 39.

12. Robert Herbert Quick, *Essays on Educational Reformers* (New York: D. Appleton and Company, 1896), p. 99.
13. Ellwood P. Cubberley, *The History of Education* (Boston: Houghton Mifflin Co., 1920), pp. 408–409.
14. Ibid., pp. 409–10.
15. M. W. Keatinge, *The Great Didactic of John Amos Comenius*, part 1 (London: A. and C. Black, Ltd., 1921), p. 13.
16. Frank Pierrepont Graves, *A History of Education* (New York: The Macmillan Co., 1910), p. 276.
17. Ibid., p. 278.
18. M. W. Keatinge, *The Great Didactic of John Amos Comenius*, part 2 (London, A. and C. Black, Ltd., 1923), p. 156.
19. Ibid., pp. 156–57.
20. S.S. Laurie, *John Amos Comenius, Bishop of the Moravians: His Life and Educational Works* (Syracuse, N.Y.: C. W. Bardeen, 1892), p. 99.
21. Cubberley, *The History of Education*, p. 416.
22. Edgar W. Knight, *Twenty Centuries of Education* (Boston: Ginn and Co., 1940), pp. 355-56.
23. Samuel G. Williams, *The History of Modern Education* (Syracuse, N.Y.: C. W. Bardeen, Publishers, 1892), p. 219.
24. John E. Wise, *The History of Education* (New York: Sheed and Ward, 1964), p. 227.
25. H. C. Barnard, *The French Tradition in Education* (London: Cambridge University Press, 1922), p. 168.
26. "St. John Baptist de La Salle," *A Cyclopedia of Education*, vol. 3, ed. P. Monroe (New York: The Macmillan Co., 1913), p. 637.
27. Graves, *A History of Education*, p. 229.
28. F. de la Fontainerie, trans., *The Conduct of the Schools of Jean-Baptiste de la Salle* (New York: McGraw-Hill Book Co., Inc., 1935), p. 35.
29. Brother Constantius, "Christian Brothers," *A Cyclopedia of Education*, vol. 1, ed. P. Monroe (New York: The Macmillan Co., 1913), p. 645.
30. W. J. Battersby, *De La Salle, a Pioneer of Modern Education* (London: Longmans, Green and Co., 1949), pp. 79–80.
31. Good, *A History of Western Education*, p. 165.
32. Fontainerie, *The Conduct of the Schools*, p. 39.
33. Adamson, *Pioneers of Modern Education*, p. 232.
34. M. Dempsey, *John Baptist de la Salle: His life and His Institute* (Milwaukee: The Bruce Publishing Company, 1940), p. 105.
35. Ibid., p. 195.
36. Battersby, *De La Salle*, p. 82.
37. "St. John Baptist de La Salle," p. 637.
38. Barnard, *The French Tradition in Education*, p. 196.
39. Frederic E. Farrington, "Rollin, Charles," *A Cyclopedia of Education*, vol. 7, ed. P. Monroe (New York: The Macmillan Co., 1913), p. 195.
40. Phil E. Hager, "Nineteenth Century Experiments with Monitorial Teaching," *Phi Delta Kappan* 40 (January 1959): 164.

41. David Salmon, "Monitorial System," *A Cyclopedia of Education*, vol. 4, ed. P. Monroe (New York: The Macmillan Co., 1913), p. 296.

42. "Monitorial System," *American Journal of Education* 10 (June 1861): 465.

43. Barnard, *The French Tradition in Education*, p. 207.

44. Charles Rollin, *The Method of Teaching and Studying the Belles Lettres* (London: W. Otridge and Son, 1810), p. 319.

45. Edgar W. Knight, *Education in the United States* (Boston: Ginn and Co., 1929), p. 124.

46. John Barnard, "Autobiography of the Rev. John Barnard," *Collections of the Massachusetts Historical Society*, 3d series, vol. 5 (Boston: John H. Eastburn, 1836), p. 178.

47. Henry Barnard, ed., *Memoirs of Teachers and Educators* (New York: Arno Press and *The New York Times*, 1969), p. 23.

CHAPTER 3

Peer Teaching in the Eighteenth Century and Educational Transition to the Nineteenth Century

INTRODUCTION

"The eighteenth century is called the age of reason, but it was also an age of benevolence, toleration, and political democracy, partly because these attitudes were considered reasonable, but also in response to humane feeling."[1] Events occurring in the eighteenth century are generally considered as a preparation for those activities that took place during the first part of the nineteenth century. For this reason, it is vital to look at the circumstances that influenced educational conditions as well as progress in the eighteenth century yet laid the groundwork for what took place in the nineteenth century. The second half of this chapter will deal specifically with those factors that directly affected educational activities at the turn of the century and for the next few decades.

The eighteenth century saw a culmination of the revolt against church control over human affairs. "Rationalism held that the world is entirely subject to natural law and ruled out everything supernatural and all revealed religion as contrary to the uniformity of nature and to natural law."[2] The concept of educating citizens for the welfare of the church and for a future life completely vanished. There was a revolt against the despotism of the church and the resulting barriers to intellectual progress.

A new humanitarian spirit of the century attempted to reform the conditions of the peasants, the criminals, and slaves, and to inculcate rulers with new interest in attempting to improve the welfare of the people they governed. Major efforts were made to raise the condition of people previously ignored.

In England, a democratic form of government had evolved and developed to a great extent. Elsewhere, democratic growth was slow. However, concepts of the natural rights of the individual, of life, liberty, and the pursuit of happiness, increasingly opposed the existing autocratic conditions in both church and state. This opposition eventually led to revolutions that took place at the close of the century and that vastly changed governments, especially in France and in America.

A new theory about the purpose of education became more prevalent. Schools were to be maintained by civilians rather than by churchmen, and they were to promote societal and state interests. Although educators and educational theorists were advancing new concepts—interest in health and physical education, in science, in efforts to aid the student to think for himself, in practical arts—these improved ideas did not receive actual application for some time. Good wrote that "the prophets of the new day were not well received and new practices were carried out in only a few schools and by small groups of innovators."[3] Barnard commented that "during this period . . . teachers of all types tended to be fettered by tradition and convention, or by routine and narrowness of outlook; though, as we have seen and as we shall see again, there were always a few who could rise above the general level and take a higher viewpoint."[4]

Evidence of the use of peer teaching was found only in France and in the British Isles.

EDUCATORS IN THE BRITISH ISLES

Educational efforts in eighteenth-century England were without state support, and were generally carried out by individuals, sometimes with church support, and by voluntary organizations. As the eighteenth century progressed, an awareness of the miserable condition of the poor became more prevalent, accompanied by a concern for the education of the children of the poor. Charity schools were established, but they reached only a small portion of the needy class. These schools provided a basic education in reading, arithmetic, and sometimes writing; often, practical skills were also taught. The intent of these schools was primarily religious and moral.[5]

Toward the latter part of the century, Sunday schools were added as a possible solution to the problem of educating the poor. These schools were aimed at those children who worked in industry during the week or the children who inhabited the streets daily. Again, the instruction was rudimentary and the stress was on the religious and moral development of the children. "The Sunday schools were the first attempt to fashion a mass education adjusted to the conditions of the changing society."[6]

It was not in these schools, however, that peer teaching was used. The schools of the poor were to utilize peer teaching in the nineteenth century, not earlier. During the eighteenth century, peer teaching could be found only in isolated incidents.

David Williams and David Manson were among the educational innovators of their day. In 1773, Williams gave up his career as a Dissenting minister and moved to London, where he began to improve his knowledge of educational matters and where he started teaching private pupils. The following year he opened a school. Most of his pupils came from well-to-do families or from well-known public schools. Although he charged a high tuition (for that era), 100 pounds a year, he still could not make ends meet because he constantly experimented with new reforms.

"Williams was determined to avoid the authoritarianism, verbalism, and concentration on the classics that he felt were defects of the average boarding or public school of his day."[7] He felt that the current attempts of committing much work to memory were mechanical, and he abhorred the students' lack of understanding of what was being studied.

Williams believed in education according to nature, and in the perfectability and educability of the child according to the rules of natural education. "Education, he wrote, was 'the art of forming a man on rational principles, and yet making him capable of entering into the community and becoming a useful and good citizen.' "[8]

Among the several unorthodox teaching methods he tried was the one of "reciprocal assistances." Similar to the subsequent monitorial method that became so popular in England in that boys taught other boys, it differed in intention and organization. The use of reciprocal assistance arose from an experiment Williams had conducted. A boy in his school had never learned to read because of some physical disability incurred early in his childhood. Williams requested that another student teach him, and he was interested to see how quickly the boy learned. This method worked better than any other Williams had tried.

Unfortunately, Williams's school, which operated far in advance of the ideas of his day, was only open for two years, and no discernible influence is apparent on English education.

David Manson was an Irishman who conducted his first school in a cowshed. For a time, he gave up teaching, but then in 1752, he returned to Belfast and started an evening school. The school eventually became so successful that he added boarding facilities.

Only one account of his methods and organizations is extant, and this is found in a supplement to his *New Pocket Dictionary*, published in 1762. Manson was "one of the first to modify the normal school routine by combining lessons with play and amusement and devising a system of pupil self-government based on a complex gradation of rank . . . In addition, his organization of one scholar instructing another anticipated the monitorial system of Bell and Lancaster."[9]

The first activity of a school day was the division of children into ranks based on their performance of some learning activity. After they had been divided into ranks, "the day's lessons proceeded, with children reciting to each other under the supervision of monitors."[10]

Elizabeth Hamilton, a Scottish writer and educationalist, in her book *The Cottagers of Glenburnie*, written in 1808, mentioned a David Manson, a schoolmaster of Belfast, who managed his school on a plan very similar to that later developed by Bell and Lancaster. She wrote that Manson published a book about his methods of teaching, but it never received much notice.[11]

Manson's school continued successfully until he died in 1792. Neither he nor Williams had any disciples, nor did they influence their contemporaries enough to have established a school of thought or practice.

Education for the Quaker poor in England was largely neglected during the latter part of the eighteenth century. This was due to little conviction among the Friends about the necessity of good schooling. However, schools were run privately for the wealthier Quakers.[12]

In 1779, Ackworth School was founded for the poorer members of the Friends Society. By 1781, there were 310 pupils who came from all over the country, a fact that indicated the urgent need for education among Quakers at that time.

Ackworth used an apprentice-teacher system. An apprentice was given a year's schooling; then he served for six years, during which time he received board and lodging, clothes, and a small amount of pay. He was responsible for much of the teaching and supervision. Apprentices were usually boys in their teens who learned of classroom teaching and management by being in the classroom.

These apprentices had been regularly used at Ackworth before Bell and Lancaster brought their "systems" into vogue. The apprentices provided most of the teachers of elementary subjects in Quaker schools until about the middle of the [nineteenth] century, when the widening curriculum made too much of a demand on their limited training.[13]

An additional mention can be found of peer teaching in England. Hager wrote that an Abbé Gaultier, who was a French refugee in England in the 1770s, established a school in London for other French refugee children.[14] Once, when his entire staff deserted, he supposedly used peer teaching to remedy the situation. Salmon and an article entitled "Monitorial System" both include Gaultier in their listing of names when reporting on the use of peer teaching.[15,16]

THE FRENCH EDUCATORS

At the turn of the century, there is record of peer teaching being utilized by a Mme. de Maintenon,[17] who was the second wife of Louis XIV. In 1686, she established a school for poor girls, which became one of the first serious attempts to educate girls.[18] Hager and Salmon both mention that Mme. de Maintenon introduced a form of monitorial system at her school at Saint-Cyr.[19,20]

Three sources refer to a Frenchman named Herbault who utilized peer teaching at the Paris Hospice de la Pitié.[21,22,23] In a book by the Count de Lasteyrie, *Nouveau Systeme d'Education*, Herbault is mentioned briefly as having used a system by which a well-taught scholar communicated instruction to the unlearned.[24]

Count de Lasteyrie wrote more extensively about the knight Paulet, who used peer teaching in a school for orphans at Vincennes in 1772. He listed four principles on which Paulet's system was based, the second one being: "To employ them reciprocally in instructing each other, by offering to the disciple the honor of becoming in his turn a master, as the highest reward of his progress."[25]

Count de Laborde also included an account about Paulet in his book on education for the poor according to the plans of Lancaster and Bell. He stated that he wished to relate the story of Paulet because it gave to France the honor of having been the first to put in use a method now in vogue in England and being adopted by France; that is, the monitorial system.

He recounted the story of the knight Paulet, from an Irish family established in France, who lived in Paris society until an incident drew him into another way of life. Paulet found a poor child deserted in the woods, took him home, cared for him, and took charge of his education. After a few weeks, the child brought two other starving orphans to Paulet. Paulet kept them also and then took in others, thus forming a school to which he dedicated his time and fortune. A generous inheritance came to his aid, and his school eventually had two hundred pupils, children of soldiers or of poor gentlemen, for whom he thought education could give a respectable rank.

Paulet, having been a soldier, thought order and regularity were essential, and his school was conducted on a sort of military fashion. He allowed the children to govern themselves, under his leadership, and he banished corporal punishment, using punishments that humiliated the culprit to the point that students would do anything to avoid it. The children taught each other. Paulet chose the most intelligent to teach the others. However, Paulet did not believe in mere memory work but tried to help students become discriminating in their studies.

Paulet's school came to the attention of the king, who assigned 32,000 francs per year to aid in meeting costs. Laborde stated that there was no doubt that if this school had been maintained, it would have served as a model for all institutions in existence. But the Revolution caused the institution to close, and it was necessary to reinvent the principle of instruction all over again, a principle, he said, so useful to society. England acquired this right to the grate-fulness of men.[26]

EDUCATIONAL CONDITIONS IN NORTH AMERICA

Knight stated that

life in the United States in the last decades of the eighteenth century was full of struggles, dangers, and deprivations. The means of transportation and of communication were meager. . . . Education was making little prog-ress. The energies of the people, almost exhausted by war, were absorbed by more immediately pressing needs.[27]

He further pointed out that the need for education was not widely felt, education being considered a privilege for the wealthy and a charity for the poor. Free education remained a dream of the vision-ary and was generally considered impractical. Illiteracy bore no stigma, and the public still felt, as they had in colonial days, that schools should be established and maintained by churches and phil-anthropic organizations.

Cubberley said that "it can hardly be said that the American people had developed an educational consciousness, outside of New England and New York, before about 1820, and in some of the States, especially in the South, a State educational consciousness was not awakened until very much later."[28]

There appears to be no record of peer teaching taking place at that time. Not until the first half of the nineteenth century, when the influence from England became extremely forceful, did peer teaching see widespread use in North America.

TRANSITION TO THE NINETEENTH CENTURY

Conditions in England

The years from the beginning of the nineteenth century to approximately the early 1830s were characterized by much social and political unrest in England. Conditions generated by this unrest had a strong influence on education of the time, which remained highly undeveloped and the subject of much controversy.

Economic conditions in England had begun to change with the onset of the Industrial Revolution, dating back to the latter part of the eighteenth century. As a result of the great development of manufacturing and commerce, England became the world leader in industry and in trade.[29] But the rise of factories and industry also contributed to social ills. The population in towns grew rapidly, mostly because of the Industrial Revolution, but also because of the gradual abolition of the open-field system. Peasants no longer were capable of being self-sufficient; the process of enclosure benefited only the industrialists.[30] As a result, the peasants flocked to the towns and became dependent on wages that could be earned in factories and mills. "Whatever the moral rights or wrongs of industrialism, it certainly altered social relationships as well as social activities. The Industrial Revolution created the wage-earning class, a vast army of workers in the mills, mines and foundries."[31]

As the influx into towns continued, there was little planning, and the proverbial English slums proliferated around the industrial areas. Sanitation was woefully inadequate. "It is important to note that this rapid and uncontrolled expansion implied a shortage of schools in the new manufacturing areas."[32]

Dobbs wrote of some problems resulting from the factory system. These were "the long hours of confinement in an unhealthy atmosphere, the absence of supervision, the constant separation of parent and child, and the general disturbance of family life."[33] Midwinter also pointed out some of the results of industrialism and town life. "Along with these conglomerations of people, packed into the dreadful confines of the nineteenth-century town, went a number of critical social ills. Disease was perhaps the most desperate issue in such places. . . . Poverty, crime and ignorance were other social problems associated with town growth."[34] The poverty resulting in the towns, which grew from the structure of the economic system as well as the class structure, was appalling.

It would be difficult to exaggerate the sordid misery of the life of the poor in England at the beginning of the century. "The problem of pauperism came upon men in its most terrible form between 1775 and 1834," wrote

Arnold Toynbee. England was stricken by a combination of calamities. The loss of America, the Napoleonic wars, a series of ruinous harvests, and a vicious method of administering the poor laws, served together terribly to undermine the resources of the country. Whatever the principal cause, no one now will call in question the misery of the poor, their sanitary neglect, demoralisation, acute want, and terrible ignorance, at the time of which we are speaking.[35]

The structure of social classes became more deeply rooted in England at the beginning of the nineteenth century and affected education.[36] Many were fearful that the education of the working class would cause them to be discontent with their lot, "disobedient, extravagant, and politically radical."[37]

The small upper ruling class, alarmed at the developments in France, became confirmed in its opposition to any general popular education aside from a little reading, writing, counting, and careful religious training, while on the other hand men of more liberal outlook felt that popular enlightenment was a necessity to prevent the masses from becoming stirred by inflammatory writings and speeches.[38]

Evans confirmed this view. He stated:

Against the backcloth of the French Revolution most of the propertied governing class feared the possible consequences of educating the poor more than the possible dangers and disadvantages of not doing so. In particular they were concerned lest the provision of the elementary education for the poor should produce a growing dissatisfaction with their lot in life at the close of the Industrial Revolution. Better to let sleeping dogs lie.[39]

Each social class viewed the education of its class in a different way, while the upper class had distinct views on what education for the lower class should be. The upper class saw education as not necessary for practical purposes but as a way to acquire social graces. "Secondary and higher education was the preserve of the well-to-do, with the very wealthy looking to the public schools and the universities and the comfortably off to the endowed grammar schools and private secondary institutions."[40]

As the middle class increased in numbers and importance, they wished to imitate the methods utilized by the upper class, relying largely on tutors and the public schools.[41]

"Elementary schooling, narrowly conceived and self-contained, was all that working class children could hope to receive."[42] "The working-class view of education was far less formed than that of the other classes. The members of this class did not question the way in which the middle and upper classes defined their own education and were only beginning to formulate their own educational needs."[43]

One reason that education for the working class and the poor was not fostered to a greater extent was that the economy did not demand well-educated workers. "For the vast majority of jobs, even when skilled, a knowledge of the three R's was just not necessary."[44] The actual purpose of schools at that time was "to impart a certain attitude towards life, and that not the upright independent attitude of a freeman. They were to prepare the poor to appreciate the social conditions which in the existing order they were designed to fill."[45]

In spite of the existing conditions described above—that is, education as the bare minimum for the working class, education not essential to the economy, the abject poverty of the working class, the insistence of class structures—many humanitarian and philanthropic causes worked to improve educational standards. Binns, Evans, and Cubberley pointed out that this was the age of philanthropy and humanitarianism.[46,47,48] Charity schools had already been founded in the seventeenth century and saw continuous growth. Because the wealthy, were anxious to keep the ranks of the poor in disciplined order, they willingly gave donations for such education, particularly as it stressed religious instruction.[49] Binns stated that there were, at this time, probably one thousand endowed schools and sixteen hundred charity schools in England.[50]

Other schools functioned on the voluntary system, and of these, the Sunday school movement figures most importantly. It was an attempt to control the vast number of poor children during the hours they were not working. Rudimentary instruction in secular education was meager, but religious instruction assumed a position of foremost importance. Attention focused on Bible study. "The various religious bodies, who provided most of the formal education available for the working class, were quite explicit on what kind of education should be provided because they had a very clear goal at which to aim. Their schools were provided for religious purposes."[51]

Many of the factors that have been discussed influenced the growth of universal education, and, eventually, the state attempted to intervene in education. The first act of intervention was passed in 1802. It dictated that factory owners were to provide instruction in the three Rs and were to ensure some religious teaching for an hour every Sunday.[52,53] "An interesting point to note is that here education was defined as a state responsibility only inasmuch as parliament should make the rules by which it was to be supplied."[54] Gradually, during the century, state involvement grew, but at this point, education for the working class and the poor was dominated by voluntary, charitable, and philanthropic organizations. Because the monitorial movement directly concerned the education of the masses, it is important to understand that context.

In the grammar schools of the time, the classics remained the basic curriculum, although history and geography were not always omitted. Private schools flourished, and these offered a more realistic, utilitarian approach through a broader curriculum.[55] These schools were largely attended by the middle and upper classes, and the monitorial movement had little connection with these schools.

Because of the growing demand for education for the working classes and the poor, a counterdemand evolved, which indicated that "the education provided should be systematized, economical, and should not teach too much. Such a system of training was now discovered and applied, in the form of mutual or monitorial instruction."[56]

Evans pointed out two of the fundamental problems that faced efforts to expand elementary education: shortage of money and shortage of teachers. The monitorial movement became the answer in meeting both these needs.[57]

Conditions in America

In the United States, there was little interest in or consciousness of education before about 1820. There were a few provisions for education in some state constitutions, but education was left largely to churches, private endeavors, and schools for the poor provided either by some private or state funds.[58]

Some reasons for this state of affairs paralleled similar conditions in England. Class distinctions were still strong, and views held by both classes hampered the growth and interest in public schools. Knight pointed out some of the prevalent thoughts of the time:

The ancient doctrine that the education of the masses would be dangerous to society was still generally held in high esteem by the classes. And the poor believed that public education would stamp them as paupers. Opposition appeared also on the part of sectarian interests, which feared that their own religious schools would be replaced. Many thoughtful people viewed education by the State as an invasion of the parental and family function.[59]

Various other factors affected educational views in the early nineteenth century. In the first decades, the control of education was left in the hands of the leaders. But gradually interest in education increased, as the idea became prevalent that education was essential for the good of the nation, and the people began to exercise more control. Interest in education increased, and this time period saw "the acceptance of the belief that national welfare and perpetuity are dependent upon the dissemination of intelligence and that the nation itself is responsible for the education thus necessitated."[60]

At the turn of the century, the lack of interest in education was also the result of the diversity in population. In 1790, nine out of ten persons were concerned with agriculture, and agricultural life led to isolation and independence. But the Industrial Revolution stimulated the growth of cities, which eventually developed an economic demand for education.

The sparsely settled territories caused problems in communication and transportation. The means by which communication could be carried out were meager, and the methods of transportation were not conducive to much travel. With this in mind, it is obvious that people could hardly be unified in idea or purpose, and major reforms were impossible.

The Revolutionary War and the beginning of a new nation did not immediately bring about great educational changes because the energies of the people, "almost exhausted by the war, were absorbed in more immediate pressing needs."[61] "The emphasis on individualism was too strong, the interest in new political and economic developments appealed too powerfully to the efforts of a newly liberated people."[62] Democracy still had to be developed even if the government was based on democratic ideals. Consequently, the working out of popular and free education had to wait for the full development of democracy in action rather than in ideal. "Self-government, now to be given a trial, was also to become educative in character. New demands for schools, which came slowly to be viewed as necessary, were to arise out of new problems of public welfare."[63]

In the first decades of the nineteenth century, the schools of the United States saw little reform. Most of them were still ungraded, one-room, one-teacher schools, with inadequate equipment, poorly trained teachers, and few materials. "The aim of course after course was the digestion of knowledge embodied in a text-book, and all too often meaning and practical application was subordinated to, if not displaced by, simple memorizing."[64] The curriculum usually consisted of rudimentary instruction in reading, writing, and arithmetic, with most of it being conducted on the individual basis.

Discipline was usually severe. When the fact is considered that students of considerable age differences were confined to one small room, often supervised by an inadequately trained teacher, it can be seen that discipline was perhaps the first and last resort to retain some semblance of order.[65]

Adding to the difficulties of maintaining a school were the problems of poor school-building construction. "Inadequate facilities only increased the discomfort of all concerned. Many a schoolroom was dangerously cold in the winter and vice versa in the summer; while an insufficient number of seats or an uncomfortable supply aggravated discomfort."[66]

The social-class structure reflected itself in the schools. The vernacular elementary school served the lower classes, while the Latin secondary school was attended by the upper classes. The American academy made its appearance at this time and served as a transitional institution from the Latin school to the public high school. "It gave opportunity to that middle class of pupils who could afford the time and cost of some schooling above the elementary but who were in many cases not preparing for college."[67]

Education was not, at this time, a function of the state. It can be seen that "even our forefathers of this period, outside of New England, scarcely considered elementary education to be a function of the State but would leave it to private initiative or local interest."[68] "The conception of education as a national process and a national force was a slow development of this early National period."[69] Education, for the most part, was the domain of churches, private individuals, incorporated school societies, and some schools for the poor provided for by state or private funds.[70]

As the forces of democracy and nationalism increased, the demands that schools exercise their patriotic duty also increased. Arguments were heard that widespread schooling would increase economic prosperity by raising the productivity of the people. Also, universal education would prevent poverty, diminish crime, and, most important, education was the natural right of each individual, and the nation should provide it for all people.[71] As the century progressed, universal public education gradually became a reality.

It is not difficult to see why monitorial instruction was widely accepted in the United States at the turn of the century. This method of instruction "made wide appeal chiefly because it promised a royal road to learning through inexpensive methods of teaching."[72] The number of children needing to be taught increased, students were gradually divided into classes, and the monitorial method made it possible to handle a large number of children in one school at a small cost.[73] Monroe pointed out several features that made this system popular, particularly in the towns and cities that were increasing in size. "It was an elaborate social machine, and mechanical devices of all kinds were then in vogue. The new democracy, as yet an experiment, put great faith in such governmental machinery. There was a general belief that most social ills could be thus cured."[74]

The monitorial instruction methods actually aided in the development of universal popular education because of the economy of the plan. Eggertsen stated that "in some cities it costs only a little more than a dollar a year a pupil for teaching on the monitorial system."[75]

Conditions in France

Of the countries on the European continent, France exhibited the most interest in the use of monitorial instruction. Perhaps this was partially a result of its own legacy of peer teaching, particularly in the century prior to the French Revolution. Other countries on the Continent adopted the monitorial system, but many of these did so largely because of the efforts of the British and Foreign School Society.

Prior to the French Revolution, most schooling had been conducted through the Catholic church. At the time of the Revolution in 1789, illiteracy remained high—75 percent of the women and 50 percent of the men were illiterate. Free schooling did not exist, nor were funds available for free education. Child labor also prevented much widespread schooling.[76]

Arnold, writing a half century after the close of the Revolution, indicated uncertainty as to the state of education in France before the Revolution. "The era approached from which dates a wholly new history for France; and it is impossible to determine accurately in what state the Revolution of 1789 found the instruction of those masses, on whom it was to confer such unbounded power."[77]

He indicated that, although schools run by religious organizations existed, and a few village schools could be found, "the instruction of the mass of the poor remained very nearly what it had been in the middle ages."[78] In this context, it should be remembered that the activities of the Jesuits and the Christian Brothers continued until they were suppressed by the Revolution. Male pointed out that, although the eighteenth century was known as the "age of reason," "French education up to the eve of the French Revolution remained under the control of the clergy."[79]

"The Revolution presented itself with magnificent promises of universal education."[80] Plans were proposed by Talleyrand, Condorcet, Mirabeau, and others. The idea was that "education should be organized by the State, should be secular, and open to all."[81] However, the programs proposed as a result of the Revolution did not take place quickly. Good explained the reasons: "The disorder of the times, the lack of resources and of an effective tax system, the lack of professional lay teachers, and the absence of a national educational consciousness delayed the establishment of universal free education for almost a century."[82] Male pointed out that "the Legislative Assembly was too engrossed in other considerations to carry through a major educational reform."[83]

When Napoleon came to power, the educational conditions were chaotic. The results of the Revolution had left France virtually without schools for about ten years.[84] Napoleon's interests lay mainly with secondary education and the training of leaders. However, he did make some provision for primary education.

Napoleon established the Imperial University, a system of administration for all grades of school. "Its functions were to govern the schools, appoint the teachers, disburse the funds, and set the school examinations."[85] Primary education was delegated to the private and church groups, now allowed to function once again, but controlled by the government. "To commit the primary instruction of France to religious corporations was at no time the intention of Napoleon. To avail himself of the services of these corporations, under the control of a lay body . . . he was abundantly willing."[86] This lay body was the Imperial University.

The Restoration government of 1815 to 1830 aided the progress of education by providing funding. "The very small annual appropriations were gradually increased and by 1830 somewhat more than half of the thirty-seven thousand communes (or townships) had established primary schools."[87] Cubberley pointed out that during the Restoration, "what had been provided was retained, and there seems to have been an increasing demand for additions and improvements, particularly in the matter of primary and middle-class schools."[88] This was the time during which monitorial schools, or *instruction mutuelle*, was introduced in France.

NOTES

1. H. G. Good, *A History of Western Education* (New York: The Macmillan Co., 1947), p. 201.
2. Ibid.
3. Ibid., p. 202.
4. H. C. Barnard, *A Short History of English Education from 1760–1944* (London: University of London Press, Ltd., 1949), p. 38.
5. Pamela Silver and Harold Silver, *The Education of the Poor: The History of a National School, 1824–1974* (London: Routledge and Kegan Paul, 1974), p. 17.

6. Ibid., p. 7.
7. W. A. C. Stewart and W. P. McCann, *The Educational Innovators, 1750–1880* (New York: St. Martin's Press, 1967), p. 38.
8. Ibid., p. 39.
9. Ibid., p. 14.
10. Ibid., p. 19.
11. James Plumptre, *The Way in Which We Should Go: A Sermon* (Cambridge, England: Francis Hodson, 1809), p. 20.
12. W. A. Campbell Stewart, *Quakers and Education* (London: The Epworth Press, 1953), p. 49.
13. Ibid., p. 88.
14. Phil E. Hager, "Nineteenth Century Experiments with Monitorial Teaching, *Phi Delta Kappan* 40 (January 1959).
15. David Salmon, "Monitorial System," *A Cyclopedia of Education* vol. 4, ed. P. Monroe (New York: The Macmillan Co., 1913).
16. "Monitorial System," *American Journal of Education* 10 (June 1861).
17. Salmon, "Monitorial System."
18. Frederic E. Farrington, "Maintenon (Mme. de), Francoise D'Aubigne, Marquise de Maintenon," *A Cyclopedia of Education*, vol. 4, ed. P. Monroe (New York: The Macmillan Co., 1913).
19. Hager, "Nineteenth Century Experiments."
20. Salmon, "Monitorial System."
21. "Monitorial System."
22. Hager, "Nineteenth Century Experiments."
23. Salmon, "Monitorial System."
24. "Monitorial System."
25. Ibid., p. 464.
26. Alexandre de Laborde, *Plan d'Education* (Londres: Berthoud et Wheatley, 1815), pp. 4–13.
27. Edgar W. Knight, *Twenty Centuries of Education* (Boston: Ginn and Co., 1940), p. 235.
28. Ellwood P. Cubberley, *The History of Education* (Boston: Houghton Mifflin Co., 1920), p. 655.
29. P. W. Musgrave, *Society and Education in England Since 1800* (London: Methuen and Co., Ltd., 1968), Chapter 2.
30. Barnard, *A Short History of English Education*, Introduction.
31. Eric Midwinter, *Nineteenth Century Education* (New York: Harper and Row, Publishers, 1970), p. 13.
32. Barnard, *A Short History of English Education*, p. xvi.
33. A. E. Dobbs, *Education and Social Movements, 1700–1850* (London: Longmans, Green, and Co., 1919), p. 46.
34. Midwinter, *Nineteenth Century Education*, p. 11.
35. Henry Bryan Binns, *A Century of Education* (London: J. M. Dent and Co., 1908), p. 3.
36. Keith Evans, *The Development and Structure of the English Educational System* (London: University of London Press, Ltd., 1975), p. 6.
37. Good, *A History of Western Education*, p. 348.

38. Cubberley, *The History of Education*, p. 620.
39. Evans, *The Development and Structure*, p. 15.
40. Ibid., p. 6.
41. Musgrave, *Society and Education*.
42. Evans, *The Development and Structure*, p. 6.
43. Musgrave, *Society and Education*, p. 11.
44. Ibid., p. 7.
45. Binns, *A Century of Education*, p. 5.
46. Ibid., p. 4.
47. Evans, *The Development and Structure*, p. 16.
48. Cubberley, *The History of Education*, Chapter 24.
49. Midwinter, *Nineteenth Century Education*, Chapter 2.
50. Binns, *A Century of Education* p. 4.
51. Musgrave, *Society and Education*, p. 11.
52. Ibid.
53. John William Adamson, *A Short History of Education* (London: Cambridge University Press, 1919).
54. Musgrave, *Society and Education*, p. 6.
55. S. J. Curtis and M. E. A. Boultwood, *An Introductory History of English Education Since 1800* (London: University Tutorial Press, Ltd., 1962), p. 105.
56. Cubberley, *The History of Education*, p. 624.
57. Evans, *The Development and Structure*, p. 17.
58. Ellwood P. Cubberley, *Public Education in the United States* (Boston: Houghton Mifflin Co., 1934), Chapter 24.
59. Knight, *Twenty Centuries of Education*, p. 245.
60. Paul Monroe, *Founding of the American Public School System*, vol. 1 (New York: The Macmillan Co., 1940), p. 187.
61. Edgar W. Knight, *Education in the United States* (Boston: Ginn and Co., 1929), p. 136.
62. Monroe, *Founding of the American Public School System*, pp. 204–5.
63. Knight, *Education in the United States*, p. 138.
64. Freeman R. Butts and Lawrence Cremin, *A History of Education in American Culture* (New York: Henry Holt and Co., 1953), p. 274.
65. Ibid., 274–75.
66. Ibid., p. 275.
67. H. G. Good, *A History of American Education* (New York: The Macmillan Co., 1956), p. 111.
68. Monroe, *Founding of the American Public School System*, p. 211.
69. Ibid., p. 205.
70. Cubberley, *Public Education*.
71. Butts and Cremin, *A History of Education*.
72. Edgar W. Knight and Clifton L. Hall, *Readings in American Educational History* (New York: Appleton-Century-Crofts, Inc., 1951), p. 133.
73. Butts and Cremin, *A History of Education*, pp. 274–75.
74. Monroe, *Founding of the American Public School System*, p. 363.
75. C. A. Eggertsen, "The Monitorial System of Instruction in the United States" (Doctoral diss., University of Minnesota, 1939), p. 76.

76. George A. Male, *Education in France* (Washington, D.C.: U.S. Department of Health, Education, and Welfare, 1963), p. 7.

77. Matthew Arnold, *Popular Education in France* (London: Longmans, Green, Longmans, and Roberts, 1861), p. 20.

78. Ibid., p. 21.

79. Male, *Education in France*, p. 8.

80. Arnold, *Popular Education in France*, p. 22.

81. Male, *Education in France*, p. 8.

82. Good, *A History of Western Education*, p. 296.

83. Male, *Education in France*, p. 8.

84. Ibid., p. 9.

85. Good, *A History of Western Education*, p. 297.

86. Arnold, *Popular Education in France*, p. 33.

87. Good, *A History of Western Education*, p. 298.

88. Cubberley, *The History of Education*, p. 596.

CHAPTER 4

Developments in Nineteenth-Century England

INTRODUCTION

The first forty years of the nineteenth century saw great efforts to promote education among the lower classes in England. As was discussed in Chapter 3, there were various substantive reasons for these educational efforts.

The French Revolution caused much alarm in England. "The nobility became justly alarmed lest the contagion of the French Revolution should spread to their shores. For the first time they seemed to have some appreciation of the extent of the ignorance and viciousness which were in their midst."[1] The nobility felt the vulnerability of their position if rank and wealth and intelligence were to lose their prestige. Consequently, there existed a widespread feeling among the upper class that much should be done to promote intelligence and reverence among the social classes where they had not existed.[2]

On the other hand, the events in France caused an opposite view toward education. Many who were inclined to help the poor in other ways saw the education of this class as a distinct danger, even to the extent of viewing elementary reading and writing instruction as harmful. "Sir Thomas Bernard described how the Society for Bettering the Condition of the Poor was founded at a time when 'the horrors of the French Revolution had renewed the prejudices against any general system of education.' "[3]

This concept of education of the poor was partly reflected by the philanthropists and humanitarians of the early nineteenth century.

"Every member of the middle class about 1800 was a philanthropist in thought if not in deed."[4] Most of these individuals felt that the children of the early nineteenth century, products of the Industrial Revolution, had to be guided through life by the efforts of the schools.[5] Their aim of education was, in general, limited "to teaching the children of the poor 'sufficient,' to influencing their behaviour without raising their aspirations beyond 'their proper stations.' "[6]

The great impact of the Industrial Revolution must be remembered for it brought about a new class of people, an industrial class, and this new class included the poverty-stricken of that age.

Along with industrialization came a great growth in population as well as a shifting in its density. The enclosures of land and the increasing competition of machinery drove men from the country into the towns; the centres of population were altered from the old agricultural south to what was becoming the industrial north. The increase in the population during the early years of the nineteenth century was striking.[7]

The industrialization of England brought about many problems: factory conditions, sanitation, housing, religion, and education.

The position of the church was weakened as the population concentrated around industrial centers, and "the education movement sponsored mainly by the churches at the beginning of the nineteenth century was built on a sense of urgency in the face of social and political danger."[8] Much was said about the "proper stations" of the poor, as is exhibited by the words of the National Society regarding the purpose for its establishment.

The sole object in view being to communicate to the poor generally, by the means of a summary mode of education, lately brought into practice, such knowledge and habits, as are sufficient to guide them through life, in their proper stations, especially to teach the doctrines of Religion, according to the principles of the Established Church, and to train them to the performance of their religious duties by early discipline.[9]

Consequently, a prevalent view of education was that it should be given as required for religious purposes, particularly for the reading of the Scriptures. "Early educational enthusiasts . . . were quick to see that the traditional social values might be safeguarded by giving the children of the labouring poor a godly and religious upbringing."[10] The matter of religion in education, however, was to become a most volatile one, and a controversy centering around the monitorial system and its relation to religion took place in the early nineteenth century.

In contrast to the religious views of education, the utilitarian philosophy was that "education was necessary for social and political ends," and the utilitarians wished to keep education free from religious teaching.[11] Utilitarianism was a dominant, influential philosophical view during the nineteenth century. Leading utilitarians such as Jeremy Bentham and James Mill espoused the monitorial movement in that it met a practical need.[12]

As a consequence of these influences, the educational needs of children of the masses received far greater attention than in previous centuries.[13] Voluntary efforts, however, were hampered by insufficient funds, and the state took no part in the educational efforts. The lack of finances, the large number of children needing education, and the scarcity of teachers, combined with social and economic influences, brought about the widespread support of an ingenious and economical system for educating the vast numbers of poor children.[14,15] This new system of schooling corresponded well with the industrial influence of the time. The system "was not unlike the new factory both in appearance and in method."[16] In view of these influences, it is not difficult to see why peer teaching, as exemplified in the monitorial systems of Lancaster and Bell, achieved such notoriety and made such great headway in the early decades of the nineteenth century.

JOSEPH LANCASTER AND THE MONITORIAL SYSTEM

Lancaster and His Early Educational Efforts

Joseph Lancaster was born in Southwark, England, in 1778. His father had been a British soldier in the American Revolution and was now a sieve maker. Early in his life, Lancaster exhibited an enthusiasm for educating the poor as well as a leaning toward religious influences. At the age of fourteen, moved by an essay on slave trade, he ran away from home and intended to go to Jamaica to teach the poor blacks to read the Bible. He was duly returned home by the captain of the ship. After that experience, he entertained the idea of becoming a Dissenting minister but was subsequently attracted to the Society of Friends. At the age of twenty he joined the Quakers. He then followed his inclination toward teaching and was an usher in a boarding school and subsequently in a day school.[17,18,19,20]

Lancaster was not satisfied with teaching in a school and wished to establish a school of his own. In 1798, he began a school for poor children in his father's home in London. His fees were extremely small, and he attracted a large number of pupils. He soon outgrew his quarters and in 1801, established a school on Borough Road. "Lancaster had many of the qualities of a great schoolmaster— enthusiasm, self-confidence, ingenuity in devising methods, insight into the nature of children, an ardent love for them, and rare power of managing them."[21]

His expenses invariably exceeded his income, and he was forced, because of the vast number of students that came to him, to solicit subscribers. Darton described him as "a poor man, and a desperately bad financier, though the best beggar in the world."[22] Because he was too indigent to pay for assistants and because he found the old methods of teaching inadequate, the idea occurred to him that boys who knew a little could teach those who knew less. David Salmon assumed that the idea probably occurred to him in 1800, and when Lancaster published the first and second editions of his *Improvements*, he had done little other than to utilize the basic monitorial concept of one student teaching another.[23] By 1805, with the third edition of *Improvements*, however, "he had evolved not only a new kind of teacher but also a new kind of teaching and a new kind of school management."[24] He knew nothing of previous attempts in peer teaching, even in England, and claimed he had discovered a new method of teaching, one that cost little.[25]

This novel plan of educating the poor aroused much curiosity and interest. The list of Lancaster's visitors grew. Lancaster said:

The school soon excited much attention and enquiry; visitors not satisfied with seeing, were anxious to take home some outlines of the system in print. Foreign princes, ambassadors, peers, commoners, ladies of distinction, bishops and archbishops, Jews and Turks, all visited the school with "wonder waiting eyes," and were equally desirous of carrying home a memorial of the interesting scenes they had witnessed. This led to a publication which had an extensive demand.[26]

Lancaster's fame grew, and in 1805, he met George III at Weymouth, the interview having been arranged by William Corston, one of the eventual founders of the British and Foreign School Society.[27] Lancaster gave an account of his educational system, presented the king with a copy of the third edition of *Improvements*, and received the pledged financial support of the royal family. From this meeting* came the well-known endorsement by George III: "I highly approve of your system and it is my wish that every poor child in my dominions should be taught to read the Bible; I will do anything you wish to promote this object."[28]

Lancaster wrote of this meeting:

The personal virtues and mind of the late king of England, George the third, were much in character like an American aloe; long in growing, longer in blowing, but blooming in beauty at last. Towards the close of a long reign, piety eminently enthroned itself in his heart, and his good wishes for his people. . . . He became the author's friend and patron, he placed his own name at the head of the list of subscribers, and influenced his family.[29]

This royal patronage confirmed Lancaster's belief of the magnitude of his discovery, and, already an unwise and prolific spender, he now spent more money in the promotion of his method of education. Salmon wrote that "his recklessness [in spending money], his extravagance, and his ostentation almost pass belief."[30] He was arrested for debt but released on a technicality. He then built two schools and a training school, established a printing press, and built

---

*William Corston, in a short biography of Lancaster, preserved an account of this meeting, which can be found in "Joseph Lancaster," *American Journal of Education*, 1861, and Binns, 1908. Copies of Corston's biography are extremely rare and virtually unattainable.

a factory for making slates.[31] These enterprises plunged him further into debt.

His inability to handle money and his personal extravagance are often mentioned. The *Edinburgh Review* listed a detailed account of his dismal financial condition and stated, "Such was the almost hopeless state of his finances early in 1808, notwithstanding the respectable patronage which he enjoyed, and the rapid progress which his great plan was making."[32] Lancaster himself appeared to be less concerned about this problem. He said:

In this pursuit great have been the personal sacrifices required of the author; but the goodness of the cause has stimulated him cheerfully to make them. Happily for the public, his efforts have been successful; and not only thousands of children are educating, but preparations are making for that of tens of thousands, to their welfare, and the satisfaction of all that love their country.[33]

Eventually, his supporters helped him liquidate his debts and formed the Royal Lancasterian Society, which later became the British and Foreign School Society.

Lancasterian Methods and Views on Education

Among the various educational agencies which were the outgrowth of the times, none was more prominent than what is known as the mutual, the monitorial, or the Lancastrian* system of instruction. It was a scheme without any foundation in philosophy, and not deserving to be called a method; and yet it was the object of an incredible amount of enthusiasm, scholars and statesmen expressing, in large public meetings and learned reviews, most extravagant praise and expectations of its results.[34]

The essence of the system was the monitor. The school was conducted by the pupils themselves. "The master instructed the monitors, who then drilled that instruction into their fellow-pupils;

---

*Both spellings, "Lancasterian" and "Lancastrian," are found in the literature related to Lancaster. He preferred the use of "Lancasterian," while it appears that "Lancastrian" was merely adopted by some as a convenience. In this paper, unless "Lancastrian" is found in a direct quotation, the spelling "Lancasterian" will be used.

the system is well described by the term familiar to its continental imitators, 'the Mutual System.' "[35] Lancaster said, "The qualification of a monitor in points of knowledge is simply to know 1st the thing to be taught—2nd the mode of teaching it."[36] "The whole school is arranged in classes; a monitor is appointed to each, who is responsible for the cleanliness, order, and improvement. of every boy in it. . . . The proportion of boys who teach, either in reading, writing, or arithmetic, is as one to ten."[37] Sidney Smith pointed out in the *Edinburgh Review* in 1807 that if there were a thousand boys, there was only one master, and the rest of the teaching was conducted by the students themselves.[38] Lancaster maintained that "a master cannot train too many monitors—if all the boys in the school were qualified to be monitors the minor class excepted, it would conduce to their own improvement."[39]

Two fundamental points in conducting a monitorial school were order and emulation.[40] Sidney Smith, in the *Edinburgh Review*, said that

it is obvious that a school like this of Mr. Lancaster's consisting of from 700 to 800 boys, would soon fall into decay, without very close attention to order and method. In this part of his system, Mr. Lancaster has been as eminently successful as in any other; contriving to make the method and arrangement, so necessary to his institution, a source of amusement to the children.[41]

Dunn described what he called a scene that visitors were not likely to forget. It was an orderly spectacle, and although the noise may have been bewildering to an observer, it was at least the noise of work, and instant quiet could be had by a mere command.[42] Salmon, however, maintained that order and quiet were not synonymous, and though claims could be made about the orderliness of the monitorial school, it must have indeed been noisy. He quoted a Mr. Baines of Carshalton, who was reminiscing as he visited the Borough Road School.

I cannot help comparing the aspect of this room with what is was thirty-seven years ago. Then I was a student here. . . . Round the room were six hundred or seven hundred boys in little drafts, singing "L-e-a-p, leap to jump." The babel was such that I remember on one occasion trying if I should be heard singing "Black-eyed Susan." I sang and no one noticed me. . . . I was Monitor of Order at the time.[43]

The system of management Lancaster used resembled a military concept of order. Children were taught a series of commands that regulated the functions of the school. Lancaster acknowledged that he relied on rewards and emulation in his system. A monitor was honored for superior work. Students were ranked by a leather ticket suspended from a buttonhole, and if a mistake was made, the boy's place and rank had to be surrendered. Many prizes were delivered for exceptional work.

Because he abhorred the cruel corporal punishment that usually existed, his system of discipline involved an elaborate series of punishments based more on ridicule and a fitting punishment to suit the crime than on physical force. He also had an elaborate series of rewards for behaviors, which were considered a deterrent to misbehavior. Sidney Smith wrote in the *Edinburgh Review* in 1807, "Mr. Lancaster punishes by shame rather than pain; varying the means of exciting shame, because as he justly observes, any mode of punishment long continued loses its effect."[44]

Lancaster himself greatly stressed the economy of his method. He said that the expense of educating a child was estimated to be one guinea per annum. "This economical plan of usefully educating a thousand scholars is done at a much less expence than any of my friends ever expected me to reduce to practice."[45] Salmon concluded that "the fact that the monitorial system, so often abandoned elsewhere after a brief trial in one or two institutions, should have flourished throughout the British Islands for some forty years may be attributed to its cheapness."[46] The initial cost was small since only a bare, simply furnished room was required. Pupils stood for most of the lessons, and materials were often copied on large posters. Students did not have books of their own; Lancaster at first used sand for students to practice writing, and only later introduced slates.

Lancaster believed that "above all things, education ought not to be subservient to the propagation of the peculiar tenets of any sect."[47] He also wrote, "I desire to avoid making the education given to such a large number of children in my institution, a means of instilling my own *peculiar* religious tenets into their minds, and prefer the more noble grounds which I have recommended."[48] He advocated teaching children to read the Bible but carefully avoided introduction of theological matters "so that the religious prejudices of the parents might not be offended."[49] It was because of these views that contention arose over the monitorial system, causing the establishment of separate educational societies.

Though aided by subscriptions and funds from his friends, Lancaster maintained that education for the poor ought to become a national concern. He said:

The rich possess ample means to realize any theory they may chuse to adopt in the education of their children, regardless of the cost; but it is not so with him whose subsistence is derived from industry: ignorance and incapacity often prevent his having proper views on the important subject of education, and when he has, slender resources as often prevent their being reduced to practice.[50]

Lancaster himself did little to further the cause of state-supported national education, yet his system paved the way for the eventual establishment of such a concept.

Lancaster expounded on his method and views of education in numerous publications. "Between the years 1803 and 1810 Lancaster published nine new works and half a dozen new editions."[51] The first book was entitled *Improvements in Education, as it respects the Industrious Classes of the Community: containing among other important particulars, An Account of the Institutions for the Education of One Thousand Poor Children, Borough Road, Southwark; and of the New System of Education in which it is conducted.* This became the most important of his writings, and, although he continued to expound on his method, no great changes were made in subsequent editions.[52]

LANCASTER'S FINANCIAL PROBLEMS AND THE FORMATION OF THE BRITISH AND FOREIGN SCHOOL SOCIETY

Between 1805 and 1808, Lancaster made extensive journeys to cities and towns, superintending the establishment of schools and arousing the interest of the citizens. His subscription lists now included supporters like Jeremy Bentham, James Mill, Henry Brougham, Josiah Wedgwood, and other "enlightened Liberals in the country, many Broad Churchmen, and most of the Nonconformist philanthropists."[53] However, the sums coming in were inadequate, largely because "he had not the vaguest notion of finance or economy."[54] Lancaster "was no man of business; and he was also extravagant and given to display."[55]

Friends now came to his aid. These were men who had already been interested in his work and who now were willing to assume his debts plus carry on the work of the school on Borough Road and other educational efforts. A committee of his creditors examined his affairs and were satisfied with his honesty. The *Edinburgh Review*, a supporter of Lancaster and his monitorial system, quoted from one of the reports of the committee of creditors and gave the following as a reason for doing so: "because this passage offers one of the most affecting pictures any where to be found, of virtuous industry, and honest, enlightened zeal, struggling against the hard necessities of a poverty occasioned by excess of charity and benevolence."[56]

Among the most influential men in rescuing Lancaster from his overwhelming debts was Joseph Fox.* Fox was a young surgeon-dentist, "not less eminent for his professional skill, than for his extensive and diversified benevolence."[57] He had heard Lancaster lecture and was much impressed. He subsequently introduced to Lancaster by William Corston, and the three men discussed Lancaster's affairs. Fox and Corston, a hat maker and a Moravian who had long been an advocate of education for poor children, formed a society dedicated to relieving Lancaster of his financial dilemma, thus making it possible for Lancaster's educational work to continue. Corston was appointed treasurer and Fox was secretary, while Lancaster was to superintend the education in all schools connected with the newly formed society as well as edit publications.[58] Soon after this arrangement, Fox and Corston were joined by four others: William Allen, who apparently assumed the position of treasurer that same year, John Jackson, a member of Parliament, Joseph Foster, and Thomas Sturge.[59] "From this time the accounts were properly kept, the trustees holding themselves responsible to the public."[60] The society took the name of Royal Lancasterian Institution for Promoting the Education of the Children of the Poor. "Lancaster's work from this time forward ceased to be the effort of

---

*Biographical sketches of the three staunchest and most loyal supporters of Lancaster—Joseph Fox, William Corston, and William Allen—are found in the *American Journal of Education*, 1861.

an individual; it had begun to take on the character of a movement."[61]

Lancaster continued his lecture tour, but, as Dunn pointed out, he remained unchanged. "He was still the victim of his impulses. The excitement of his mind never subsided. The repression of his extravagance was to him an intolerable interference. One by one he quarrelled with his friends."[62] In July 1810, the committee of the society found that debts were increasing while the work was spreading. The formation of a larger committee was necessary. They sought cooperation from "benevolent persons whose situations in life give them influence in order . . . to place the establishment upon a permanent footing."[63] Lancaster did not consent to this larger group, but, by this time, matters were out of his hands. "The Committee realised that the money it collected was given to it for the promotion of education; Lancaster thought that it was given to him for his own use—that the Committee had the privilege of increasing his income but not the right of regulating his expenditure."[64]

Donations began to increase, and the new support was encouraging to the committee. On May 17, 1811, the first anniversary dinner was held at the Freemason's Tavern, and the duke of Kent, a strong supporter and subscriber, presided. From this occasion comes a sample of the high esteem held by the public for the monitorial system and for Lancaster as well. Isaac Brandon wrote a poem that was recited at the dinner. Of monitorial instruction, he said:

O bless'd Instruction! now thy temples rise,
Virtue shall spring like incense to the skies!
Thy searching powers the mental mines explore
And gems of Genius shall be lost no more!
Each tender flower shall feel thy fostering care,
Nor waste its sweetness more on desert air!

Lancaster was included in the eulogy also.

Honour'd the man, and deathless be his name
Whose schools now rise his monuments of fame:
Marble will moulder, that his worth may trace
But these rever'd shall live from race to race![65]

Brandon referred to the progress both of the children in the monitorial schools and of the monitorial movement itself.

System of Genius! whose effect sublime
Seems to enlighten without aid of Time;
Like that vast engine's mighty speed and power
Which stamps the coin by myriads in an hour!

Lancaster's actions continued to astonish and confuse his supporters, and bitter disputes about his financial ventures finally brought about further changes in the organization of the society that had supported him. In 1813, the name of the society was changed to British and Foreign School Society. "That marks the final abandonment of the Lancasterian name, with which, and the undue emphasis it laid upon a single striking personality unfitted for national eminence, harm as well as good had been wrought."[67]

Lancaster complained that the committee had "usurped his glory and 'chowsed' him out of his property."[68] On April 16, 1814, he severed all connection with the society that had originally been founded for the propagation of his system of education. He later wrote bitterly about the friends who had attempted to help him. "Popularity and love of power, had induced *interested* men to render his [Lancaster's] institution pecuniary services, which they volunteered to administer."[69] He accused his friends of betraying him, "the unsuspecting." But then he said, "He triumphed over his enemies—carried on his work with success, and finally suffered by his confidence in false friends."[70]

The British and Foreign School Society continued to establish schools under the monitorial system. The society "was founded on the principle that the religious education of the children of the poor by day schools is a *social* duty of Christian citizens possessed of light and of means beyond the general body of their fellow countrymen."[71] The schools were open to children of any denomination. No distinctive religious instruction was given, although pupils were required to attend a Sunday worship service.[72] In 1839, the Committee of Council on Education was formed, and the British and Foreign School Society received a grant of 5,000 pounds to establish a normal school. The society expanded the school already established on Borough Road, where Lancaster had years before begun the training of his monitors at a model school.

In 1839, the society reported that they were "by no means disposed to bind themselves exclusively" to the monitorial system but would be willing to use other methods united with the monitorial system.[73] Eventually, this system was superceded by the pupil-teacher method.

ANDREW BELL AND THE MADRAS SYSTEM

Bell and the Development of the Madras System

Andrew Bell was born in St. Andrews, Scotland, in 1753. Dunn characterized him as "a plodding industrious boy, fond of his books, but hating school on account of the tyranny which he witnessed and endured. 'Oh, it was terrible'; he said, 'the remains of feudal severity. I never went to school without trembling; I could not tell whether I should be flogged or not.' "[74] In 1769, he entered the university of his city and, presumably, left with a degree. He sailed for Virginia in 1774 and, for several years, served as tutor to wealthy families. He "learned there, it is to be supposed, something of the skill in teaching which he afterwards showed."[75]

Bell returned to England in 1781 and, eventually, felt it advantageous to combine teaching with preaching. Through the aid of a friend who interceded for him, he was ordained as minister of the Church of England. After a short ministry in Leith, he felt there was no hope for advancement, so he decided to try India as a better place in which to accomplish his ambitions.

Although Bell's biographer, Robert Southey, stated that a friend thought it fitting that Bell be granted a doctor's degree from the University of St. Andrews so that he could be properly dignified for future success in India, other evidence indicates that Bell requested this honor himself.[76] He asked that he be distinguished with the honorable title of D.D. "His mind, he wrote, was above his fortune and above his birth, and the fees would be duly paid."[77] He was surprised and disappointed when the diploma granted was that of M.D., "a designation of questionable value to one who had neither pursued nor studied the art of medicine."[78] "It would have been some consolation for the new-made physician if he might have pre-scribed for them. As he could not have this pleasure he merely refrained from thanking them."[79]

Bell arrived in Madras, India, in 1787. Within a short time, he was appointed to several regimental chaplaincies, "all of which were accepted by the greedy pluralist without compunction."[80] Darton added his comment, "In Madras, it is to be feared, he became a pluralist chaplain."[81] Leitch offered the opinion that most of the offices to which he was appointed were sinecures, but none of them "sine salaries."[82] In addition to these duties, some of which were no doubt performed by proxy, he accepted the posi-tion of superintendent of the Military Male Asylum at Madras, a charity school and asylum for children of English soldiers and native wives. To his credit, Leitch said, "a good salary was offered to him but this . . . he firmly and persistently declined, as he considered the task of instructing the young to be one of his chief duties as a clergyman."[83]

Bell found much satisfaction in this position as manager and teacher. "He threw far more energy into his work than the masters liked. They had taken to teaching because they could not find any-thing better to do, and their incapacity was equalled only their obstinacy."[84] Bell noticed that the students appeared to be making little progress, and an unreasonably long time seemed to be spent in teaching their letters. One day he happened to pass a native school and saw the children tracing their letters in the sand spread before them on the ground. Immediately, he thought of this as a way to make the lessons more interesting as well as more convenient since no slate or copybook was needed. He determined to adopt this way of teaching. "His teachers, four in number, proved to be very obtuse in laying hold of the new device. But worse than all, they were quite stubborn, opposing the innovation and refusing to carry out the doctor's design."[85]

Since his teachers would not help him, he selected an eight-year-old boy to teach the others according to his ideas. John Frisken accomplished the job to the satisfaction of Dr. Bell, and soon the system spread. Bell eventually "dismissed his teachers and organ-ized the whole school under boy-instructors solely, who were them-selves taught by the superintendent."[86] The school prospered and became popular, even to the point that the government saw it as an economical way to teach in other schools.

Bell liked India. "Both the civil and military authorities were friendly; he liked his work; he was making money fast, and he thought the climate 'delightful.' "[87] But by 1794, he found that his health was being affected and he decided to return to England. Before leaving Madras, he presented an account of his work to the directors of the asylum, which was eventually published in London in 1797, entitled *An Experiment in Education, made at the Male Asylum, Madras; suggesting a System by which a School or Family may Teach itself under the Superintendence of the Master or Parent.*

The president of the charity that supported the school thought that the system was most beneficial and that it should be spread to other areas. The report by Bell was circulated, stressing that the "Military Male Orphan Asylum had flourished under *a system of tuition altogether new* . . . which they recommended as deserving the attention of those who interest themselves in the welfare of the rising generation."[88]

For some time, *An Experiment in Education* attracted little attention. "As a commerical transaction the pamphlet was a failure. The number sent with the author's compliments to men of position and influence must have exceeded the number sold."[89] The first school to adopt the system was St. Botolph's, a charity school in London. The system spread slowly, and Bell, now a rector at Swanage, was content to let it do so without much effort on his part. He remained at Swanage until approximately 1805, when he was drawn out by the controversy precipitated by Mrs. Trimmer.

In 1812, he was appointed superintendent of the schools organized by the National Society. He toured the Continent in 1816, "examining wherever he went any school considered exceptional and generally finding fault with what he saw."[90] On this journey, he visited Johann Pestalozzi at Yverdun, Switzerland, and one of the pupils of Pestalozzi, W. H. Ackermann, wrote a report of the visit. He recounted how Bell toured the school, but "nothing seemed to please him."[91] Whatever he observed, he condemned. "Thus it seemed impossible to give to the great pedagogue, who seemed boxed up in his own system, as much as an idea of the truth, that instead of giving his pupils an immense number of receipts, it was immeasurably better to develop their thinking power and power of application."[92] On the second day of the visit, Bell and Pestalozzi were to exchange their ideas on education in front of a large audience. Ackermann called them the "two most noted and dissimilar school men of their time; two schoolmasters of world-renown, as diametrically opposed to each other in their principles, as well as in their finances."[93]

Bell refused to accept, or even consider, Pestalozzi's principles of education, and maintained that his system was better. Upon leaving Yverdun the next day, Bell said to Ackermann, "Well, now I have seen the method of your Pestalozzi. Believe me, in twelve years from now nobody will speak of it; but mine will have spread all over the globe. Come back to me to England; you will make your fortune. With Pestalozzi's maxims and mode of teaching you will never succeed."[94]

Bell died in 1832 and was buried "where he wished and where he thought he ought to be, in Westminster Abbey."[95] He had been successful financially as well as professionally, and he bequeathed a large sum for the establishment of schools based on the Madras system, as well as for the foundation of a Madras College of St. Andrews.[96]

Bell's Methods and Views on Education

Soon after Bell returned to London, his first book, *An Experiment in Education*, was published in 1797. The book went through four editions, each increasing in length. Had not Lancaster's *Improvements in Education* appeared on the scene, it seems likely that Bell's first edition would have remained the only edition. However, as the controversy between the two systems of education grew, Bell felt obliged to continue publishing and adding to his book. Salmon outlined the progression of these volumes and their contents.[97]

By 1792, Bell's monitorial system had evolved to such a point that he was able to write from India and give details of his methods in letters to friends. These letters, preserved and organized by his biographer, Robert Southey, the poet laureate of England, and by Southey's son Charles, who completed the task begun by his father, indicate that, although Bell took great interest in his position as superintendent, there was no mention at first of any new or specific method of instruction. In May 1792, however, he wrote to Dr. Adamson of St. Andrews:

I believe I have mentioned the school with which I am charged. The orphans educated here are bound out to any art or trade by which they may be useful to themselves and society. We have already saved from perdition, and given to the world, a number of apprentices, clerks, apothecaries, sailors, mechanics, etc. In the course of two years I have had boys taught to speak, and write, and spell English, and to advance in arithmetic.[98]

Bell then continued his letter with the first comments on his new method: "The conduct of the school, which is entirely in my own hands, is particular. Every boy is either a master or a scholar, and generally both. He teachers one boy, while another teaches him. The success has been rapid."[99]

Bell wrote to Mr. Dempster describing what was taught in his school. "We profess to teach only to read, to write, to spell, and to cipher."[100] However, if a boy had progressed beyond the rudiments of instruction, Bell taught him bookkeeping, geometry, or whatever else the boy needed to fit him for a profession.

As Bell continued to work and improve his system, he became increasingly more aware of its importance, particularly as he perceived it. To a Dr. Rudd he wrote about the hardships he encountered in establishing the system, but he then added:

I have already seen its happy effects, and feel a pleasing consciousness of having done what has seldom been done—reared a work in some respects new, and differing from all institutions of the kind I know of—and having done this by means of such agents as are always at command. The progress of my pupils is beyond what you would believe in Europe.[101]

In this letter, Bell indicated the newness of his discovery. Later he wrote, "This System has no parallel in scholastic history."[102] However, Bell probably was unaware that the system had already been utilized in India much earlier. Sutton found that "the idea was already very old when Christian F. Schwartz, the revered missionary and educational advisor to the king in Tanjore, had organized such schools half a century before [Bell]."[103]

Bell's aim for educating the poor, for whom his system was at first devised, was to teach the rudiments of reading, writing, and arithmetic, and the ultimate object was "to make good scholars, good men, good subjects, and good Christians; in other words, to promote the temporal and spiritual welfare of our pupils."[104] Gill questioned those aims, however. The "rudiments of learning" were indeed rudimentary. As Gill stated, they "embraced only mechanical reading and writing, with some knowledge of the fundamental four."[105] Apparently, Bell thought it was sufficient for his students to learn to read the Bible. Gill pointed out that "it seems ludicrous in this connection to speak of 'good scholars,' when the ability to read the Bible well does not give the ability to read even a newspaper."[106]

Nevertheless, even though much criticism was directed to Bell's system in later years, the conditions under which he first established his system, and the students under his care, must be remembered. His great aim then was "to redeem the children from the stigma under which they laboured, and the fatal effect which that stigma produced, and to render them good subjects, good men and good Christians."[107]

Most of Bell's contemporaries would admit that he had a difficult task and that he had to work with the most unpromising materials. "It was an established opinion that the half-cast children were an inferior race, both in moral and intellectual faculties, as if a certain mulish obliquity of nature had been produced by crossing colours in the human species."[108]

Bell himself felt that his aim was being accomplished. He wrote his sister that he could not "conceal my joy and satisfaction in observing that since the late dereliction of our masters, the school has improved beyond what it had ever before done in the same period. . . . The more the boys teach themselves and one another, the greater I have always found their improvement."[109]

Later, Bell was to attach even greater significance to his system. His book in 1823, *Mutual Tuition and Moral Discipline,* stated that his system "is essentially discriminated from all others by the inherent principles. . . . It also differs materially from them in the laws by which it is regulated, and in the practices which it employs." He added, "Nor is it less strikingly distinguished by the results, which it has produced. Its success has been as remarkable, as its nature is popular. . . . No founder of any school, ancient or modern, ever lived to witness so wide a spread of his system."[110]

Bell's system consisted of a rather complex arrangement. "Each class is paired off into tutors and pupils. The tutor sits by the side of his pupil, and assists him in getting their common lesson."[111] Thus, the tutor assisted one child, with all children becoming tutors for the class below them. The assistants took charge of the class and aided the tutors and acted as examiners. The teacher had charge of the class and directed the activities of the assistant. They may have been responsible for one or more classes. The sub-ushers and ushers were to inspect the school and supervise the organization. The schoolmaster was to direct and conduct the entire system. Bell arranged his school into forms, or classes, "each composed of as many scholars as having made similar progress unite together. The scholar ever finds his own level, not only in his class, but in the ranks of the school."[112]

Bell continually stressed the basic fact on which his system was founded.

This system rests on the simple principle of tuition by the scholars themselves. It is its distinguishing characteristic that the school ... is taught solely by the pupils of the institution under a single master, who, if able and diligent, could, without difficulty, conduct ten contiguous schools, each consisting of a thousand scholars.[113]

In another volume, he again said, "To sum up the whole: The Madras System consists of conducting a school, by a single Master, through the medium of the scholars themselves."[114] He stressed that, by this means, the mind of the child would be exercised, his memory improved, and the scholar constantly busy, and happily so. The system would aid students in acquiring good habits of method, order, and good conduct, and allow them to work to their fullest capacity.

Nor did he fail to stress the economy of his system. He stated that his system, "of which economy forms a striking feature, brings along with it a strong recommendation to general circulation."[115] In another volume, he mentioned the "expeditious and cheap means, which it furnishes of training up the inferior orders of Society in moral and religious principles, and in habits of useful Industry."[116]

Bell remained convinced of the importance of his discovery. He wrote in 1823:

When the Madras Asylum was the only school on this system, the Author was wont to say, "You will mark me for an enthusiast; but if you and I live a thousand years, we shall see this System of Education spread over the world." Little did he then imagine that he should have lived to witness the progress already made towards the event to which he looked forward.[117]

MRS. TRIMMER AND THE GREAT CONTROVERSY

In 1804, Lancaster wrote to Bell with the intention of discussing various aspects of education. He presented a number of topics that he would like to discuss, asked for further information, and closed with, "It is with great respect I subscribe myself thy obliged friend and admirer."[118] Bell answered cordially, adding that he had heard of Lancaster's fame and progress.

Lancaster traveled to Swanage late that year and visited with Bell for several days. When the third edition of *Improvements in Education* was published in 1805, Lancaster said, "I am indebted to Doctor Bell, late of Madras, for the preceding information on the subject:* I have reduced it to practice, and find it does honour to its benevolent inventor; to which I have added several valuable improvements."[119]

Up to this point, the relations between Lancaster and Bell were friendly. "Lancaster might have continued to praise Bell for inventing the monitorial system, and Bell might have continued to praise Lancaster for showing the possibilities of such a system, but for the intervention of Mrs. Sarah Trimmer."[120] As Adamson wrote, "The two men were forced by circumstances into rivalry."[121]

Mrs. Sarah Trimmer, born in 1741, was about sixty years of age by this time. She had been an active promoter of Sunday schools, an author of a number of books for children, and editor of a magazine, *The Guardian of Education.*[122] Apparently, Mrs. Trimmer first became alarmed about Lancaster's increasing fame and notoriety as a result of Lancaster's audience with King George III in 1805 and the resulting comment made by the king, "It is my wish that every poor child in my dominions should be taught to read the Bible."[123] The fact that Lancaster had a policy of not teaching any particular creed alarmed Mrs. Trimmer even further.

Mrs. Trimmer began to correspond with Bell, stating that Lancaster was building on his foundation, that he should lay claim to

---

*Apparently, the subject of pronouncing syllables.

being the founder of the system, and that it should be introduced into the charity schools. Bell replied, giving an account of his meeting with Lancaster in December 1804, saying that Lancaster appeared to copy him on every point, and adding that he refused to become a subscriber to Lancaster's undertakings.[124] Mrs. Trimmer appealed to Bell's vanity, and it appeared to him, through her efforts, that he would be unfaithful to his church if he did not enter into the controversy and into attempts to establish his system in the schools.

Both Lancaster and Bell subsequently claimed to have invented the monitorial system. This issue, however, had no public interest until, through Mrs. Trimmer's efforts, it became "the occasion of a dispute between Church and Dissent, that attained great prominence in the press and in political and ecclesiastical society."[125] Jarman stated that "in reality the quarrel represented a deeper struggle between the Church of England and the Nonconformists for the control of education, a struggle which gravely hampered the work of making a national system."[126] Darton expressed the opinion that, in terms of public awareness, the matter "was not much more than an open wrangle over little points of priority" until Mrs. Trimmer intervened.[127]

The fact that these worthies worshiped in different churches, that the one followed the established Anglican rite, and was even an ordained Anglican man of God, while the other was a Quaker, bore inevitably on the controversy, turning it in the course of time into a war of sects as well as pedagogues."[128]

Following her correspondence with Bell, Mrs. Trimmer published *A Comparative View of the New Plan of Education* in 1805. She approved of the mechanical parts of Lancaster's plan and called it "so excellent a method," but she said that, because of her apprehensions, she required "deliberate consideration before it is adopted by the members of the Established Church, namely that which relates to Religion and Morals."[129] She could see merit in adopting Lancaster's system in the charity school because it might be applied to religious instruction. She criticized Lancaster's religious instruction because it only required the students to attend a church on Sunday. She said that "it should be remembered, that religious education is an EVERY DAY BUSINESS."[130] Children from the "lower orders" probably did not receive adequate guidance from their parents, and they could not possibly gain a comprehensive knowledge by attending church on Sunday only. This should be done consistently in the day schools.

Mrs. Trimmer also had strong views on the place of the poor in society. She argued that boys who were elevated in rank at Lancaster's schools through his system of rewards might become dangerous to society. By becoming nobles in a school, they might wish to, in the future, become nobles in society and take the place of the hereditary nobility.

"The publication of the *Comparative View* was the first overt act in a seven years' war."[131] Pamphlets, sermons, articles, and newspaper letters followed. The Whigs, Sidney Smith, and the *Edinburgh Review* sided with Lancaster and defended him. The *Quarterly Review*, the Tories, and the Anglican church sided with Mrs. Trimmer and defended Bell. In 1806, shortly after the appearance of *A Comparative View*, Smith wrote a review of the book that appeared in the *Edinburgh Review*. He called Mrs. Trimmer "cruel" and "silly" and said that the main reason for this book was "to prove that the church establishment is in danger, from the increase of Mr. Lancaster's institutions."[132] He denied that Lancaster's instruction "is any kind of impediment to the propagation of the doctrines of the church; and if Mr. Lancaster was to perish with his system to-morrow, these boys would positively be taught nothing; the doctrines which Mrs. Trimmer considers to be prohibited would not rush in, but there would be an absolute vacuum." He defended Lancaster by saying that in no Protestant country of the world had the education of the poor been so neglected, and Lancaster had called the attention of the public to this evil. He accused Mrs. Trimmer of denying that this evil existed. He further called her "uncandid and feeble" and said, "But our principal argument is, that Mr. Lancaster's plan is at least better than the *nothing* which preceded it. The authoress herself seems to be a lady of respectable opinions, and very ordinary talents; defending what is right without judgment, and believing what is holy without charity."[133]

In commenting on the situation, Lancaster wrote an opinion about Mrs. Trimmer, which he appended to a statement about the notoriety and public attention his method was receiving. He said that most of his ideas were accepted with

animation and delight, except one instance of bigotry in a poor aged female, who dreamed the church was in danger, and the bishops asleep at their posts, and therefore she strove mightily to awaken them to as much vigilance as would prevent any Quaker running away with the church steeple, though he might not know what to do with such an uncouth and cumbersome thing afterwards.[134]

Attacks on Lancaster's unsectarianism continued from the pulpit. In 1809, Reverend James Plumptre mentioned "two benevolent individuals" who "have had a most astonishing effect" on education.[135] He spoke favorably of Lancaster and his achievement and said, "We respect the benevolence, and the sincerity, and the piety of this good man; but we conceive him to be in an error, to which we cannot concede." In addition, "If he cannot assent to our creed, neither can we give it up, and assent to his."[136] Besides, this caused his system to be alien to the needs of the church.

The height of the dispute came in 1811. Mrs. Trimmer died in December 1810, but by now, the controversy had grown to such proportions that her demise caused no slackening of the dispute. Her role was assumed by the Cambridge Lady Margaret professor, Dr. Herbert Marsh. He saw Lancaster's plan as efficient, but in spirit and method, it was not congruent with what he thought the national plan should be. "The danger facing Anglicans was that 'children educated in such seminaries [the Lancasterian or British schools] would acquire an indifference to the Established Church.' "[137]

Dr. Marsh was asked to preach the sermon at the annual meeting of the Society for Promoting Christian Knowledge (SPCK) at St. Paul's Cathedral. The society dated back to 1697 and was the means through which Anglicans had provided educational facilities at the charity-school level. He stated that the church had already laid a foundation for religious education, that the church had authority to conduct religious education, and that the religion established by law in England must be considered the national religion. If national education was not conducted along the principles of the national religion, the principle of self-destruction would take over. Educational effects could not be neutral. If children were educated without certain principles of religion, they would eventually not choose any religion, or if they did choose, would probably select the wrong one. If the Dissenters wished, they could educate the children according to their own dissidence. The church had to uphold its sovereign authority. Finally, why should the church adopt a method of education that was unorthodox, when they had a perfectly suitable one right at hand?[138]

The *Edinburgh Review* then commented that "the sermon of Professor Marsh is intended as a recommendation of Dr. Bell's plan in preference to Mr. Lancaster's on this single ground, that Dr. Bell is a churchman, and Mr. Lancaster a sectary. This consideration comprises the *whole* of the superiority which he claims for that reverend person."[139] The *Review* also wrote that Marsh took it for granted that the Dissenters were trying to work for the downfall of the church, which was not so. Lancaster and his supporters were devoted to teaching "the first elements of knowledge—elements equally necessary to the churchman and the dissenter, and altogether independent of the forms of faith which they enable the infant mind to imbibe."[140]

After this sermon, in which Marsh spoke so strongly against Lancaster, "finding his utterances exciting much attention, roared again in a series of letters to the *Morning Post*."[141] Marsh wrote, "I feel myself compelled to stand forward in vindication of a cause, in which, from a late defence of it, I am materially involved."[142] "If the mechanism of the new system, as practised by Dr. Bell, is not inferior to the mechanism, as practised by Mr. Lancaster, the members of the Establishment can have no hesitation in preferring the former to the latter."[143] If the mechanism was not inferior. then it could be combined with religious instruction of the church. "This is the *real state* of the question."[144] "The cause, therefore, of Dr. Bell, is the cause of the Establishment; and a Professor of Divinity in an English University can never employ his pen on a more worthy subject, whatever be the vehicle of his defence."[145]

The *Quarterly Review* continued the polemic. In an article published in 1811, the anonymous writer (sometimes thought to be Dr. Marsh) attacked Dissenters and suggested that they have their own schools if they wish. It also attacked Joseph Fox, saying, "It is to be hoped this gentlemen manages his 'key-instrument' more skillfully than his pen, and that he does not sometimes take hold of the wrong tooth as well as of the wrong argument."*[146] The attack extended to Sidney Smith as well, calling him "a judge more conspicuously gifted . . . with a sense of ridicule than of justice,"[147] and saying that he was "less violent than Mr. Joseph Fox, because he is more malicious."[148]

The *Edinburgh Review* countered with an article, "Education of the Poor," also in 1811, and thought to be written by Sidney Smith. The article pointed out that the issue, or "the present state of the question," was that "Mr. Lancaster is a dissenter; and he does not, together with the branches of education . . . teach a fourth branch . . . the doctrines of the church."[149] Mr. Bell's plan was called "more limited in its efficacy, infinitely inferior in economy, crude and imperfect in many of the most essential parts, still it comes off a right stock, and is wholly in regular, episcopalian hands."[150] Further, the opponents of Mr. Lancaster were accused of having

restored the lost invention of the Romish priesthood—that the "white man's book" is not to be entrusted with safety to any but the already enlightened few; and that it were better for nations to remain in outer darkness than be illuminated with the dangerous and uncertain lights which beam from the very sources of Inspiration![151]

The *Edinburgh Review* stated its reluctance at being carried into a controversy. Its wish, the article said, was that the most effectual means be used in educating the poor. "We were disposed to concur in Sir. T. Bernard's benevolent wish, that one half of the poor might be educated by the one plan, and the remainder by the other."[152] Nevertheless, the need to counter the attack made by the *Quarterly Review* was strongly felt.

FORMATION OF THE NATIONAL SOCIETY

Dr. Marsh had started a movement toward establishing a society that would oppose the work of Lancaster's committee, and four months after his sermon in St. Paul's Cathedral, the National Society for Promoting the Education of the Poor in the Principles of the

---

*This statement refers to the fact Joseph Fox was a déntist.

Established Church was founded. This was, in effect, the education committee of the Church of England.

The society was set up to be a direct counterpart "to the nonsectarian Lancasterian Society, on the basis that education must be conducted according to the tenets of the Church of England."[153] Founders of the National Society stated: "By means of this organization, all who desire the promotion of sound popular education are enabled to meet together for the advancement of a great common object, on the broad and comprehensive ground that they are members of the National Church."[154] The National Society intended to increase the number of schools and promote a good system of education by training teachers, inspecting schools, and supplying schoolbooks and materials. "The National Society was more than a merely advisory body. . . . Its aim was heroic; nothing less than shouldering the whole burden of the national education at a time when that burden was increasing very rapidly."[155]

The National Society was successful from the beginning. By 1816, one hundred thousand children were taught in schools connected with the society. By 1821, the number had grown to three hundred thousand.[156] By 1831, the number had increased even more to 900,412 children receiving instruction in the monitorial schools.[157] In 1839, the National Society also received a grant of 500 pounds from the Committee of Council on Education to be used in establishing a normal school (an equal grant was given to the British and Foreign School Society).

"There can be no question that in 1811 definite religious teaching had won the day. . . . England then was no place for radicalism or free thought, and the younger society could honestly claim the title of 'National' for itself and its aims."[158]

PROPONENTS AND USERS OF THE SYSTEM

Jeremy Bentham and the Chrestomathia

Jeremy Bentham, born in 1748, was a utilitarian philosopher and a reformer of English law who had an influence on English politics and on social legislation dealing with education.[159] In 1816, Bentham published a book, *Chrestomathia: being a collection of papers explanatory of the design of an institution, proposed to be set on foot, under the name of the Chrestomathic Day School or Chrestomathic School, for the extension of the New System of Instruction to the higher branches of learning for the use of the middling and higher ranks of life.* The new system Bentham referred to was the monitorial, or mutual, system of instruction of Bell and Lancaster, which he admired. In an Appendix to *Chrestomathia*, he wrote that the new instructional system needed only an allusion since it was so universally recognized. The impetus for this book arose from the need to create new kinds of education for the growing middle class.[160] "It offered an architectural, administrative and pedagogic blue-print for a new type of 'day school.' "[161]

The title, *Chrestomathia*, or the reference to the Chrestomathic School, was derived from two Greek words, indicating something conducive to useful learning.[162] This book brought attention to a growing idea—that of extending monitorial instruction beyond the mere rudimentary skills. "Deliberately setting aside all existing educational practice, Bentham embarked on a survey of the whole field of human knowledge, including the most recent advances in science and technology."[163] He outlined his scheme in intricate detail, formulating tables for the fields of knowledge that he systematized. Bentham included the sciences, mechanics, chemistry, physics, history, geography, languages, and mathematics, and all these were justified "by reference to their utility in normal life. Knowledge, in his view, must serve a social function. . . . All other knowledge is useless."[164]

Bentham's ideas of management of the school reflected the ideas of Bell. "Like any other factory, the school is to save time by mass-production and to economize money by employing 'teachers' (the monitors) whose special merits are that they are 'tractable' and 'unpaid.' "[165] Maximum efficiency of learning was the main concern, and Bentham defined forty-three principles that would ensure maximum efficiency.

Bentham's proposed Chrestomathic School never materialized. However, he can be credited with making a proposal to extend the monitorial system to the higher branches of education, or, as a review of his *Chrestomathia* said, "But the honour of proposing to try the experiment, and of digesting a plan of instruction for the New School, has been reserved for the illustrious author of the

Chrestomathia."[166] In addition, when the middle class began to start educational institutions of their own, they had available this theory of education, which they used as a foundation.[167]

Robert Owen of the Lanark Mills

Robert Owen's life, from 1771 to 1858, "covers the traditionally accepted time-span of the Industrial Revolution, and he accepted the existence and implications of industrial change."[168] In 1799, Owen became the active head of the New Lanark Mills in Scotland. The usual social conditions existed at these cotton mills when he took charge: children as young as five were bound as apprentices for a period of nine years; they worked twelve to thirteen hours a day; virtually no educational effort was made; and what little was taught was done at the end of the lengthy working day. Owen tried to remedy these conditions: he did not employ children younger than ten; he limited the adult working day to twelve hours; and he opened a school. The school, called the Institution for the Formation of Character, doubled as a day school for small children and as an evening school for the young workers and parents.

At first, Owen was an admirer of the monitorial system. He subscribed a thousand pounds to the Lancasterian system's funds, and he offered the same amount to the National Society on the condition that it open schools without any distinction of creed.[169] If the society refused to do this, the amount would be reduced by half. The National Society accepted the 500 pounds, but Owen believed that as a result, the society became more lenient on this matter.[170] Owen saw the importance of the monitorial system as a preparation of the public mind to accept his own educational theories. The usefulness of the system was a social one; "To remove from the population 'gross ignorance and extreme poverty, with their attendant misery' and to make the workers 'rational, well disposed and well behaved.' "[171]

Because Owen praised the monitorial system, it was commonly thought that his school would be a Lancasterian school. In 1811, the *Edinburgh Review* wrote that "one [school] is now building at the Lanark cotton mills, to contain no less than 1000."[172] By 1814, however, he made it clear that his school would not function on the mechanical system of the monitorial method. At this time, he began to denounce the "mockery of learning." The children in his care were not to have a curriculum that was aimed at teaching them their place in society. "In future they should have the best possible curriculum and be trained in the most rational habits, with the object of becoming rational beings and useful members of society."[173] By this, Owen made a decisive break with the old philanthropic attitude as put into practice by the systems of Lancaster and Bell.

Why this change in Owen's thinking took place is not certain. He may have been in touch with some of the more progressive educational thinkers of his time. In later years, he visited Switzerland and met Pestalozzi and Fellenberg. When Owen's school opened in 1816, the schools of the National Society and of the British and Foreign School Society were at the height of their popularity. "The genius of Owen lay in his break with this system and the introduction of the working-class child to the methods of education according to nature."[174] Owen's school, including his infant-school idea, came at a time when the defects of monitorial methods were beginning to be noticed. "It gave a new and somewhat deeper philosophical interpretation of the educational process. . . . It also contributed its share toward awakening a sentiment for national action."[175]

THE HILLS AND HAZELWOOD

While Bentham's Chrestomathic School never was established, a form of utilitarian theory in practice could be seen at the Hazelwood School. Thomas Wright Hill opened the first school, Hill Top, in 1803, but greater educational fame is attached to the Hazelwood School, the location to which Hill Top was moved because of the need for larger premises. At Hazelwood, Hill's son, Rowland, assisted in the management of the school, and it became "a school very much in the radical and utilitarian tradition."[176]

Hazelwood was a middle-class school for sons of successful industrialists. The students were trained to educate themselves, and they were also given charge of the administration of discipline. The principles of Lancaster and Bell had some influence, but the system was used with caution.

A careful employment of the then popular mutual system was made, the boys being grouped in small classes whenever a boy became an instructor, and a master supervised his doings. But the Hills were aware of the limitations of such a plan; the monitors merely "heard" the repetition of a lesson.[177]

Hazelwood was an example of the growing middle-class concern for an improved education of their own children. The increased desire for a more practical education is significant of the middle-class attitude of the time. Unfortunately, the Hills did not attempt to gain a group of followers or spread their system into many schools, and no one copied Hazelwood, "which was probably the most remarkable piece of educational and social planning" during the nineteenth century.[178]

OTHER ADHERENTS TO AND SUPPORTERS OF THE SYSTEM

Although the monitorial system was widespread and had great popularity, it is not the purpose of this study to list all the schools that used it or all the individuals who supported its use and advocated its adoption. However, a few outstanding cases must be included, either as examples of schools where the system was used or as examples of prominent individuals who were involved with the educational activities of their times.

In 1809, Sir Thomas Bernard wrote a book about education for the poor, and in 1812, he wrote about the Barrington School. Bernard was a philanthropist who eventually became Chancelor of Durham diocese, and he was one of the chief organizers in 1798 of the Society for Bettering the Condition of the Poor. Bernard advocated the reduction of expense in conducting schools in which Bell's system was used, and compared the expenses of running charity schools with those of Bell's schools. He pleaded that the poor should not be deprived of general instruction because of lack of funds.[179] Bernard said that "the reader will not easily and correctly appreciate the value of Dr. Bell's method, until he has attended to the difficulties, which have been in general considered as impediments to the progress of instruction, and has examined the manner in which Dr. Bell has obviated them."[180] He then listed some of these "difficulties," among them he listed "the want of qualified and intelligent schoolmasters."[181]

Bernard saw the monitorial system as a means of overcoming this difficulty because of "the simple principle of tuition by the pupils themselves."[182] He thought the strength of the system was that, not only did the masters have many able assistants, but "the teachers acquire knowledge by instructing others." He also stated that "the main-spring of the machine is kept in action, by the faculties of the scholars being thus employed and stimulated."[183]

Samuel Whitbread, an eminent brewer and a member of Parliament, introduced a bill in 1807 "for the establishment of schools throughout the land to supply machinery by which all children were to be entitled to two years' schooling between the ages of seven and fourteen years."[184] He spoke before the House of Commons and said:

I believe the greatest reform that could take place in this kingdom would be to impart instruction to every man in it. A system of education has lately been formed, so simple, so cheap, and so effective, that the discovery of it is a great benefit to the world at large, and the discoverer, Mr. Joseph Lancaster, is entitled to very considerable praise.[185]

The bill was rejected.

After the death of Whitbread in 1815, Lord Brougham became the main leader in the parliamentary struggle for national education. As early as 1810, Brougham had tried to make the Lancasterian movement a public one. Though he failed, he was able to secure the establishment of a committee to investigate the education of the poor in London.[186]

The report, which was completed in 1818, led Brougham to describe England as the worst-educated country in Europe. Only a fourth of the children were being educated, and most for a short time only. It was estimated that over one and a half million children never went to school at all, and the report also stated that, because of the increasing population and the demand for child labor, the situation would get worse.[187] Brougham maintained that conditions had been even more deplorable before schools were established on the Bell and Lancaster systems, when only about 5 percent of the population were receiving an education.[188] Although this bill did not pass either, Brougham's continued efforts received much credit in the eventual establishment of national education.

Bishop Shute Barrington founded a school in Bishop Auckland in 1810. His desire to create a school was prompted by the many poor children in his town who aroused his pity. Prior to this, he had already shown interest and sympathy for the poor, and he was the first president of the Society for the Bettering of the Condition of the Poor.

The bishop was anxious to introduce a school into his diocese that was based on the principles of the new mode of instruction—the monitorial system. But, he maintained, that if it were done properly, the students who were to be monitors should have some training. He established a college at Bishop Auckland for educating masters, ushers, and teachers, which eventually became one of the two normal schools sponsored by the National Society. Following the opening of the training school, Bishop Barrington then had a free school built.[189] "In its size, organization and equipment it was undoubtedly one of the best of the schools founded on the Bell system."[190]

Attempts to transplant the monitorial system into secondary education occurred early. In 1810, James Pillans undertook "with some trepidation the rectorship of the Edinburgh High School."[191] He was "appalled by the difficulties" that he faced as rector, and yet he was "catching that enthusiasm which in teaching goes far to supply the deficiency of genius."[192] He was at the time considering improvements yet doing so cautiously. He said, "I am aware of the danger of dashing too precipitately into new schemes and think it better to do the old well than, by attempting the new prematurely to fail in both."[193] One of the systems he was considering was the monitorial system. He became an enthusiastic proponent and admirer of the system and had it incorporated a year after he assumed rectorship. An assistant wrote that it had "converted a laborious and often irksome profession into the most easy and delightful employment possible."[194]

The Quaker school at Ackworth and the use of apprentice teachers was discussed in Chapter 3. The monitorial system was tried there between 1822 and 1834. As Stewart said, the system "was given a cautious probationary period at Ackworth."[195] Quaker schools in general tried the Lancasterian methods during the period from about 1820 to 1845.

Joining members of Parliament, church officials, and others in commending the monitorial system were two of the great writers of that era. William Wordsworth joined the eager supporters of the monitorial system. "He was an enthusiastic supporter of that system as it was propounded by Bell and maintained by the Church of England."[196] He did not, however, espouse the utilitarian educational ideas, and in 1843, he wrote that so little progress had been made "in diminishing the evils deplored or promoting the benefits of education."[197] Samuel Taylor Coleridge called the monitorial system an "incomparable machine," a "vast moral steam engine."[198]

Although the monitorial system was dying out by the 1840s, records of its adoption during that time do exist. William Ellis was a businessman, an educator, and a follower of the utilitarian philosophy. He criticized the popular school curriculum that taught traditional subjects, and maintained that the expanding industrial society needed a new curriculum. "Ellis's strategy was to found and equip a number of schools in which social science would not be merely another subject in the curriculum but the very staple of the education given."[199] He opened the first Birkbeck School in 1848, named in honor of Dr. Birkbeck, pioneer of Mechanic's Institutes. His teaching methods were eclectic. "These included 'the monitorial system of Bell and Lancaster, the collective-lesson system of Stowe, and the arrangments incident to the object-lesson system of Pestalozzi.' "[200] The monitorial system was used to save on the expense of teachers' salaries. Ellis made a lasting mark between 1850 and 1880 as "teacher, educational thinker, and philanthropist of a characteristically radical-capitalist stamp."[201]

Barbara Bodichon was impressed by her friend William Ellis, and she was probably somewhat influenced by his educational thinking. She opened a day school for boys and girls in 1854 and caused consternation by her experimental ways. Bodichon strongly believed in the education of women. She also mixed children of different social classes in her school. However, the clergy objected to her nondenominational religious teaching.*

One possible fault of the school was a too slavish adherence to the monitorial system, which had been copied from William Ellis's school. It was used almost entirely in reading and arithmetic, but even the careful instruction of the monitors and the close supervision of the Head could not eliminate the mechanical monotony inherent in this form of teaching.[202]

THE MONITORIAL SYSTEM IN OTHER PARTS OF THE BRITISH ISLES

In 1811, the *Edinburgh Review* reported that in Scotland, there were already at least fifteen Lancasterian schools in operation, the largest being in Glasgow.[203] Lancaster wrote in 1821 that a number of schools had been established at Edinburgh, Glasgow, Ayr, Aberdeen, and other towns.

In 1825, John Griscom, the American traveler, wrote that the new system was making less progress in Scotland than in England, but he attributed this to the fact that the schools were superior to those in England, "which rendered a change less necessary." He also added that "among a people whose habits are much adverse to fluctuations, the adoption of any new scheme was much less to be expected. Nevertheless, the system of Lancaster (and probably that of Bell) is making its way in Scotland."[204]

As for Ireland, the 1811 article in the *Edinburgh Review* stated that they had less precise information but believed that at least nine or ten large schools had been opened. In 1821, Lancaster wrote that "schools have been established very extensively, and that of Belfast in particular is fit for a model for the three kingdoms."[205]

Griscom also reported on Ireland. He said, "But the most remarkable and cheering instance of the rapid progress of this invaluable system occurs in Ireland."[206] He stated that the model school in Dublin, which he visited in 1819, seemed to be the best monitorial school in Europe. He also visted a school in Belfast.

---

*A more complete account of both Ellis and Bodichon can be found in Stewart and McCann, 1967, chapters 18 and 20.

Balfour reported that monitors were used in the Dublin Model School from the very beginning of its establishment, and that in the National schools, monitors were the chief source of eventual teachers.[207] In 1845, a year before pupil-teachers were introduced in England, that system was utilized in Ireland and developed in the next ten years.

EVALUATION AND CRITICISM OF THE MONITORIAL SYSTEM

The early nineteenth-century monitorial system received mixed reviews almost since its inception. Lancaster thought that he had discovered the *best* system of education and that his system was also the least expensive.[208] Bell took great pride in his system as well, as is exemplified by his statements in *Mutual Tuition and Moral Discipline*. He said, "Its success has been as remarkable as its nature is popular."[209]

In 1811, *The Philanthropist* praised the Lancasterian system for "the extraordinary manner in which the talents of boys are drawn forth."[210] The article also approved of the constant activity it gave children's minds, the pleasure of the duties involved, and the exceptionally rapid progress made by students. It also found commendable the order introduced into the school through this system.

A distinguished visitor from America, John Griscom, found much to comment on, mostly in a positive vein, when he visited the British Isles in 1818–1819. In his reports on European education, he recounted a visit to the Borough Road School, Lancaster's training school for monitors.

My excellent friend, W. A. took me today to the Borough-road school, where we spent an hour, in observing the operations of this improved and most important method of conveying instruction to the children of the poor. This school is intended as a model for others, both in the construction of the building, and in the management of the classes. I can only say, that we were highly gratified with the indications of neatness, order and skill, in its appearance, as in the performance of the scholars. The Lancasterian principles of instruction, or the art of managing very large schools at a very small expense, is evidently gaining ground, not only in England, but in other countries, and it may doubtless be regarded, as the most valuable practical discovery in relation to human happiness with which the world has been recently blessed. Great credit is certainly due to Joseph Lancaster for the extraordinary ingenuity which he displayed in the mechanism of his system, and still more extraordinary perseverance with which he urged the adoption of his mode of instruction, throughout the kingdom. Had there been as much discretion in his subsequent deportment, as there was of talent and benevolence in the early part of his career, he might still be entitled to the high eulogium once bestowed upon him by the Prince Regent, that "he was doing more good than any man alive." But whatever may have been his merits, scarcely less is due to my friend A. and his deceased coadjutor, Dr. Fox, for their disinterested and noble efforts to preserve the Lancasterian system from sinking beneath the pressure of pecuniary embarrassment, in the early stages of its advancement.[211]

In 1819, Griscom reported on a school he visited in Manchester.

Having no where seen, in England, one of the national, or Bell's schools, in operation, my friend D. conducted me this morning to one of the two which are established in Manchester. The mode of instruction differs essentially from the plan of Lancaster, and certainly possesses some features which are very valuable. It is less mechanical, and it exercises, to a great extent, the judgment and understanding of the pupils. Much stress is laid upon an acquaintance with the scriptures; and the method of instruction is better devised for making the children thoroughly acquainted with them. It is a more expensive mode than the other.[212]

Another American traveler to Europe was A. D. Bache, who wrote an extensive report in 1839. Regarding the elementary schools of Great Britain, he said, "The schools for the instruction of the people during week days are still miserably deficient, both in number and kind, and as yet there appears no prospect of concert of effort to bring about a better state of general education."[213] He commended the British and Foreign School Society and the National Society for having done the most for elementary education. "I visited schools in connexion with both, or following their methods, and as might have been expected, found their model schools established in London, in general, the best specimens of their views."[214] Bache qualified his praise, however. After having visited the Borough Road School, he wrote, "The success is limited, however, by the capacity of the method itself, and I cannot hold up even this improved form of it as a model for imitation." He referred to the system of mutual instruction as belonging "to a very unadvanced grade of public education."[215]

The report of the Committee of Council on Education for 1845 by F. C. Cook took an even sterner view of the shortcomings of the monitorial system. "We cannot reflect upon the age or acquirements of monitors without being struck with the absurdity of expecting any good results from the use of such materials."[216] It gave further examples, citing the fact that any knowledge of geography or history that the more intelligent might possess was not called for. Also, the character of the religious instruction in the National schools was said to contribute to the students' confusion of the holiest things with what was inconsequential. The report stated that the insufficient supply of qualified teachers and the incompetence of monitors are "defects which ought no longer to be permitted to exist."[217]

Vaille, writing in 1881, commented that the failure of the system was simply a matter of time, and yet it had accomplished a purpose that may not have been achieved by a better system.

The idea of real instruction for masses had just dawned upon society. The great need then was for an engine to demonstrate its possibility, and to arouse enthusiasm in its behalf. To succeed, such an engine must be not only effective, but economical as well; and if it could possess novelty, so much the better.[218]

Vaille also credited Lancaster with organizing the first model and training school, the Borough Road School. In addition, he said that Lancaster laid the ground work for the pupil-teacher system, adopted in 1846 and still in use at the time when Vaille was writing.

Writing in 1889, Gill stated that the advantages of the monitorial system over the individual system utilized prior to Lancaster and Bell's time were obvious. The school was turned from a place of idleness and mischief to one of "healthy excitement." [219] He further said that although monitors, as teachers, could possibly instruct their peers because of their understanding of each other's language and style, this should only take place if the situation was one where mere memory or fact teaching was involved. "No wise teacher will refuse to avail himself of such services as they [monitors] can render. But the limits of their power should be well understood. They can instruct, but not educate."[220]

David Salmon wrote a biography of Joseph Lancaster in 1904. When referring to the monitorial system, he said, "For practical imitation Lancaster offers as little to the teacher of the present day as Noah offers to the captain of a Cunarder, but his methods possess sufficient historical interest to justify a brief description."[221] Perhaps this reflects some of the more severe criticism that was, at times, leveled at Lancaster.

In 1912, Graves, writing a volume on great educators, referred to both Lancaster and Bell as "vain and pedagogically ignorant." Neither, he felt, deserved much praise as an educational reformer. "The monitorial systems overemphasized repetition in the teaching process and treated education purely from the standpoint of routine. The monitorial method was not real instruction, but a formal drill. It had no principles."[222] But Graves did commend the monitorial system for awakening the English nation to the need for education for the poor. "The societies afforded a substitute, though a poor one, for national education in the days before the government was willing to pay for general education . . . and they became the avenues through which such appropriations as the government did make were distributed."[223]

Cubberley also commended the monitorial system for exerting an influence on an awakening interest in education. "It increased the number of people who possessed the elements of an education; made schools much more talked about; and aroused thought and provoked discussion on the question of education."[224] In addition, the training and model schools set up by both societies marked the beginning of normal-school training in England.

Barnard wrote in 1949 that the monitorial movement aided in popularizing elementary education. Besides, "its system of dividing the pupils into groups—instead of the master teaching a few pupils separately while the rest wasted their time—was something of an innovation which has proved of permanent value."[225]

In 1962, a small book was published by the City of Chichester in England to commemorate the founding of the Lancasterian School for Girls in 1812. Two years before, in 1810, Lancaster had lectured in Chichester, after which the town resolved to establish a school based on his plan. It was to reach the poor children for whom an education was not provided by the existing charities. The 1962 history of the school stated:

To understand the significance of this venture it must be realised that in 1812 the government assumed no responsibility for the education of children. . . . Although the system developed by Joseph Lancaster is subject to serious criticism in the light of later experience, his organization successfully fulfilled a desperate need and set the pattern for 19th century elementary education in England.[226]

Writing on educational theory in 1964, Brauner said, "The Lancasterian monitorial system produced quick and decisive results against absolute illiteracy."[227] He pointed out the mechanical way in which drill in the rudiments of reading, writing, and figuring was conducted. In addition, Brauner stated that the monitorial method influenced the normal schools that began in that period. Two misconceptions have remained: "1) that teaching consists of imparting bits of factual knowledge; and 2) that to impart such knowledge, one need know only as much as is to be imparted."[228]

Meyer said that, from the current point of view, the monitorial schools were "transparently defective."[229] Yet he pointed out some favorable aspects also. Because of the large number of students with whom the monitorial system dealt, attention had to be given to the classroom and its equipment, such as lighting, ventilation, blackboard, and desks. The monitorial system also brought to public attention the advantages to be gained from trained teachers.

Godsden found fault with the cheapness and mechanical methods of the monitorial system, and he said that they "formed an unfortunate legacy which the system bequeathed to the elementary school."[230]

Selden pointed out that Lancaster demonstrated that "organization was in and of itself a good idea, and his practice of grouping students by a combination of age and ability was to become standard."[231] Above all, Lancaster made schooling available to the poor when they otherwise would have received none, thus contributing to the idea that education is a fundamental right.

Finally, Evans wrote that the monitorial school was a decided improvement over the schools previous to it. Children obtained a superficial knowledge of reading, writing, and arithmetic and were taught discipline. Monitorial schools also popularized the idea of universal education. However, he listed three detrimental factors of the system: (1) little worthwhile education resulted; (2) denominational rivalry increased; and (3) it set the standard for elementary schools that developed in the later nineteenth century by mechanical methods, low standards, large classes, cheapness, and narrow educational ideas.[232]

KAY-SHUTTLEWORTH AND PUPIL-TEACHERS

After the monitorial system had been functioning for approximately thirty years, it came under increasingly severe criticism. The working class became more aware of the need for education, particularly as the right to vote was granted to them, and they became dissatisfied with the shallowness of the education provided. The monitorial system was also criticized because much useful knowledge was neglected and the cultivation of greater reasoning power was ignored. The problems were frequently considered to exist because of the use of children as teachers.

In 1839, the government set up the Committee of the Privy Council for Education, which was to consider "all matters affecting the education of the people," and to supervise all educational grants.[233] At the same time, Her Majesty's inspectors were appointed since inspection of schools was a condition of all educational grants.

The first secretary of the committee was Dr. James Kay-Shuttleworth. He had graduated from medicine at twenty-three and had worked among the poor in Manchester. His writings called attention to the miserable condition of the victims of the Industrial Revolution, and in 1835, he was appointed assistant poor-law commissioner. He felt that education was one of the chief means of aiding the poor.

He had for long regarded education as the key to reform, and had advocated schools, libraries, mechanics' institutes, and instruction in science and domestic economy, as a means of helping the workers to help themselves. His work as a poor-law official convinced him more strongly than ever that the education of the poor was a national responsibility.[234]

Kay-Shuttleworth had made an extensive study of the schools in England and on the Continent. "His study of the educational methods . . . convinced him that the monitorial system was a failure. He called it 'monitorial humbug.' "[235] By this time, the late 1830s, criticism was being leveled at the monitorial system because of the "poor standards of reading, writing, and arithmetic achieved under the rote-learning monitorial process, and concern was being expressed at the prevalence of bribery and corruption among the monitors."[236] Critics said that the majority of the students made little or no progress, and Kay-Shuttleworth's own inspectors reported likewise.

In Norwood, Kay-Shuttleworth began to put into practice some of the reforms he advocated. At the School of Industry, which was run along monitorial lines, he introduced a pupil-teacher system, inspired by his observations of a similar system in Holland. He selected the most promising of the monitors and apprenticed them to the schoolmasters. The experience at Norwood made him aware that no real progress would take place in universal education without qualified teachers. "The weakness of the monitorial system was becoming manifest and some attempt to train an adequate number of teachers was imperative if a national system of any kind was to be set up."[237]

A plan for a state normal school had been rejected by Parliament, so Kay-Shuttleworth determined to establish his own. With a friend, E. C. Tuffnell, he set up Battersea Training College in 1840. In this school were a number of monitors who were to be trained to be pupil-teachers, their ages ranging from fourteen to twenty-one, and also older men between twenty and thirty were taught.[238] "Everything was done to discourage the rule-of-thumb, monitorial methods, which were inculcated in the British and Foreign School Society's training college at Borough Road."[239] Although successful, the college ran into financial difficulties and, in 1843, had to be turned over to the National Society.

The National Society preserved the curriculum, with the exception of adding religious instruction, and Battersea proved an inspiration for an increase in the number of normal schools. "The rapid development of training colleges in the forties shows an increasing realisation at this period of the limitations of the monitorial system, and of the truth that educational efficiency in the last resort depends on competent teachers."[240]

By 1846, the education grant had reached nearly 100,000 pounds a year, and the Committee of the Privy Council for Education decided to proceed with further developments. That committee introduced the pupil-teacher system. Apprentices were to be paid with government funds. Thirteen-year-olds were chosen to serve for five years. At the end of the apprenticeship, pupil-teachers could compete for Queen's scholarships. Successful candidates would receive an additional three years of training at normal schools. College-trained teachers received proficiency grants from the government in addition to a salary.[241] By 1859, "The new system had produced over 7,000 trained certificated teachers, whilst twice as many pupil-teachers were in the schools. Significant inroads were made into the shortage of teachers and monitorial methods began to retreat before the advance of class teaching."[242]

Barnard presumed that Kay-Shuttleworth "regarded the pupil-teacher system as merely a temporary and opportunist method of bridging the gap between the employment of monitors and the introduction of an efficient scheme for training adult teachers."[243] However, it indicated progress, and Kay-Shuttleworth's proposals met with much support.

The pupil-teacher system suffered a setback by the Revised Code of 1862, which narrowed the scope of their work and training and which decreased funding. Various changes continued to be made in the program, but by the 1880s, the system began to break up. In the early twentieth century, it was so modified that it no longer resembled peer teaching.

NOTES

1. E. O. Vaille, "The Lancastrian System. A Chapter in the Evolution of Common-school Education," *Education* 1 (January 1881): 265.
2. Ibid.
3. Pamela Silver and Harold Silver, *The Education of the Poor: The History of a National School, 1824–1974* (London: Routledge and Kegan Paul, 1974), p. 7.
4. F. J. Harvey Darton, "Bell and the Dragon," *Fortnightly Review* 85 (May 1909): 898.
5. Silver and Silver, *The Education of the Poor*, p.9

6. Ibid.
7. T. L. Jarman, *Landmarks in the History of Education* (New York: Philosophical Library, 1952), p. 239.
8. Silver and Silver, *The Education of the Poor*, p. 8.
9. Ibid., pp. 8–9.
10. John Hurt, *Education in Evolution: Church, State, Society and Popular Education, 1800–1870* (London: Rupert Hart-Davis, 1971), p. 14.
11. Jarman, *Landmarks*, p. 245.
12. W. H. Burston, "The Utilitarians and the Monitorial System of Teaching, in Education and Philosophy," *The Yearbook of Education*, ed. G. Z. F. Bereday and J. A. Lauwerys (New York: World Book Co., 1957), p. 384.
13. P. H. J. H. Gosden, comp., *How They Were Taught: An Anthology of Contemporary Accounts of Learning and Teaching in England, 1800–1850* (New York: Barnes and Noble, 1969), p. 1.
14. Ibid.
15. S. J. Curtis and M. E. A. Boultwood, *An Introductory History of English Education Since 1800* (London: University Tutorial Press, Ltd., 1962), p. 7.
16. Silver and Silver, *The Education of the Poor*, p. 10.
17. Darton, "Bell and the Dragon."
18. Curtis and Boultwood, *An Introductory History*.
19. James Leitch, *Practical Educationists and Their Systems of Teaching* (Glasgow: James Maclehose, 1876).
20. David Salmon, ed. *The Practical Parts of Lancaster's Improvements and Bell's Experiment* (London: Cambridge University Press, 1932).
21. Ibid., p. viii.
22. Darton, "Bell and the Dragon," p. 898.
23. Salmon, *The Practical Parts*.
24. Ibid., p. ix.
25. Curtis and Boultwood, *An Introductory History*, pp. 7–9.
26. Joseph Lancaster, *The Lancasterian System of Education* (Baltimore: Wm. Ogden Niles, Printer, 1821), p. 2.
27. Hurt, *Education in Evolution*, p. 15.
28. Salmon, *The Practical Parts*, p. ix.
29. Lancaster, *The Lancasterian System*, p. 2.
30. Salmon, *The Practical Parts*, p. ix.
31. Curtis and Boultwood, *An Introductory History*, p. 8.
32. "Education of the Poor," *Edinburgh Review* 19 (November 1811): 4.
33. Joseph Lancaster, *The British System of Education* (Georgetown, Washington, D.C.: Joseph Milligan, 1812), pp. v–vi.
34. Vaille, "The Lancastrian System," p. 265.
35. John William Adamson, *A Short History of Education* (London: Cambridge University Press, 1919), p. 244.
36. Joseph Lancaster, *Manual Folio*, Box 4 (in Lancaster Collection of the American Antiquarian Society, Worcester, Mass), p. 63.
37. Joseph Lancaster, *Improvements in Education as it Respects in Industrious Classes of the Community*, 3d ed. (Clifton: Augustus M. Kelley, Publishers, 1973), p. 37.

38. Ellwood P. Cubberley, *Readings in the History of Education* (Boston: Houghton Mifflin Co., 1920), p. 525.

39. Lancaster, *Manual Folio*, p. 68.

40. Darton, "Bell and the Dragon," p. 899.

41. Cubberley, *Readings*, p. 524.

42. Henry Dunn, *Sketches* (London: Houlston and Stoneman, 1848).

43. David Salmon, *Joseph Lancaster* (London: Longmans, Green, and Co., 1904), p. 10.

44. Cubberley, *Readings*, p. 525.

45. Lancaster, *Improvements in Education*, p. 9.

46. David Salmon, "Monitorial System," *A Cyclopedia of Education*, vol. 4, ed. P. Monroe (New York: The Macmillan Co., 1913) p. 297.

47. Lancaster, *Improvements in Education*, p. viii.

48. Ibid., pp. xii–xiii.

49. Leitch, *Practical Educationists*, pp. 160–61.

50. Lancaster, *Improvements in Education*, p. vii.

51. Salmon, *The Practical Parts*, p. xxvii.

52. Ibid., p. xxviii.

53. Darton, "Bell and the Dragon," p. 906.

54. Ibid.

55. H. C. Barnard, *A Short History of English Education from 1760–1944* (London: University of London Press, Ltd., 1949), p. 67.

56. "Education of the Poor," p. 5.

57. Dunn, *Sketches*, p. 67.

58. Henry Bryan Binns, *A Century of Education* (London: J. M. Dent and Co., 1908).

59. Dunn, *Sketches*, p. 70.

60. Ibid.

61. Binns, *A Century of Education*, p. 31.

62. Dunn, *Sketches*, p. 17.

63. Salmon, *The Practical Parts*, p. xii.

64. Ibid.

65. Isaac Brandon, *Instruction: A Poem* (London: Richard Taylor and Co., 1811), p. 7.

66. Ibid., p. 10.

67. Binns, *A Century of Education*, p. 65.

68. Salmon, *The Practical Parts*, p. xiii.

69. Lancaster, *The Lancasterian System*, p.3.

70. Ibid., p. 4.

71. "British and Foreign School Society," *American Journal of Education* 10 (June 1861): 373.

72. Barnard, *A Short History of English Education*.

73. Salmon, "Monitorial System," p. 297.

74. Dunn, *Sketches*, pp. 22–23.

75. Darton, "Bell and the Dragon," p. 896.

76. Dunn, *Sketches*, Chapter 2.

77. Salmon, *Joseph Lancaster*, p. 20.

78. Dunn, *Sketches*, p. 26.
79. Salmon, *Joseph Lancaster*, p. 20.
80. Dunn, *Sketches*, p. 27.
81. Darton, "Bell and the Dragon," p. 897.
82. Leitch, *Practical Educationists*, p. 122.
83. Ibid., pp. 122–23.
84. Salmon, *The Practical Parts*, p. xvii.
85. Vaille, "The Lancastrian System," p. 266.
86. Ibid.
87. Salmon, *The Practical Parts*, p. xviii.
88. "Bell and Lancaster's System of Education," *Quarterly Review* 6 (October 1811): 269.
89. Salmon, *The Practical Parts*, p. xliv.
90. Ibid., p. xx.
91. L. R. Klemm, "An Interview Between Pestalozzi and Dr. Bell," *Education* 7 (April 1887): 560.
92. Ibid.
93. Ibid., pp. 560–61.
94. Ibid., p. 562.
95. Salmon, *The Practical Parts*, p. xxii.
96. "A Thing That India Has Taught Europe," *The American Review of Reviews* 40 (July 1909): 114–15.
97. Salmon, *The Practical Parts*, Introduction.
98. Robert Southey, *The Life of the Rev. Andrew Bell*, vol. 1 (London: J. Murray, 1844), p. 177.
99. Ibid.
100. Ibid., p. 178.
101. Ibid.
102. Andrew Bell, *Mutual Tuition and Moral Discipline* (London: G. Roake, 1823), p. 2.
103. Robert B. Sutton, "Historical Report from Madras," *School and Society* 92 (Summer 1964): 321.
104. Andrew Bell, *The Madras School* (London: T. Bensley, 1808), p. 7.
105. John Gill, *Systems of Education* (Boston: D. C. Heath and Co., 1889), p. 163.
106. Ibid.
107. "Bell and Lancaster's System," p. 269.
108. Ibid., p. 265.
109. Southey, *The Life of Andrew Bell*, p. 193.
110. Bell, *Mutual Tuition*, p. 2.
111. Bell, *The Madras School*, p. 15.
112. Ibid.
113. Ibid., p. 2.
114. Bell, *Mutual Tuition*, p. 22.
115. Bell, *The Madras School*, p. 3.
116. Andrew Bell, *Instruction for Conducting a School* (London: John Murray, 1813), p. 8.
117. Bell, *Mutual Tuition*, p. 8.

118. Charles Cuthbert Southey, *The Life of the Rev. Andrew Bell* (London: J. Murray, 1844), p. 126.

119. Lancaster, *Improvements in Education*, pp. 58–59.

120. Salmon, *The Practical Parts*, p. xxiv.

121. Adamson, *A Short History of Education*, p. 246.

122. David Salmon, "Trimmer, Mrs. Sarah," *A Cyclopedia of Education*, vol. 5, ed. P. Monroe (New York: The Macmillan Co., 1913).

123. C. A. Eggertsen, "The Monitorial System of Instruction in the United States," (Ph.D. diss., University of Minnesota, 1939), p. 39.

124. John Miller Dow Meiklejohn, *An Old Educational Reformer, Dr. Andrew Bell* (Edinburgh and London: William Blackwood and Sons, 1881), pp. 42–43.

125. Adamson, *A Short History of Education*, p. 251.

126. Jarman, *Landmarks*, p. 257.

127. Darton, "Bell and the Dragon," p. 904.

128. Adolph E. Meyer, *The Development of Education in the Twentieth Century*, 2d ed. (New York: McGraw-Hill, 1965), p. 282.

129. Sarah Trimmer, *A Comparative View of the New Plan of Education* (London: T. Bensley, 1805), p.6.

130. Ibid., p. 10.

131. Salmon, *The Practical Parts*, p. xxvii.

132. Sydney Smith, "Review of Sarah Trimmer's Comparative View," *The Edinburgh Review* 9 (1806): 183.

133. Ibid., p. 184.

134. Lancaster, *The Lancasterian System*, p. 2.

135. James Plumptre, *The Way in Which We Should Go: A Sermon* (Cambridge, England: Francis Hodson, 1809), pp. 19–20.

136. Ibid., p. 22.

137. Hurt, *Education in Evolution*, p. 16.

138. "Andrew Bell and the Madras System of Mutual Instruction," *American Journal of Education* 10 (June 1861): 481–82.

139. "Education of the Poor," p. 26.

140. Ibid., p. 32.

141. Darton, "Bell and the Dragon," p. 907.

142. Herbert Marsh, *A Vindication of Dr. Bell's System of Tuition* (London: Law and Gilbert, 1811), p. 5.

143. Ibid., p. 6

144. Ibid., p. 7

145. Ibid., p. 8.

146. "Bell and Lancaster's Systems, p. 295.

147. Ibid., p. 288.

148. Ibid., p. 297.

149. "Education of the Poor," p. 3.

150. Ibid., p. 23.

151. Ibid., p. 21.

152. Ibid., p. 2.

153. Brian Simon, *Studies in the History of Education, 1780–1870* (London: Lawrence and Wishart, 1960), p. 149.

154. "National Society," *American Journal of Education* 10 (June 1861): 499.
155. W. H. G. Armytage, *Four Hundred Years of English Education* (Cambridge, England: Cambridge University Press, 1970), p. 91.
156. Darton, "Bell and the Dragon," p. 907.
157. Ellwood P. Cubberley, *The History of Education* (Boston: Houghton Mifflin Co., 1920), pp. 625–26.
158. Darton, "Bell and the Dragon," p. 908.
159. Michael E. Sadler, "Bentham, Jeremy," *A Cyclopedia of Education*, vol. 1, ed. P. Monroe (New York: The Macmillan Co., 1913), p. 364.
160. Simon, *Studies in the History of Education*, p. 79.
161. Armytage, *Four Hundred Years*, p. 92.
162. "Review of Jeremy Bentham's Chrestomathia," *Westminster Review* 1 (January 1824): 56.
163. Simon, *Studies in the History of Education*, p. 79.
164. Ibid., p. 80.
165. John William Adamson, *English Education* (London: Cambridge University Press, 1930), p. 103.
166. "Review of Jeremy Bentham's Chrestomathia," p. 56.
167. Simon, *Studies in the History of Education*, p. 84.
168. W. A. C. Stewart and W. P. McCann, *The Educational Innovators, 1750–1880* (New York: St. Martin's Press, 1967), p. 53.
169. Binns, *A Century of Education*, p. 50.
170. Stewart and McCann, *The Educational Innovators*, p. 58.
171. Ibid., p. 59.
172. "Education of the Poor," p. 8.
173. Stewart and McCann, *The Educational Innovators*, p. 60.
174. Ibid., p. 55.
175. Cubberley, *The History of Education*, p. 631.
176. Stewart and McCann, *The Educational Innovators*, p. 100.
177. Adamson, *English Education*, p. 52.
178. Stewart and McCann, *The Educational Innovators*, p. 271.
179. Thomas Bernard, *Education of the Poor* (London: W. Bulmer and Co., 1809).
180. Ibid., p. 20.
181. Ibid., p. 27.
182. Thomas Bernard, *The Barrington School* (London: W. Bulmer and Co., 1812), p. 51.
183. Ibid., pp. 51–52.
184. Cubberley, *Readings in the History of Education*, p. 536.
185. "Joseph Lancaster," *American Journal of Education* 10 (June 1861): 358.
186. Armytage, *Four Hundred Years*, p. 93.
187. Keith Evans, *The Development and Structure of the English Educational System* (London: University of London Press, Ltd., 1975), Chapter 2.
188. Jarman, *Landmarks*, p. 257.
189. Francis R. Brunskill, "Bishop Barrington's Educational Experiment," *The London Quarterly and Holborn Review* 168 (January 1943).
190. Stewart and McCann, *The Educational Innovators*, p. 231.

191. Lewis F. Anderson, "The System of Mutual Instruction and the Beginnings of High School," *School and Society* 8 (November 1918): 572.
192. Ibid.
193. Ibid.
194. Salmon, *Joseph Lancaster*, p. 14.
195. W. A. Campbell Stewart, *Quakers and Education* (London: The Epworth Press, 1953), p. 97.
196. Adamson, *English Education*, p. 108.
197. Ibid., p. 109.
198. Armytage, *Four Hundred Years*, p. 90.
199. Stewart and McCann, *The Educational Innovators*, p. 329.
200. Ibid., p. 333.
201. Ibid., p. 341.
202. Ibid., p. 312.
203. "Education of the Poor."
204. John Griscom, *Monitorial Instruction. An Address, Pronounced at the Opening of the New York High School* (New York: Mahlon Day, 1825), p. 30.
205. "Education of the Poor," p. 7.
206. Griscom, *Monitorial Instruction*, p. 31.
207. Graham Balfour, *The Educational Systems of Great Britain and Ireland* (Oxford: Clarendon Press, 1898), p. 19.
208. Salmon, *Joseph Lancaster*, pp. 12–13.
209. Bell, *Mutual Tuition*, p. 2.
210. Cubberley, *Readings in the History of Education*, p. 526.
211. John Griscom, *A Year in Europe*, vol. 1 (New York: Collins and Co., 1823), pp. 105–106.
212. John Griscom, *A Year in Europe* vol. 2 (New York: Collins and Co., 1823), p. 532.
213. Alex Dallas Bache, *Report on Education in Europe* (Philadelphia: Lydia B. Bailey, 1839), p. 174.
214. Ibid.
215. Ibid., p. 175.
216. Gosden, *How They Were Taught*, p. 7.
217. Ibid., p. 8.
218. Vaille, "The Lancastrian System," p. 272–73.
219. John Gill, *Systems of Education* (Boston: D. C. Heath and Co., 1889), p. 165.
220. Ibid., pp. 176–77.
221. Salmon, *Joseph Lancaster*, p. 7.
222. Frank Pierrepont Graves, *Great Educators of Three Centuries* (New York: The Macmillan Co., 1912), p. 242.
223. Ibid., p. 243.
224. Cubberley, *The History of Education*, p. 629.
225. Barnard, *A Short History of English Education*, p. 68.
226. Grace Hine, *The Lancastrian School for Girls, Chichester, 1812–1962* (The Chichester City Council, 1962), p. 2.
227. Charles J. Brauner, *American Educational Theory* (Englewood Cliffs, N.J.: Prentice-Hall, 1964), p. 154.

228. Ibid., p. 155.
229. Adolph E. Meyer, *An Educational History of the Western World*, (New York: McGraw-Hill, 1965), p. 284.
230. Gosden, *How They Were Taught*, p. 1.
231. Judith Selden, "Learning by the Numbers," *American Education* 11 (May 1975): 27.
232. Evans, *The Development and Structure*, p. 18.
233. Barnard, *A Short History of English Education*, p. 115.
234. Ibid., p. 116.
235. Curtis and Boultwood, *An Introductory History*, p. 59.
236. Stewart and McCann, *The Educational Innovators*, p. 182.
237. Barnard, *A Short History of English Education*, p. 118
238. Curtis and Boultwood, *An Introductory History*, pp. 58–63.
239. Barnard, *A Short History of English Education*, pp. 118–19.
240. Ibid., p. 119.
241. Silver and Silver, *The Education of the Poor*, p. 74.
242. Evans, *The Development and Structure*, p. 22.
243. Barnard, *A Short History of English Education*, pp. 122–23.

CHAPTER 5

Peer Teaching on the Continent in the Nineteenth Century

INTRODUCTION

The nineteenth century was a period in which the state gradually assumed control over education, a situation caused by a new political philosophy, revolutions for democracy, and the Industrial Revolution. "A new political impulse now replaced the earlier religious motive as the incentive for education, and education for literacy and citizenship became, during the nineteenth century, a new political ideal that has . . . spread to progressive nations all over the world."[1] Knight identified another cause for the increased emphasis on education. He stated that "nationalism gained strength in the late eighteenth and the early nineteenth century in the major European countries. . . . Under its influence education came increasingly to be employed as an instrument for promoting patriotism and for the achievement of national ends."[2]

Pollard pointed out that the leaders in education during that period were philanthropists, or humanitarians, and that despite differences in adoption of method, they agreed on two points: "that the victims of want would have to be helped if a more reasonable future were to be opened up for Europe, and that it paid better to have intelligent human beings than ignorant beasts of burden."[3] Education was widely considered the foundation on which the welfare of the common people would be developed, and leaders throughout western Europe agreed on this, even though, in places, educational aid and plans were only verbal.[4]

Although control of education gradually slipped away from the church, those most influential in the progress of education were believers in Christianity. Pollard pointed out that the impetus of education in that era was not religious, but that "many people who interested themselves in the possibilities of education, even those among them who played minor roles, were frequently devout Christians."[5]

At the turn of the century, war was also an influence on the educational reforms attempted in many European countries. "It would seem indeed that wanton destruction caused many fine spirits to cherish learning as the only rewarding thing in a world of confusion and to strive with all their might to ensure its survival."[6] The American and French revolutions had increased a sense of nationalism in European countries, and new political ideas were promoted, particularly as they concerned the common man.

In most European countries, the demand for education, especially at the elementary level of instruction, was satisfied by the monitorial method, particularly the Lancasterian system. Pollard pointed out that Europe could not afford, nor was it ready to accept, the reforms of Pestalozzi and, consequently, adopted a means by which children could be cared for in great numbers. "Lancasterian schooling was important in the educational history of several . . . European countries, where the system was taken up avidly by reformers and progressive statesmen."[7] Pollard made this evaluation:

The dissemination of the Bell-Lancaster system through England, France, Spain, Greece, Italy, Denmark, Sweden and Norway constitutes one of the most amazing educational movements of all time. True one may say that its success was due to its comparative effectiveness at a time when cheapness was the prime consideration, and that it weakened in its influence in proportion as nations were prepared to spend more money on education, but the fact remains that it was by far the most widely spread method of instruction used on the Continent in the twenty years succeeding Waterloo.[8]

The monitorial system made great headway, and by 1831, a report in the *American Annals of Education* stated that Belgium, Denmark, Sweden, Norway, Russia, and parts of Italy had established monitorial schools.[9] Later that same year, another report stated that Denmark had two thousand monitorial schools, Sweden had eighteen hundred, and schools of that kind had also been introduced in Spain and Sardinia. In addition, the method was increasingly adopted in France, where, at one time, the government had interfered with its progress.[10] "This system succeeded best in areas where there were powerful forces for social reform and no firmly established national school system."[11] In countries where public support was widespread and where a school system existed, monitorial instruction was used only sporadically or not at all.

The British and Foreign School Society was instrumental, to a great extent, in spreading the monitorial system. Often the society worked in connection with missionary societies "to spread the monitorial gospel."[12] The society's yearly reports mentioned schools being established in Haiti, Jamaica, the Bahamas, Egypt, Malta, Ceylon, India, Australia, and Africa, as well as in western European countries, which will be discussed in this chapter.

It is interesting to note that the monitorial system that came from England was not the only type of peer teaching used on the Continent. Switzerland could claim the use of peer teaching prior to the advent of monitorialism in England. Holland established a system of pupil-teachers that was eventually adopted by England.

In the first half of the nineteenth century, a number of prominent American travelers visited western European countries and reported in detail on the educational conditions. John Griscom traveled in 1818 and 1819 and wrote a book on his experiences. In 1836, A. D. Bache, president of Girard College of Orphans, visited educational institutions in Europe that were established particularly for orphans and wrote an extensive report to the trustees of his institution. The report, published in 1839, included, not only educational institutions for orphans, but also discussed methods and systems throughout European countries. He wrote, "After completing a tour through some of the institutions of Ireland, Scotland, and England, I crossed to the Continent, and visited, in turn, the principal schools of France, Switzerland, Holland, Belgium, and the chief States of Germany, making also a rapid visit to Italy."[13] Monroe stated that "this voluminous work was on the whole exceedingly valuable. The discussion was confined to the presentation of essential facts, but these facts were very illuminating to those interested in the current problems of American education."[14]

In 1837, the educator Calvin E. Stowe reported on his European visit to the Ohio legislature. Horace Mann wrote about European conditions in his seventh annual report. Henry Barnard, secretary of the Board of School Commissioners of Connecticut, published in 1839 a report of his 1835–1836 visit to Europe, his first annual report. Barnard later used this information, as well as material gleaned from subsequent visits, in a volume published in 1854, *National Education in Europe.* "It covers all European countries and gives a wealth of detail concerning methods, types of teaching, subjects of study, nature of school buildings, and in fact practically every topic concerning education which could be of either professional or general interest."[15] In 1872, Barnard published a more comprehensive work, two volumes entitled *National Education*, which included information sent to him by European educators.

These reports not only preserved first-hand accounts of early nineteenth-century education in Europe but also influenced American education. Kaestle stated, "One of the most influential forces of all those at work in behalf of public education in the United States during the second quarter of the last century . . . arose out of reports on education in Europe."[16] These influences showed in developments in state control and support of education, the training of teachers, and the idea of compulsory attendance.[17]

MUTUAL INSTRUCTION IN FRANCE

Peer teaching had been used in France prior to the Lancasterian influence in the second decade of the nineteenth century. In fact, the French Committee of Public Instruction reported to the National Convention in 1792 and advocated the adoption of "moniteurs," "enabling four classes to be taught by one teacher at the same sitting." The spokesman of the committee stated, "The attempts of the most capable children to teach their schoolmates what they themselves know, and to inculcate it upon them, will instruct themselves more effectively than would their master's lessons."[18]

In 1810* an influential member of the nobility, the duc de la Rochefoucauld-Liancourt, had translated Lancaster's *Improvements* into French, and from that point on, the monitorial system began to receive publicity in France.[19,20] La Rochefoucauld had fled to England at the time of the French Revolution, and he expressed gratitude for the kindness the British had shown to him. He remained an enthusiastic promoter of the monitorial system.[21]

France received further promotion relative to the monitorial system through Benjamin Shaw, the member of the British and Foreign School Society who later crusaded for the system in the United States. Shaw had lived in Paris for several months, having been sent there by the society to publicize the benefits of the system.[22,23] Shaw was described by Lasteyrie as "a distinguished member of the English Society, who, animated by a zealous and enlightened philanthropy, came as soon as circumstances allowed to France, in order to labor for the spread of the new system, and by his experience and advice to aid those who wished to organize it in France."[24]

It was in 1814, however, that major efforts were made in France on behalf of the adoption of mutual instruction. Napoleon had abdicated on April 11, 1814, the first Treaty of Paris had been signed by May 30, and communication between European countries was facilitated. Four members of the Society for the Encouragement of National Industry were sent to England to investigate the monitorial system. Salmon explained that the society had been established to promote the development of mechanical arts and new inventions, "but as the training of the child was the most promising method for promoting the industry of the adult, the opening of schools became an object of desire." Schools, however, could not function without funds, and the state had spent money on war, leaving nothing for education. "Still, something could be done if a plan for reducing the cost of maintenance were devised, and the Society learned with much interest that such a plan was being tried with success in the British Islands."[25]

---

*Pollard set the date as 1815, but other sources agree with the 1810 date.

The four members of the deputation were the Count de Laborde, the Count de Lasteyrie, Francois-Edmé Jomard, and Jean-Baptiste Say.[26] Karaczan reported that the four men were surprised at the success of the method in England.[27] They attended the biannual meeting of the British and Foreign School Society and visited the Borough Road School and the Central School at Baldwin's Gardens (the normal school of the National Society). Upon their return to Paris, Jomard wrote a report of his impressions, and Laborde wrote a book on the monitorial system, as did Lasteyrie. Say, who was more interested in political economy, only mentioned the monitorial system in his book.[28] Laborde related his experiences and extolled a method of education that could be utilized anywhere without taxation of the people.[29] Lasteyrie limited his description of the method to one chapter, and he avoided any mention of the controversy on the question of monitorial instruction that was taking place in England.

In Paris, the deputation resolved to form a new society that would be dedicated to advancing the education of the lower classes. At about the same time, Napoleon returned from Elba, and his minister of interior, Carnot, presented a report to him about the new society, the Society for Elementary Instruction, and its aims. A committee was formed to study the most feasible methods of education and to establish an experimental school. On this committee were the Baron Gérando, Laborde, Lasteyrie, Jomard, and the Abbé Gaultier.* The school opened in June 1815 under the direction of Rev. Francis Martin of Bordeaux, a Protestant who had been sent to the Borough Road School for training.[30,31]

Although the first meeting of the new society had been held on the eve of the battle of Waterloo, the change in government had little effect on its work. "Martin's became a model school under the government, the royal family subscribed to the funds, and other schools were rapidly organized in Paris."[32] Karaczan reported that the method was thriving in all parts of France, and he guessed that

---

*The Abbé Gaultier (see Chapter 3) taught in England during the French Revolution, having there found some of his students who were also in exile. He returned to France in 1801, and in 1815, according to Pollard, he visited England again to study the monitorial system.

by 1816, there were eighty monitorial schools in France.[33] The Restoration government made little headway in financing education, but in 1816, it granted 50,000 francs for primary schools. Salmon said that the decree accompanying the grant, which provided primary education for every canton, was "little more than a pious wish,"[34] and yet it must have had some effect because fifteen hundred monitorial schools opened before 1820.

It was not long, however, before a controversy over monitorial instruction, similar to the one in England, began in France. In late 1816, the clerical reactionaries began to oppose the monitorial method, no doubt because of the prevalence of Protestant teachers in monitorial schools. Salmon stated that "it was only a method of organization and instruction, and it might be employed with the same facility in a Catholic school as in any other. But it was suspect in its origin and in the horrible liberality of the Society which had done most to promote it." The result was that all Protestant teachers were to be dismissed, and that the simultaneous method employed by the Christian Brothers was to take precedence. Salmon said that the number of monitorial schools declined, but Binns and Kaestle maintained that the number of schools increased.[36,37,38,39] Griscom wrote:

The cry of danger to the Catholic Church has been listened to, the schools have to struggle under the weight of clerical displeasure, and the society seems to be threatened with annihilation. The spirit of the system has, notwithstanding, proved to be congenial with the tastes of the French people; many of the schools were in excellent order, and some parts of the general scheme of mutual instruction have been improved by the ingenuity and learning of the Savans [sic] of that country.[40]

Griscom also reported in his book that he had visited the school of the Abbé Gaultier "and found him with a class of boys, composed of the monitors of different schools. This excellent man is a warm friend and promoter of the system of mutual instruction, as they here call the plan."[41] Griscom also met and visited with Count Lasteyrie and wrote that they had interesting conversations relative to schools. Lasteyrie, Griscom said, exerted himself "notably in the cause" of mutual instruction.[42]

By the 1830s, interest in monitorial instruction began to wane. Victor Cousin, while visiting in Holland in the late 1830s, wrote that "the system of mutual instruction is still popular in France, to a degree that is truly lamentable," and "unhappily, the system of mutual instruction survived the struggles which preceded the revolution of 1830, but simultaneous instruction is gradually making progress, and the eyes of honest and disinterested persons will be opened."[43] In 1839, Bache reported that there were two leading methods in the public schools, the simultaneous and the mutual instruction methods. He found that "those on the plan of mutual instruction were inferior to the English model."[44]

In spite of its shortcomings, the mutual instruction method, as the monitorial system was called in France in order to disassociate with the foreign element, became an incentive for the establishment of mass education.[45,46]

THE SWISS EDUCATORS

Napoleon, in the last decade of the eighteenth century, annexed several cantons of the Swiss Confederation and, in 1798, decreed the establishment of a Helvetic Republic to be organized along French ideas. By the end of 1799, Switzerland was a land occupied and virtually ruled by France.[47] Numerous Swiss cantons fought the French armies, and "amongst the Swiss Cantons which offered the most energetic resistance to the encroachments of the French Directory, Unterwalden stood in the first rank."[48] Silber stated that "the Roman Catholic population had been incited by their priests to oppose the democratic Constitution and were ruthlessly punished by the French with slaughter and devastation. Hundreds of people were killed, and children lost their parents and their homes."[49]

Johann Heinrich Pestalozzi was sent to Stanz by the French to establish a school for the orphaned and poor children. He arrived in Stanz late in 1798 or early in 1799 (sources vary on the date). "The Government assigned him for his school an empty convent, in which some alternations were indispensable. When it became known that the convent was open, even before the kitchen, school and bedrooms were completed, poor orphan children flocked thither in large numbers."[50] Pestalozzi worked in Stanz against immense odds. He had no assistant, although he had about eighty children in his care.[51] Krüsi described the situation:

The inhabitants of the town were governed by priests, from whom little help and sympathy could be expected. Add to this the general devastation of the country, the want of food, shelter, and other necessaries of life, the absence of school furniture and apparatus, and the reader can judge whether it offered many inducements to a man fifty-three years of age, of frail physical constitution, and weary from disappointment and care.[52]

Pestalozzi had been unsuccessful as a minister, but he had not lost sight of his aim to serve his own countrymen. He wrote:

I saw the unfortunate condition of all mankind, especially of my own countrymen, in all its hollowness. I saw indulgence despoiling the highest moral, spiritual, and civil interests, and sapping the lifeblood of our race as never before in the history of Europe. I saw finally the people of our nation steeped in poverty, misery, and universal want. From youth up the purpose of my life has been to secure to the poor of my country a happier fate by improving and simplifying their educational privileges.[53]

Barnard wrote that Pestalozzi's experience at Stanz "gave a distinct and tangible aim to his deep inward longing to serve his fellow creatures; it became the vision of his dreams, the object of all his plans."[54]

Pestalozzi wrote of his experiences in a lengthy letter to his friend Gessner, a bookseller. In this letter is evidence that Pestalozzi used peer teaching. He said:

The number and inequality of my children rendered my task easier. Just as in a family the eldest and cleverest child readily shows what he knows to his younger brothers and sisters and feels proud and happy to be able to take his mother's place for a moment, so my children were delighted when they know something that they could teach others. A sentiment of honour awoke in them, and they learned twice as well by making the younger ones repeat their words. In this way I soon had helpers and collaborators amongst the children themselves. . . . These child-helpers, whom I had formed from the very outset, and who had followed my method step by step, were certainly much more useful to me than any regular schoolmasters could have been.[55]

A passage from Pestalozzi's *How Gertrude Teaches Her Children* also points out his use of peer teaching:

Children taught children. . . . This self-activity, which had developed itself in many ways in the beginning of learning, worked with great force on the birth and growth of the conviction in me, that all true, all educative instruction must be drawn out of the children themselves, and be born within them. To this I was led chiefly by necessity. Since I had no fellow-helpers, I put a capable child between two less capable ones; he embraced them with both arms, he told them what he knew, and they learned to repeat after him what they knew not.[56]

Leitch quoted Biber in clarifying a misunderstanding that Pestalozzi's system was the same as that of Lancaster and Bell. Biber defined the difference as follows:

Pestalozzi employed one child to teach another. This is mutual instruction, no doubt. Bell and Lancaster employed one child to teach another: this, too, is mutual instruction; but Pestalozzi awakened in one child a consciousness of his powers and a tendency to mental self-activity; and the child so awakened he called in to assist him in awakening other children in the same manner and by the same means. Pestalozzi led his children by the love which they bore him, by the moral ascendency which he gained over them; so that, whithersoever he led the way, they were willing to follow; and in the same manner he taught his children to treat one another. Bell and Lancaster, on the contrary, drill one child through an artificial machinery of lifeless tasks, and the child so drilled they employ to drill others in the same manner and by the same means.[57]

Pestalozzi's experience at Stanz lasted only until June 1799, when the French appeared again in Stanz and closed his school. Although Guimps wrote that in Stanz was the "birth of a great, fruitful, and salutary reform,"[58] there is no further evidence that could be found relating to Pestalozzi's use of peer teaching.

Pestalozzi did meet Bell, however. In 1815, Bell visited Yverdun, but he could find nothing of merit in Pestalozzi's system. "Whatever we may think of Bell as an educationist, he was certainly a poor prophet. On leaving Yverdun, he said, 'In another twelve years mutual instruction will be adopted by the whole world and Pestalozzi's method will be forgotten.' "[59]

Jean-Baptiste Girard was born in Fribourg, Switzerland, in 1765. He was a member of the Order of St. Francis, "a scholar of some stature and an able teacher."[60] In 1799, he sent to Albert Stapfer, Minister of Arts and Sciences, a plan for the organization of national education, and Stapfer subsequently invited him to come to Berne. There, Girard saw the many vagrant children, results of the Revolution, and determined to build a primary school for them. He went to Pestalozzi in Burgdorf, seeking counsel. Pestalozzi encouraged Girard to do what he himself had done in Stanz. Toward the end of 1803, Girard was able to establish a school in Berne. Then he was recalled to his hometown, Fribourg. The Franciscans had been asked to direct a new school, and they were willing, provided Girard would return. Girard became director of the primary schools in Fribourg in 1804 and continued until 1823.

Pollard reported that Girard had difficulty in deciding which method of education to use. Finally, he "came to use by turn the direct spoken word of a master supplemented by the services of monitors."[61] By 1815, "he had succeeded in bringing his school to the forefront in the battle against ignorance. That in itself was a remarkable achievement, but what was even more remarkable was the fact that he did so whilst relying on the services of monitors."[62] Leitch called Girard "the benevolent founder of mutual instruction in Switzerland" and said, "When he met with difficulty in explaining any word or subject to a child, he often called in a boy more advanced to aid him, and usually found him to succeed entirely, even when all his own efforts had failed."[63]

Girard did not hear of the work of Bell or Lancaster until 1815, when he read the accounts written by Lasteyrie and Laborde. He determined to become more acquainted with monitorial instruction as practiced in England, and he adopted several features, particularly those of Bell's system. He also relied on the ideas of Pestalozzi. "To him, therefore, special consideration must be given, for not only did he bring the mutual method to a high level of efficiency, but also devised an educational compromise which was quite without parallel in Europe."[64]

In 1818, John Griscom from New York visited Fribourg and, although he did not meet Girard personally, was introduced to his school. He verified the success Girard experienced and said, "The

Lancasterian plan of instruction, came opportunely to his aid; but he was rather a 'Belliste,' than a 'Lancasterian.' "[65]

By 1823, Girard and his methods of instruction had aroused opposition from the Jesuits in Fribourg and from the bishop of the diocese. Mutual instruction was declared to be "defective in religion and morals."[66] Girard was dismissed and sent to Lucerne to teach philosophy.[67]

Actual monitorial schools were established in a few places in Switzerland. Griscom visited a school in Geneva in 1818 and wrote that the methods used were similar to what he had seen in England.[68] Karaczan listed schools in Geneva, Carrouge, and Lausanne.[69]

When Barnard published his book *National Education in Europe* in 1854, he wrote that teachers in Switzerland were assisted by monitors in teaching the more mechanical parts of instruction. The monitors were chosen from the advanced pupils and stayed with the teacher until they were ready to go to a normal school. Barnard felt this was an advantage because "Swiss teachers have often been engaged in schools, and in school management, from their earliest years."[70] Although it was better to have experienced teachers, Barnard stated, monitors were useful if such teachers were not available.

ADOPTION OF THE SYSTEM IN THE SCANDINAVIAN COUNTRIES

The French Revolution had a decided influence on Denmark and on Frederick VI, particularly in awakening an interest in education. In 1789, a committee was appointed to reorganize the school system. This committee, the High Commission of Schools, formulated what became the school law of 1814, which provided for the establishment of elementary schools in villages and towns, higher education in the towns, and made attendance compulsory.[71,72]

Even before 1814, interest had been shown in monitorial instruction. In 1811, a prisoner of war had been returned to England for training by the British and Foreign School Society, and the society also arranged for a Dane to lecture on the monitorial system in Denmark, Sweden, and Prussia. A Mr. Feldborg was admitted to the Borough Road School for training in 1814.[73]

In 1816, Frederick VI learned of the monitorial movement through reports sent from the French embassy in Copenhagen. His interest was further aroused in 1818 by Captain Josef Nicolai Abrahamson, a young officer who had been in northern France and who had become acquainted with the method of mutual instruction. In France, Abrahamson "had conceived the idea that, by means of it, he could confer a signal benefit on the poor children of his native land."[74] With the king's permission, Abrahamson began a model school in Copenhagen. The apparent success of the school was encouraging, and in 1822, "the method of mutual instruction was recommended for all elementary schools."[75] A report by Abrahamson in 1826 to the king stated that monitorial instruction had been applied to the lowest classes of the schools. "Reading, writing, computation, and geography, these constitute the first elements of knowledge, the aim of instruction in the lower classes, the end which is to be attained by monitorial instruction."[76] Abrahamson listed the advantages of mutual instruction as follows:

Economy in the materials;
Rapidity of progress;
Satisfaction of masters and pupils;
Advancement of morality;
Good preparation for higher studies;
Relief to the masters.[77]

Abrahamson also stated that 1,707 schools had opened voluntarily, adding that "the King wisely issued no orders for the general introduction of this useful institution."[78]

In 1831, the *American Annals of Education* printed a notice that Abrahamson had reported the progress of mutual instruction in Denmark and that since 1823, 2,575 schools had opened. The entire number of schools in operation was 2,814.[79]

Pollard wrote that the monitorial system continued to be used in Denmark until 1837, while Arnett and Smith said that it was extensively employed until 1841.[80,81] Kaestle wrote that "in Denmark and Sweden, the monitorial movement had a large impact and a relatively placid history, constituting an early phase of public school development."[82]

Educational reform did not take place in Sweden, until after 1800, and was largely the result of the introduction of the monitorial system into Denmark.[83] Barnard reported that organized popular schools increased between 1800 and 1842, but what gave education a new impulse was "the discussions which grew out of the controversies of the Bell and Lancaster methods in England and Denmark."[84]

Count Jacob de la Gardie had lived in London and had observed the monitorial schools there. In 1821, he published a report that attracted the interest of the Swedish king, Gustavus IV. The king sent one of his secretaries, J. A. Gerelius, and a government official, H. Svensson, to London. "On their return they became, with de la Garde,* the leading spirits of a society which was established in 1822 to promote the construction of monitorial schools throughout Sweden."[85]

Bogoslovsky reported that in Sweden, the monitorial system "offered such practical savings in time and money and was within such easy reach of everybody it seemed heaven-sent, at least for the poorer communities."[86] Knowledge of the monitorial system came at a time when the public wanted more educational facilities, and it offered the best solution to the problem.

The monitorial system was officially recognized by royal decree in 1824. "Societies to aid in its introduction were organized in Stockholm and Gottenburg, and two Normal and Model Schools, one at the capital and a second at Lund, were established. . . . By these means the system was rapidly and almost universally nationalized."[87] By 1841, there were approximately five hundred schools, but after the law of 1842 made education a national concern, cheapness was no longer a factor, and the use of monitors declined.[88] The law of 1842 made the support of schools obligatory by local municipalities, and compulsory attendance was adopted.

Barnard made the following evaluation:

Deficient as this system was soon shown to be, especially in the hands of inefficient teachers, who converted it into a mere mechanical agency for

---

*The name "de la Gardie" is spelled by Pollard as "Garde." He is the only one to do so.

the most rudimentary memorizing, it accomplished much good in bringing the popular schools into some uniformity, and in establishing some agencies for arousing public and parental interest, which were afterwards turned to better account.[89]

In Norway, the monitorial system enjoyed a certain amount of popularity. "Indeed there can be little doubt that in Norway, as elsewhere in Western Europe, the mutual method was soon recognized as a singularly inexpensive means of instructing the offspring of the poor."[90]

Pollard reported that in 1814, a monitorial school was opened at Larvik by a teacher named Sölling who had studied in England. William Allen visited Norway in 1818, and his lectures aroused much interest. A year later, Bishop Christian Sörenssen visited the Borough Road School and wrote a book on his observations. E. F. G. Bohr, a disciple of Abrahamson, began several monitorial schools in various parts of Norway.[91]

PEER TEACHING IN HOLLAND

The common people of Holland had few educational opportunities until 1784, when a Mennonite clergyman organized the Society of Public Good, whose object was promoting elementary instruction in the city of Groningen. This aided in the inauguration of a movement for public education.[92]

In 1806, the same year in which Holland came under the rule of Napoleon, a school law was formulated that became the basis of public education in Holland.[93]

This early measure settled for the Netherlands the principle of public inspection of schools. It provided for the appointment of school inspectors who were to constitute in each province a permanent school board. The largest communes were required to form local school boards. No school could be established without the special permission of the provincial or communal authorities. The course of primary instruction comprised reading, writing, arithmetic, Dutch, French or other modern language, geography, and history. Schools were to be entirely independent of ecclesiastical influence. The schoolbooks were to be authorized by the school boards. Nobody was allowed to teach without passing the prescribed examinations.[94]

After the fall of Napoleon, when the kingdom of Netherlands was established, a decree was issued, which designated the school law of 1806 as the basis of all public education.

Mutual instruction never made much headway in Holland. In 1836, Victor Cousin from France visited Holland and studied the educational system. He recorded his conversation with van den Ende, who, in 1816, had established the first normal school in Haarlem. They discussed mutual instruction, Cousin having noted that he had not yet seen a single monitorial school. Van den Ende replied, "Nor will you. . . . And this by no means arises. . . from our not being sufficiently acquainted with that system; we have studied it well and it is because we have studied it, that we have laid it aside."[95]

The Society of Public Good had, early in the nineteenth century, offered a prize for the best essay on the advantages and disadvantages of simultaneous instruction and mutual instruction. Visser, the inspector of schools in Friesland, had been granted the prize. In his paper, "the system of mutual instruction is analysed in its most minute details, and is proved to be unsound on every point which bears upon education in the proper sense of the term."[96] Bache concluded that "this excellent dissertation which was published and widely distributed by the society, no doubt contributed to form or to strengthen the opinion which prevails at this day."[97]

Mutual instruction was not totally excluded, however, as the tenth article of the regulations, formulated also in 1806, stated. "When the master shall think it advisable, he shall reward the most advanced and most orderly pupils, by appointing them to teach certain things to the least advanced among the other scholars."[98] Cousin added that he could recommend such a practice.

On the one hand it is no disadvantage to those who are taught, because the instruction is confined to the most easy things, . . . and on the other hand, it is very useful to the teachers themselves; for in order to instruct another, we must know the thing well ourselves, and thus the little schoolmaster teaches himself very profitably. . . . The head master and the undermaster are in this way a little relieved, and can apply themselves with more care to their different employments. Mutual instruction, within certain limits, is sound in principle, it is only the extravagant length to which it is carried which renders it vicious and irrational.[99]

Cousin visited another teacher, L'Ange, and while in his class-room was surprised to see a twelve-year-old boy teaching reading to some younger students. Cousin asked L'Ange if he was an assistant; the answer was that he belonged to the most advanced class. Cousin related the conversation.

"He is then a monitor," I replied, "and you adopt the plan of mutual instruction." "God forbid," said Mr. L'Ange with a smile,—"but we are eclectic here; we do not proscribe any useful practice, to whatever general system it may belong. Thus, when a child is found to possess the talent of teaching, and intends to become an assistant, and ultimately a teacher in a primary school, . . . we see no objection to entrusting a pupil of this description, not to teach, but to hear the lessons, in the more easy parts, repeated."[100]

According to Cousin's account, he and L'Ange continued to discuss monitoral instruction, and the latter assured him that the system had been tried and found lacking, particularly when applied to moral and intelligent beings. Neither could L'Ange find reason for it in the schools of the poor. "For the poor have especial need of *education*, and you cannot *educate* by a plan of mutual instruction; you can *instruct* only by it."[101]

Horner, who translated Cousin's book into English, stated in the introduction that monitoral instruction "has been tried and rejected throughout Germany and Holland, the two countries of Europe where the education of children has been the most studied and the most successfully carried into effect."[102] Mann wrote in his 1844 report that "nothing of it remains in Holland."[103]

Bache also wrote that "the method of mutual instruction is not at all favoured in Holland."[104] He added that "the only approach to the monitorial system in the schools of Holland is, that pupils who have an inclination to teach, and who will probably become teachers, are put in charge of the lower classes of a school."[105]

Instead of monitorial instruction, Holland utilized a pupil-teacher system, one that England eventually copied. Students served an apprenticeship, which began when they were approximately fourteen and lasted until they were sixteen or eighteen years of age. They served as assistants and were given instruction for one hour each evening.[106] Cousin reported that the best students in the upper class were selected, and "those only are apprenticed who have distinguished themselves by assiduity and good conduct, and who have manifested a desire, approved of by their parents, to devote themselves to the instruction of youth."[107] Barnard said, "Not only is theoretical instruction given, but actual practice in teaching; the pupils being employed in the schools of the city, for the purpose of accustoming them to their duties as teachers."[108] Pupil-teachers received a salary for their services. L'Ange also told Cousin that "our assistants, who are in fact masters, are not entrusted with any thing beyond simple repetitions."[109] It was the purpose of the pupil-teacher system to supervise carefully the learning and teaching activities of the apprentices.

USE OF THE MONITORIAL SYSTEM IN OTHER COUNTRIES

As mentioned earlier, Horner said that Germany had tried monitorial instruction and had rejected it.[110] Binns wrote that the British and Foreign School Society had sent Schwabe, the foreign secretary of the society, to northern Germany in 1814; however, "the method seems to have been widely discussed but to have made little progress in these quarters."[111] Karaczan also said that the method had not taken hold in southern Germany, and he lamented on the conditions that prevented monitorial instruction from being adopted.[112] Mann wrote, in 1844, that nothing remained of monitorial instruction in most of the German states.[113]

Barnard quoted Kay-Shuttleworth as saying that the results of experiments with monitorial instruction "were so unsatisfactory that they soon occasioned a powerful reaction in the contrary direction."[114] Barnard felt that this rejection had not been entirely satisfactory in the country schools and that German states should study the system of mutual instruction as used in Holland and France.

The only German state that is on record as having used monitorial instruction is Prussia. Karaczan wrote in 1819 that the method had found many admirers there. Mann said in 1844 that only a few poor schools in Prussia used it. Prussia eventually developed a highly organized and well-planned system that had many admirers among educators in other nations. Perhaps for this reason, there is scarcely any mention of mutual instruction.

The German states in the late eighteenth century and the nineteenth century were more keenly interested in education and pedagogical methods, and they had established educational systems based on that of Pestalozzi. Monitorial instruction appears only to have been experimented with and never adopted seriously.

One interesting fact, however, is presented by Seeley. In a book on the school systems of Germany in the late nineteenth century, Seeley said, "In some schools where there is a large number of pupils one of the best pupils is taken as a monitor or helper. It is his duty to have charge of those doing seat-work, assisting, overseeing, and keeping them at work. He also assists in looking over exercise-books and is a great assistance to the teacher."[115]

In Russia, the early nineteenth century brought about a surge of philanthropic causes and efforts similar to those experienced in the British Isles and on the Continent. Zacek stated that the education of the masses became one of the concerns of the philanthropists. She said:

Not least among their concerns was the spread of literacy and the rudiments of learning among the Russian masses. For many members of this generation interest in popular education was natural, for only thereby could the moral development of the masses be furthered. The government, too, displayed considerable interest in broadening education on the lower level, both for moral and practical reasons.[116]

Alexander I became czar in 1801, and his governmental plans included a general system of public instruction. "In 1802 he replaced the Schools Commission by a 'Ministry of Popular Enlightenment,' and to this body the control of public education . . . was committed."[117] After the invasion by Napoleon in 1812, a reactionary movement took place, which caused the abandonment of many liberal policies. However, Alexander's interest in education did not falter.

In establishing education for the masses, a chronic problem that could not be ignored was the lack of trained teachers. A Central Pedagogical Institute was established in St. Petersburg as a partial solution, and the monitorial system was adopted as an additional aid in coping with this shortage.[118]

Salmon speculated that Alexander I had heard of monitorial instruction from Quakers who had settled in St. Petersburg.[119] In 1813, he commissioned Joseph Hamel to report on the monitorial schools of England. Hamel had been sent to Europe to study economic and industrial developments, and he had sent news of the monitorial system back to Russia. He later published a detailed account of the system. The czar himself came to London in 1814 and, while there, met William Allen and discussed monitorial instruction with him. Binns reported that Allen drew up a scheme for monitorial instruction for the czar and his country.[120] In 1815, Allen wrote to the Russian ambassador, Count Lieven, stating the advantages of the system. He proposed that three or four young Russian men should be sent to the Borough Road School for training and then return to Russia, where one of them would conduct a model school in St. Petersburg. Allen said in his letter:

When we contemplate the amazing power of such an instrument as this, we must see that its peculiar field of operation would be in large and populous districts, where the poor are numerous, and that it may, with the divine blessing, do more toward diminishing crime and misery, than could be effected by any penal laws; and I cannot but hope, that when thy illustrious and enlightened master, the Emperor of Russia, shall have time to consider the nature of the thing, and its bearings upon the happiness of millions, his benevolent mind will be disposed to give it a trial in his dominions.[121]

According to Binns, Allen subsequently visited St. Petersburg and attempted to aid in the opening of more monitorial schools.[122] Zacek reported that Lancasterian activity in Russia was encouraged by Allen's visit, which she said took place in the winter of 1818–1819.[123]

Four Russians were sent to the Borough Road School, as suggested by Allen, and "upon their return they taught at the Central Pedagogical Institute in St. Petersburg, and soon there were over 200 Lancasterian schools in Russia."[124] In 1825, Griscom stated that a model school existed in St. Petersburg, attended by two hundred boys.[125] The monitorial system was used in Russian military schools,[126] and many nobles, "from flattery or conviction, established schools on their estates."[127]

Zacek said that "Lancasterianism in Russia served as a catalyst of varying views of education."[128] Although some still believed that educating the masses was dangerous, others felt that a certain amount of education was vital for the encouragement of "spiritual enlightenment." Still others "saw in the Lancastrian movement a powerful instrument for civic training and for the social and economic progress of the masses."[129]

Alexander I died in 1825 and was succeeded by Nicholas I, a more autocratic ruler who extended authority over all aspects of government and over education as well.[130] Johnson stated that in efforts to carry out all regulations mandated by the government, the office of monitor was created. Among the duties of the monitor were "seeing to it that their charges prepare the lessons given them and review what they learn; and in their free time occupy the pupils with reading, or set them to translating or making abstracts of what they have read."[131]

The actual monitorial system expired with the czar Alexander I, and Kaestle reported that the only schools remaining were a monitorial school for foreigners in St. Petersburg and some in scattered places in Siberia.[132] According to Zacek, however, in 1827, there were still over two hundred schools, both civilian and military. Zacek also supported the conclusion that the Lancasterian movement died out in Russia, not so much because of the inherent deficiencies, but because of the political activities and reactions that took place in the 1820s. At that time, "official tolerance and encouragement of private Lancastrian activity was quickly extinguished. The régime returned once more to its familiar hostility toward voluntary organizations which, it was feared, might begin to demand a broader scope for their activity and become more political."[133]

A young Greek, Georgios Cleobulos, studied in Paris in 1818, became acquainted with the mutual instruction system, and determined to establish such schools in his country. Barnard reported that Cleobulos "prepared in his own language the necessary books and wall tablets, and after his return from Paris, gave instruction in the system at Bucharest and afterwards at Syra to a number of Greeks, who immediately, as teachers, introduced it into the common schools of several cities."[134] The system spread through many Greek cities and to the Ionian Isles as well.[135] These islands were under British control until 1859, and the British and Foreign School

Society was active in promoting the Lancastrian methods there. In 1854, forty thousand children were being educated in Lancasterian schools on the islands, and "the system survived after Greece annexed the islands."[136]

William Allen visited Greece in 1819–1820 and was successful in arousing interest in monitorial instruction. Even while Greece was experiencing the seven years' war, 1821–1828, an educational system was discussed, and in 1828, "the movement for a national system of education became general."[137] Schools were opened in many towns, and the Lancasterian system was used in them. In 1872, Barnard reported that "the monitorial system is pursued in all the common schools."[138]

Napoleon withdrew from Spain in 1812, and the constitution drawn up in that year provided for increased educational efforts in that country. Elementary schools were to be established throughout the country, and higher-education institutions were to be created according to need. Apparently, the law had little effect because Packard and Smith reported that "the government did little for the promotion of popular education during the nineteenth century."[139]

The Lancasterian method was introduced in Spain in 1817 by Thomas Kearney, an Englishman who had trained at the Borough Road School. Pollard reported that he "quickly interested King Ferdinand in its possibilities for rendering instruction available to the children of the poor."[140] Kaestle reported that a royal decree established the system throughout Spain. While the system appears to have flourished for a time, it soon ran into clerical and political opposition. By 1835, only one school remained in operation. However, in 1836, two Spaniards reportedly trained at the Borough Road School and returned to Madrid to begin a new model school.[141]

Fanti reported that in the early nineteenth century, very little was done to promote public education in Italy.[142] Griscom mentioned in 1825 that "a number of the most eminent of the nobility and learned men of Tuscany" were interested in the monitorial system.[143] Pollard said that a number of liberal thinkers "extolled the system of mutual teaching," reorganized existing schools in Tuscany, began an official newspaper through which to spread news of the system, and soon the monitorial methods had spread to Lombardy and Piedmont.[144] Apparently, it continued in these areas until 1844.

Kaestle reported that Lancasterian schools existed in Florence, Naples, and Tuscany at least for a decade.[145] According to Griscom, a society existed in Florence, with the purpose of promoting the monitorial system.[146]

NOTES

1. Ellwood P. Cubberley, *The History of Education* (Boston: Houghton Mifflin Co., 1920), p. 711.
2. Edgar W. Knight, *Twenty Centuries of Education* (Boston: Ginn and Co., 1940), p. 372.
3. Hugh M. Pollard, *Pioneers of Popular Education, 1760–1850* (Cambridge, Mass.: Harvard University Press, 1957), p. 129.
4. Knight, *Twenty Centuries*, p. 375.
5. Pollard, *Pioneers of Popular Education*, p. 130.
6. Ibid.
7. Carl F. Kaestle, ed. *Joseph Lancaster and the Monitorial School Movement: A Documentary History* (New York: Columbia University, Teachers College Press, 1973), p. 31.
8. Pollard, *Pioneers of Popular Education*, p. 110.
9. "Monitorial Schools in Europe," *American Annals of Education* 1 (February 1831): 84–85.
10. Ibid.
11. Kaestle, *Joseph Lancaster*, p. 33.
12. Ibid.
13. Alex Dallas Bache, *Report on Education in Europe* (Philadelphia: Lydia B. Bailey, 1839), p. 4.
14. Paul Monroe, *Founding of the American Public School System*, vol. 1 (New York: The Macmillan Co., 1940), p. 238.
15. Ibid., p. 239.
16. Edgar W. Knight, ed. *Reports on European Education* (New York: McGraw-Hill Book Co., Inc., 1930), p. 2.
17. Kaestle, *Joseph Lancaster*.
18. W. H. G. Armytage, *The French Influence on English Education* (London: Routledge and Kegan Paul, 1968), p. 33.
19. Kaestle, *Joseph Lancaster*, pp. 30–31.
20. Henry Bryan Binns, *A Century of Education* (London: J. M. Dent and Co., 1908), pp. 90–94.
21. Pollard, *Pioneers of Popular Education*, p. 103.
22. C. A. Eggertsen, "The Monitorial System of Instruction in the United States" (Doctoral diss., University of Minnesota, 1939), pp. 42–43.
23. David Salmon, "The Monitorial System in France," *Educational Review* 40 (June 1910): 31.
24. Ibid. p. 40.
25. Ibid., p. 31.

26. David Salmon, "Monitorial System," *A Cyclopedia of Education*, vol. 4, ed. P. Monroe (New York: The Macmillan Co., 1913), pp. 297-98.

27. F. F. Karaczan, *Der Wechselseitige unterricht nach der Bell-Lancasterschen Methode* (Kaschau, Germany: Otto Wigand, Buchhandler, 1819).

28. Salmon, "The Monitorial System in France," pp. 32-33.

29. Alexandre de Laborde, *Plan d'Education* (Londres: Berthoud et Wheatley, 1815).

30. Salmon, "Monitorial System," pp. 297-298.

31. Binns, *A Century of Education*, pp. 90-93.

32. Ibid., P. 92.

33. Karaczan, *Der Wechselseitige unterricht*.

34. Salmon, "Monitorial System," p. 298.

35. Salmon, "The Monitorial System in France," p. 44.

36. Ibid, pp. 46-47.

37. Salmon, "Monitorial System," pp. 297-298.

38. Binns, *A Century of Education*, p. 93.

39. Kaestle, *Joseph Lancaster*, pp. 30-31.

40. John Griscom, *Monitorial Instruction. An Address, Pronounced at the Opening of the New York High School* (New York: Mahlon Day, 1825), p. 34.

41. Knight, *Reports on European Education*, p. 31.

42. John Griscom, *A Year in Europe*, vol. 1 (New York: Collins and Co., 1923), p. 279.

43. Victor Cousin, *On the State of Education in Holland*, trans. L. Horner (London: John Murray, 1838), pp. 33, 34.

44. Bache, *Report on Education in Europe*, p. 200.

45. Salmon, "The Monitorial System in France," p. 47.

46. Kaestle, *Joseph Lancaster*, p. 31.

47. W. L. Langer, *An Encyclopedia of World History* (Boston: Houghton Mifflin Co., 1948), pp. 408-10.

48. Henry Barnard, *National Education*, vol. 2 (New York: E. Steiger, 1872), p. 19.

49. Kate Silber, *Pestalozzi, The Man and His Work* (London: Routledge and Kegan Paul, 1960), p. 111.

50. Hermann Krüsi, *Pestalozzi: His Life, Work and Influence* (Cincinnati: Wilson, Hinkle and Co., 1875), p. 30.

51. Roger de Guimps, *Pestalozzi, His Life and Work* (New York: D. Appleton and Company, 1897), p. 448.

52. Krüsi, *Pestalozzi: His Life, Work and Influence*, p. 20.

53. Levi Seeley, *History of Education* (New York: American Book Company, 1899), p. 259.

54. Barnard, *National Education*, 2:20.

55. Guimps, *Pestalozzi, His Life and Work*, pp. 168-69.

56. Johann Heinrich Pestalozzi, *How Gertrude Teaches Her Children*, trans. L. E. Holland and F. C. Turner (London: George Allen and Unwin, Ltd., 1915), pp. 17-18.

57. James Leitch, *Practical Educationists and Their Systems of Teaching* (Glasgow: James Maclehose, 1876), pp. 79–80.
58. Guimps, *Pestalozzi, His Life and Work*, p. 148.
59. Robert Herbert Quick, *Essays on Educational Reformers* (New York: D. Appleton and Company, 1896), P. 352.
60. Pollard, *Pioneers of Popular Education*, p. 112.
61. Ibid., p. 114.
62. Ibid., p. 120.
63. Leitch, *Practical Educationists*, p. 141.
64. Pollard, *Pioneers of Popular Education*, p. 110.
65. Knight, *Reports on European Education*, p. 36.
66. John William Adamson, *A Short History of Education* (London: Cambridge University Press, 1919), p. 256.
67. John William Adamson, *English Education* (London: Cambridge University Press, 1930), pp. 120-21.
68. Griscom, *A Year in Europe*, 1:362-63.
69. Karaczan, *Der Wechselseitige unterricht.*
70. Henry Barnard, *National Education in Europe*, 2d ed. (New York: Charles B. Norton, 1854), p. 176.
71. L. D. Arnett and A. T. Smith, "Denmark, Education in," *A Cyclopedia of Education*, vol. 2, ed. P. Monroe (New York: The Macmillan Company, 1913) pp. 295-96.
72. Barnard, *National Education*, p. 468.
73. Binns, *A Century of Education*, pp. 88-89.
74. Pollard, *Pioneers of Popular Education*, p. 109.
75. Barnard, *National Education*, 2:468.
76. J. N. Abrahamson, "Mutual Instruction in Denmark," *American Journal of Education* 2 (November 1827): 695.
77. Ibid., p. 696.
78. Ibid., p. 694.
79. "Mutual Instruction in Denmark," part 2, *American Annals of Education* 1 (July 1831): 332.
80. Pollard, *Pioneers of Popular Education*, pp. 108-110.
81. Arnett and Smith, "Denmark, Education in," pp. 295-96.
82. Kaestle, *Joseph Lancaster*, p. 31.
83. Ellwood P. Cubberley, *Readings in the History of Education* (Boston: Houghton Mifflin Co., 1920), p. 370.
84. Barnard, *National Education*, 2:501.
85. Pollard, *Pioneers of Popular Education*, p. 109.
86. Christina Bogoslovsky, *The Educational Crisis in Sweden* (New York: Columbia University Press, 1932), p. 25.
87. Barnard, *National Education*, 2:502.
88. Salmon, "Monitorial System," pp. 297-98.
89. Barnard, *National Education*, 2:502.
90. Pollard, *Pioneers of Popular Education*, p. 110.
91. Ibid. p. 109.

92. Anna Tolman Smith and C. H. Pluggé, "Netherlands, Education in," *A Cyclopedia of Education*, Vol. 4, ed. P. Monroe (New York: The Macmillan Co., 1913), pp. 415-18.

93. Cubberley, *The History of Education*.

94. Smith and Pluggé, "Netherlands, Education in," p. 417.

95. Cousin, *On the State of Education in Holland*, p. 35.

96. Ibid.

97. Bache, *Report on Education in Europe*, p. 206.

98. Cousin, *On the State of Education in Holland*, p. 170.

99. Ibid., pp. 170-71.

100. Ibid., pp. 72-73.

101. Ibid., p. 73.

102. Leonard Horner, "Preliminary Observations," in Victor Cousin, *On the State of Education in Holland* (London: John Murray, 1838), p. xliv.

103. Horace Mann, *Annual Reports on Education* (Boston: Horace B. Fuller, 1868), p. 278.

104. Bache, *Report on Education in Europe*, p. 206.

105. Ibid., p. 207.

106. Smith and Pluggé, "Netherlands, Education in," pp. 415-18.

107. Cousin, *On the State of Education in Holland*, p. 66.

108. Barnard, *National Education*, vol. 2, p. 414.

109. Cousin, *On the State of Education in Holland*, p. 73.

110. Horner, "Preliminary Observations," p. xliv.

111. Binns, *A Century of Education*, p. 89.

112. Karaczan, *Der Wechselseitige unterricht*.

113. Mann, *Annual Reports*, p. 278.

114. Henry Barnard, ed., *Organization and Instruction of Common Schools in Germany* (New York: F. C. Brownell, 1861), p. 90.

115. Levi Seeley, *The Common-school System of Germany and Its Lessons to America* (New York: E. L. Kellogg and Co., 1896), p. 102.

116. Judith Cohen Zacek, "The Lancastrian School Movement in Russia," *The Slavonic and East European Review* 45 (July 1967):343.

117. Anna Tolman Smith, "Russia," *A Cyclopedia of Education*, vol. 5, ed. P. Monroe (New York: The Macmillan Co., 1913), p. 230.

118. Zacek, "The Lancastrian School Movement in Russia," p. 342.

119. Salmon, "Monitorial System," pp. 297-98.

120. Binns, *A Century of Education*.

121. William Allen, "William Allen to the Russian Ambassador," *Joseph Lancaster and the Monitorial School Movement: A Documentary History*, ed. C. F. Kaestle (New York: Columbia University, Teachers College Press, 1973), p. 142.

122. Binns, *A Century of Education*.

123. Zacek, "The Lancastrian School Movement in Russia," p. 346.

124. Kaestle, *Joseph Lancaster*, p. 32.

125. Griscom, *Monitorial Instruction*, p. 35.

126. Karaczan, *Der Wechselseitige unterricht*.

127. Salmon, "Monitorial System," p. 298.
128. Zacek, "The Lancastrian School Movement in Russia," p. 355.
129. Ibid., p. 356.
130. Smith, "Russia," pp. 230-31.
131. William H. E. Johnson, *Russia's Educational Heritage* (Pittsburgh: Carnegie Press, 1950), p. 91.
132. Kaestle, *Joseph Lancaster*, p. 32.
133. Zacek, "The Lancastrian School Movement in Russia," p. 367.
134. Barnard, *National Education*, 1:554.
135. Pollard, *Pioneers of Popular Education*, p. 108.
136. Kaestle, *Joseph Lancaster*, p. 32.
137. Anna Tolman Smith and M. B. Hillegas, "Greece, Education in Modern," *A Cyclopedia of Education*, vol. 3, ed. P. Monroe (New York: The Macmillan Co., 1913), p. 162.
138. Barnard, *National Education*, 2:556.
139. R. L. Packard and A. T. Smith, "Spain, Education in," *A Cyclopedia of Education*, vol. 5, ed P. Monroe (New York: The Macmillan Co., 1913), p. 381.
140. Pollard, *Pioneers of Popular Education*, p. 107.
141. Kaestle, *Joseph Lancaster*, pp. 31-32.
142. Aristide Fanti, "Italy, Education in," *A Cyclopedia of Education*, vol. 3, ed. P. Monroe (New York: The Macmillan Company, 1913), p. 500.
143. Griscom, *Monitorial Instruction*, p. 34.
144. Pollard, *Pioneers of Popular Education*, p. 108.
145. Kaestle, *Joseph Lancaster*.
146. Griscom, *Monitorial Instruction*.

CHAPTER 6

Development of Peer Teaching in North America in the Nineteenth Century

INTRODUCTION

During the first decades of the nineteenth century in the United States, communication and transportation increased and improved considerably. "The opening of the Southwest, the development of commercial relations between that section and the older sections of the South and East, and the rapid growth in population in the entire Western region made better means of communication necessary."[1] Turnpikes, roads, rivers, and canals were greatly improved, particularly by the states themselves, thereby advancing communication between regions. Transportation received an additional impetus, with an increased use of the steamboat and the railroad.

These factors are relevant to this study because better means of communication and transportation spurred the development of a social consciousness. "Places formerly remote were brought closer together, economic interdependencies were established, isolation was in part broken down, ideas were now more readily exchanged, and men were able to take another step in their emancipation from the limitations of the primitive conditions which had so long surrounded them."[2]

Added to the growth of communication and transportation, and the resulting social consciousness, was an awakening among the laboring class of the United States. Cities had grown rapidly and profusely during the decades prior to 1830. Knight dated the beginning of the Industrial Revolution in the United States as 1789, when the first cotton mill was established in Rhode Island. Factories proliferated, and workers were needed for these factories.

Thousands of men, women, and children were drained off from the farms and firesides, and to these were added other thousands from Europe. They came into new and strange grievances. Unrest was inevitable. New social problems were inevitable. The problems of ignorance concentrated in congested communities, of pauperism, of delinquency and dependency, of vagrancy and crime, now appeared to an alarming degree for the first time in American life. Neither science nor law offered the workers protection from the destitution and disease, vermin and vice, that were certain results from long and unregulated hours of labor.[3]

Factory working conditions resembled those in England during this period of time: the working days were long, averaging fifteen to sixteen hours; two-fifths of the workers were children between the ages of six and seventeen; and only one-sixth of these children, it was estimated, could read or write.

The laborers began to unite, although it was not until 1842 that their right to unionize was first recognized. The working class and their spokesmen viewed education as a remedy to many of these social evils, although even among them, opinion was not unanimous.

The great majority of children received virtually no schooling during the first decades of the century. Eggertsen pointed out that public schools were almost nonexistent in the Middle Atlantic states, and charity schools were few.[4] Graves stated that

public and free schools were generally lacking outside of New England, and the facilities that existed were meager and available during but a small portion of the year. In all parts of the country illiteracy was almost universal among children of the poor. This want of school opportunities was rendered more serious by the rapid growth of American cities.[5]

During the first half of the forms century, many forms of financial support for schools were utilized, such as "tuition fees, rate bills, indirect taxes of many kinds, permanent public-school funds, or 'literary' funds, and lotteries."[6] It was not until about 1860 that many of the principles proposed during the first half of the century finally took shape; that is, public support, free universal education, government control and support, and the training of teachers.

It was into this setting that the Lancasterian system of education was introduced, mostly through humanitarian agencies such as the free-school societies that formed in many cities. These societies "came to regard the system of Lancaster, because of its comparative inexpensiveness, as a godsend for their purpose."[7] Kaestle discussed the basis of the adoption of the monitorial system:

In the United States the enthusiasm for monitorial schooling derived not from revolutionary fervor but from anxieties about changing social conditions, particularly in the cities. Low wages and foul tenements were degrading the urban working class, but reformers generally attributed poverty and crime to faults of character. The distance between social classes was increasing, and tension mounted proportionately. Voluntary organizations like the New York Free School Society tried to reach the growing number of poor children in the cities whose parents were not associated with any church and thus were not served by denominational charity schools. The appearance at this time of the Lancasterian system, with its appeal of economy, activity, and order, plus its nondenominational emphasis, was fortuitous.[8]

Graves pointed out that, besides the economical factors that favored the Lancasterian system, its effectiveness was also to be noted. Prior to the adoption of the Lancasterian system, "the whole organization and administration were shiftless and uneconomical, and a great improvement was brought about by the carefully planned and detailed methods of Lancaster."[9]

The societies were mainly interested in providing an education for the poor; consequently, their schools were considered pauper schools. Financial support for the schools did not necessarily come from the founders and members of the societies; state and city appropriations were secured for their work. "In this way, the members of the societies had control of the kind and amount of education given the lower classes, and set the amount of taxation necessary to furnish that education, but did not have to pay the cost of the instruction directly out of their own resources."[10]

Eggertsen pointed out one factor that is, at times, overlooked and that, in turn, brought about the decline of the monitorial system in the United States. He said, "The classes for whom it was designed had no part in its introduction."[11] Persons from the upper class as well as humanitarians fostered its adoption.

The monitorial system came to the attention of Americans in various ways: American philanthropists visited the monitorial schools of England; the British and Foreign School Society sent representatives to America; publications were received from England; teachers were trained there who migrated to America; and Lancaster himself came to the United States. It should be noted, however, that the first recorded decision to adopt the system came in 1805, but Lancaster did not arrive in America until 1818.

The features of the plan were essentially similar to those used in English schools, although many aspects were adapted to American conditions.[12] Eggertsen stated that "after borrowing the initial idea, American educators did not follow all English practices, but adapted procedures to fit American educational conditions."[13] A manual of the monitorial system published by the *American Journal of Education* provides an example of the American adaptation of the system. The introduction stated that a formal defense of the system was not necessary because of the favorable reception the system had received and because of its successful use. "The directions given in the following manual are founded upon a knowledge of all the improvements which have been made upon the new system since the first promulgation, and the experience of several years in the instruction of elementary and other schools."[14] One difference between the American and European form of monitorial instruction was that in the American schools, books were advocated, and children, generally, did not read from cards. Monroe described the system as follows:

This was a scheme of school support and of schoolroom organization as well as of method, but all three features were distinctive and very popular during a period extending over almost half a century. . . . It was an elaborate social machine, and mechanical devices of all kinds were then in vogue. The new democracy, as yet an experiment, put great faith in such governmental machinery. There was a general belief that most social ills could be thus cured.[15]

While much controversy developed in England over the merits of the Lancasterian system and the one promulgated by the National Society and Bell, there was little problem of decision in the United

States. "In the United States, where complete freedom in religion obtained, the system of Dr. Bell and the National Society found little footing."[16] Cubberley said, "It was the Lancastrian plan which was brought to this country, Church-of-England ideas not being in much favor after the Revolution."[17]

The Lancasterian system, which included nondenominational religious instruction, attracted many supporters because of this factor. Quaker philanthropists were committed to helping others outside their membership and thus could show themselves to be integrated members of society. Others who wished to see religion separated from charity schooling systems and who wished to develop public schools were also promoters of this nondenominational religious education. "Thus, a feature of the system which had been an impediment to success in England, where there was a solid Church establishment, became an important asset in America, where religious establishment was anathema."[18]

The Lancasterian schools also partially met a crucial need for teachers during the first decades of the century. "The hierarchical organization of a Lancasterian school provided a built-in apprenticeship."[19] While the system eventually received much criticism, it did provide one means by which teachers were trained. Many of the prominent monitorial school teachers (for example, John Lovell of New Haven, Robert Ould of Georgetown, and Lemuel Shattuck of Detroit) had been students in Lancaster's school, or were students of his students.

Until about 1825, the monitorial system was used solely in the elementary schools. After that time, however, it was increasingly promoted as a way of making higher education available to the people. A possible reason for this growth was that Jeremy Bentham had, in 1818, presented to each of the state assemblies a copy of his book *Chrestomathia*. With the book came a letter to the governors stating that *Chrestomathia* would aid in applying monitorial instruction to the higher classes of learning, as well as to the higher social classes.[20]

LANCASTER IN AMERICA

When Lancaster was forty, some of his friends made it financially possible for him to go to America. He arrived in New York in the fall of 1818. "On his arrival in the United States he was everywhere welcomed as the friend of learning and humanity."[21] Salmon stated that "he had come among a people prepared to do him honour."[22] Governor DeWitt Clinton of New York was among those who were on hand to meet him. "Clinton invited him to Albany, and 'introduced him to the leading persons in the chief towns on the Hudson.' "[23]

Lancaster went to Philadelphia in October, and Salmon reported that "the officials vied with each other in paying him attentions."[24] He was asked to organize a model school that would train teachers for other Philadelphia schools.[25] Hardly had Lancaster begun his work in Philadelphia when he went on a tour that included Washington, D.C.

Lancaster himself considered his presence in the United States as an affair of national significance. After official receptions in New York, Albany, and Philadelphia, he visited Congress on the 26th of January, 1819, when the House of Representatives passed a resolution: "That Joseph Lancaster, the friend of learning and of man be admitted to a seat within the Hall."*[26]

The resolution was passed on a motion by Burwell Bassett, representative from Virginia.

Lancaster returned to Philadelphia, but there he "proved so arrogant and untractable that the controllers, already annoyed with him on several counts, declined to renew his contracts after May 24, 1819. The schoolmaster thereupon found himself without a position and with several staunch enemies in the Quaker City." McCadden added that he had "worn out his welcome" in Philadelphia.[27]

Lancaster had come to America with hopes of receiving great recognition, particularly since his ideas and methods had preceded him. For some time, he was honored and his lectures were well attended. Even a man as eminent as John Adams wrote to a friend, "I have heard friend Lancaster with pleasure: he is an excellent scholastic and academic disciplinarian. I was really delighted and enlightened by the lecture."[28] In turn, advocates of his system also hoped to spread the use of monitorial methods because the founder was now among them. However, Lancaster soon had difficulty in

*Lancaster also gave an account of this visit in his *Epitome*.

his relationships, partly because Quakers in England had warned their counterparts in America of his problems, and also because of "the childlike volatility of Lancaster's own character, which all his tribulations had not been able to stabilize."[29] He soon discovered that "he was not indispensable to the Lancasterian movement,"[30] and that "he had little to offer that was new."[31] The Lancasterian plan had already been widely used, and it had proponents and opponents.

Lancaster left his family in Philadelphia and went on a lecture tour through Massachusetts and New Hampshire. While on this tour, he composed various letters to eminent Americans, which were compiled in a pamphlet entitled *Letters on National Subjects.*[*32] These letters were addressed to Burwell Bassett, a member of the House of Representatives; Henry Clay, Speaker of the House of Representatives; and James Monroe, President of the United States. All had previously heard him lecture in Congress. The first letter to Bassett was entitled "National Institutions" and referred to Lancaster's ideas on the founding of a Washington National Museum, which would serve as a repository of national collections, natural artifacts, and other items he believed would be donated. This institution would promote scientific education. To Clay, he said that this was the moment to ban ignorance and promote education, and to Monroe, he gave practical suggestions for the education of Indians. The final letter was again to Bassett, and the Lancasterian system of education was proposed as a way to achieve universal education in America.

Lancaster settled in Baltimore early in 1820 and established a Lancasterian Institute, where two former pupils were his assistants—Richard M. Jones, who eventually married his daughter Elizabeth, and John E. Lovell, later of New Haven fame. He wrote that he finally "decided on settling in Baltimore, and raising there a Lancasterian Institute, which shall be a seminary for training teachers, and a perfect model of the system of education; extended to the

---

*McCadden stated that Lancaster composed the letters while on this particular tour. However, the letters were published in 1820, the year in which he moved to Baltimore. Since he mentioned Baltimore in the second letter to Bassett, perhaps the letters were written after his move to that city.

higher branches of learning."[33] Lancaster was concerned that his system was being modified in the United States, and he believed that through his institution, he could show the "perfect model." During his stay in Baltimore, he also wrote *The Lancasterian System of Education with Improvements.* Lancaster stayed in Baltimore only until 1824. His financial matters grew increasingly worse, and he became ill. During that time, his wife also died.

In 1824, he received an invitation from General Simon Bolivar "to inaugurate a wide educational scheme on the Lancasterian plan of instruction in Venezuela, at a most handsome salary."[34] He had declined a similar invitation a few years earlier, thinking his enemies in England were trying to be rid of him, but now he accepted eagerly. The experience in South America was a failure (See Chapter 7), and he returned to America in 1827. He spent a short time in Philadelphia and was aided by his friends Roberts Vaux and Robert Ralston.

In 1827, Lancaster went to Trenton and opened a school, which again met with failure. Six months later he traveled to Montreal.*When he left there four years later, "he left behind him the usual trial of unpleasantries—including debts and a suit for libel."[35]

Lancaster spent a brief time in New Haven, where he wrote *Epitome of Some of the Chief Events and Transactions in the Life of Joseph Lancaster.* This autobiographical sketch was published in 1833. "In the *Epitome* Lancaster's self-pity is matched only by his supreme immodesty. After cataloguing his private and public griefs, he states that 'A singular concentration of powers has been found and admitted to exist in Joseph Lancaster.' "[36]

Lancaster settled in Philadelphia once again, where he continued to lecture and where he conducted another Lancasterian Institute. In 1838, he returned to New York. There is a record of a letter he wrote from New York to William Corston in England. By this time, he had opened communication with his former supporters in England, and they had raised an annuity for him. In the letter, he declared his intention of visiting England soon. However, on October 23, 1838, he was run over by a horse and carriage in the streets of New York and died two days later.[37]

---

*His experiences in Montreal are included in a later section of this chapter.

Kaestle wrote that Lancaster

> could not find a permanent position that suited his vanity and obstreperous nature.... Lancaster was always planning great things and never doing them; he projected new institutions and publications but used them primarily as devices to get salary advances, loans, and subscriptions. He probably petitioned more famous people for hand-outs than any man of his day.[38]

Salmon wrote that "his death was untimely in a double sense; it need not have come at sixty, and for his reputation's sake it should have come at thirty. At thirty some of his defects of character had not appeared, and those that had appeared might still pass for virtues in disguise; and at thirty all his creative energy was exhausted."[39]

However, Lancaster's direct and indirect contributions to American education have not gone unnoticed. Cubberley wrote that "the Lancastrian system of instruction, coming at the time it did, exerted a very important influence in awakening a public interest in and a sentiment for free schools.... It marked a long advance in the direction of free public education."[40]

THE MONITORIAL MOVEMENT IN NEW YORK

The School Societies of New York City and Their Influence

In 1805, New York was the largest city in the United States, with a city and county census numbering over 60,500 people. The state of education was dismal. Only five charity schools existed, and these were exclusively for the children of members of religious denominations for whom the schools had been established. The majority of the poor population had no education available to them, while a few private schools existed for the upper classes. However, New York was not unique among the large cities of the United States for its "inadequate and inferior educational opportunities during the first quarter of the nineteenth century."[41] Cities began to form school societies in an effort to provide an education for "poor children as do not belong to, or are not provided for by any religious society."[42] These school societies were financed by subscription and organized by philanthropic citizens.

The earliest school society was the New York Free School Society, organized in 1805. Early in that year, a group of twelve individuals met to plan the formation of a society that would support a free school. "At later meetings a memorial to the legislature asking for incorporation of such a group was drawn up."[43] The legislature passed an act of incorporation on April 9, 1805. The lengthy title of the society also identified its usefulness: "The Society for Establishing a Free School in the City of New York, for the Education of such poor Children as do not belong to or are not provided for by any Religious Society."[44] The names of individuals who formed the society began with DeWitt Clinton, later governor of the state, and included "a representation of the best elements of the old English, Dutch, and other families."[45] Clinton was elected president of the society.

A year was spent in raising money, and the school finally opened in May 1806. Many of the founders of the society were Quakers, so it may have been natural that they "should be influenced by the much heralded work of their fellow Quaker in London."[46] "Careful inquiries made by the Trustees had caused them to be very favorably impressed by the system of instruction introduced a few years before in England by Joseph Lancaster."[47] Reigart pointed out that "it was, in great measure, due to the 'limited state of funds' that the society introduced . . . the monitorial system."[48]

The Free School Society relied on its first secretary, Benjamin Perkins, for details of the plan. Perkins had visited London in 1802 and, in 1807, had published the first American edition of *Improvements in Education*. It could be assumed that the first teacher employed by the society in 1806, William Smith, had learned the system in London since the school was the first to be established on the Lancasterian system in American. Reigart stated that Perkins probably "continued to give his advice grounded on what he had witnessed in practice."[49]

There were several reasons for the adoption of the Lancasterian system. Bourne stated that "the trustees of the Society believed that they were introducing to the people of the United States a system of great value, specially adapted to the necessities of the underlying masses of society. Whatever, therefore, could increase its efficiency and multiply its powers, was adopted as fast as circumstances or means allowed."[50] Reigart listed the following reasons:

That without royal patronage or the stimulus of religious controversy, America should rival England in the adoption and extension of so mechanical a system of instruction as the one just described would seem incomprehensible at this date were it not for the evidence of the extremely inferior and inadequate school facilities in our cities before the introduction of the Lancasterian system. To supply instruction to the thousands of neglected children there was at hand a ready-made plan, remarkably cheap in operation, and, with all its faults, apparently superior in method and discipline to the schools of the day.[51]

Reigart also wrote that "the adoption of this system . . . was due primarily to its cheapness, and to the impression made by the completeness of its organization. It appeared to be particularly adapted to charity schools such as were proposed by the society."[52]

How the system was judged is perhaps best exemplified by extracts of an address made by Mayor DeWitt Clinton in 1809 at the opening of a new building of Free School No. 1. He said, "I confess that I recognize in Lancaster the benefactor of the human race. I consider his system as creating a new era in education, as a blessing sent down from heaven to redeem the poor and distressed of this world from the power and dominion of ignorance."[53] In 1818, as governor of the state, he addressed the legislature and stated:

Having participated in the first establishment of the Lancasterian system in this country; having carefully observed its progress and witnessed its benefits, I can confidently recommend it as an invaluable improvement, which, by wonderful combination of economy in expense and rapidity of instruction, has created a new era in education. The system operates with the same efficacy in education as labor-saving machinery does in the useful arts.[54]

In December 1818, Lancaster arrived in New York and was warmly welcomed by the trustees of the Free School Society, as well as by other prominent citizens. The society allowed him the use of one of their schoolrooms for his lectures on "the System of education invented by him."[55] Boese stated, "His lectures . . . were well attended, and did much to strengthen the hands of the friends of public instruction. A new energy seems to have been infused into the Society itself."[56] Palmer wrote, "His arrival seemed to give a new impetus to the advocates of his method of instruction."[57] Lancaster's arrival was instrumental in the compilation of a new manual of the system, and in 1820, the manual was published. The preface stated the purpose of publication:

The Trustees of the Free-School Society of New-York, believing that the interests of elementary education would be much advanced by the introduction of the Lancasterian System, in whole, or in part, into all the common schools in the State; offer the privilege of their establishments, for the gratuitous instruction of teachers, or persons intending to become so, in the peculiarities of that mode of tuition. As a further mean for the promotion of this desirable object, the Trustees now present to the public a Manual of the improved Lancasterian System of Instruction, as practiced in their schools.[58]

Reigart said that "the trustees took every means to maintain that purity of their chosen system. In 1818, they imported a teacher, Charles Picton, from the parent school in London."[59] Bourne, however, said that while the Lancasterian system was the basis, it was "modified and improved materially in the schools of the Society."[60] Palmer also said that the monitorial system had been modified.[61]

In 1826, the Free School Society changed its name to the Public School Society of New York. Its new charter permitted attendance by children whose parents were able to pay. "Immediately there was a decrease in attendance because many parents were 'too poor and too proud to confess their poverty,' and in 1832 the schools were again made entirely free to all."[62] Cubberley reported that the society

organized free public education in the city, secured funds, built schoolhouses, provided and trained teachers, and ably supplemented the work of the private and church schools. By its energy and its persistence it secured for itself a large share of public confidence, aroused a constantly increasing interest in the cause of popular education, and was granted financial aid in its work by both the city council and the legislature.[63]

Schools based on the monitorial system were established throughout the state of New York, including Albany, Troy, Buffalo, and Long Island.[64] An annual report by A.C. Flagg, superintendent of common schools for the state, suggested in 1827 that the present school system could be greatly improved "by the gradual introduction of the system of mutual instruction."[65] A factor involved in this proposal was that "the system of mutual instruction is admirably adapted to fitting persons to become teachers."[66] Flagg also stated that common schools could be improved by the establishment of normal schools, and he said:

The trustees of the "Public School Society" in the city of New-York, have recommended the establishment of a central school for the education of instructors on the monitorial plan. The monitorial schools in the city of New-York are of the first order; and the proposed institution would afford the means of supplying the public schools with teachers well versed in that mode of instruction.[67]

The Boston School Committee heard a report in 1828 by an investigating committee that had visited the New York system. The report listed numerous advantages in the use of the system, including, "It makes learning less irksome. . . , it gives to instruction more interest. . . , it keeps attention awake. . . . "[68] Advantages to the master were also listed, such as "aiding him by the number of assistants he can employ, and, by relieving him from the constant necessity of direct supervision of every individual."[69] The report stressed that "it is an immense saving both of time and money, in consequence of the far greater numbers that can be taught as well by this mode, as a smaller number can by the former."[70]

Another society had been formed in New York in 1785, the Manumission Society, which, in 1834, merged all its schools with the Public School Society. In 1787, the Manumission Society established the New York African Free School for black pupils, which adopted the monitorial system in 1809. A history written by Andrews in 1830 about the free schools spoke very favorably about the Lancasterian system.

The Association of Women Friends for the Relief of the Poor was another society that opened a school for poor children in 1801. Its purpose was similar to that of the Free School Society: the school was for those children whose parents belonged to no religious society and who could not be admitted to a charity school in the city. It could be assumed that this school and others established later used the monitorial system because these were also merged with the Public School Society.[71]

In 1836, the *American Annals of Education* printed an article that included a discussion on the merits of mutual instruction in common schools. Participants were largely from New York, with one from New Jersey. In general, the consensus was favorable toward the Lancasterian system. Hedges from New Jersey stated:

While in every mechanical branch we have great and numerous inventions to save labor and time, to economise often in comparative trifles, how little do we find of this description in the business of keeping school! The greatest improvement of this kind ever introduced into our country. . . was the monitorial or Lancasterian system of instruction.[72]

If the system was condemned at times, most participants felt it was because of misuse by those utilizing it. Samuel W. Seton, an agent of the New York Public Society, made an interesting point. He said, "We do not want Lancaster's principles or methods alone. Bell and Lancaster's system is what we need. Bell is the soul, while Lancaster is the body. . . . In the New York public schools we begin with Lancaster's system alone.[73] However, he added, changes had been made over the years, and some important modifications had been introduced, although he did not define them.

The Public School Society continued its function until 1852. In the meantime, the society had conflicts with religious groups, and partly for this reason, the New York City Board of Education was created, thus providing a foundation for the public-school system.[74] When the Board of Education was established, the monopoly that the Public School Society had held in public education was discontinued. "The new schools were called Ward Schools, each ward being practically a school district. The monitorial system was not adopted, a larger proportion of class rooms and teachers was provided and higher salaries were paid."[75] In 1852, the Public School Society ceased its work, and its properties were transferred to the city school board.

Reigart said the following in summary:

Seldom has any educational experiment had a trial so complete and adequate, and few have resulted in so signal a failure. A self-perpetuating body of most enlightened and distinguished citizens, holding a monopoly in public education in the metropolis, adopted a system which seemed to promise "a new era in education," maintained this system as nearly as possible "in its original purity," and retained towards it an unshaken confidence even after its mechanical nature and its educational inadequacy had become almost universally recognized.

The history of the Lancasterian movement in New York City and in the United States tends to confirm the position of the United States Commissioner of Education that we are not an inventive people in educational affairs. It required a trial of nearly half century to prove that the scheme of an ignorant, but talkative, London schoolmaster was a failure so far as practical results were concerned, and that it was without foundation in sound theory.[76]

Reigart did find it possible to defend the system, however. He listed a few ways in which he found it to be beneficial.

In place of the crippled soldier and the needy mistress of the Dame School the new system supplied young and enthusiastic teachers and monitors trained to control large groups of children. . . . In contrast with the unorganized and uneconomical methods of the schools of the times, the Lancasterian school presented a model of system and order, and an organized scheme of classification and promotion. . . . In contrasting the discipline of the modern schools with the brutality associated with the schoolmaster of a hundred years ago, great credit must be given to the monitorial system for the stress laid upon moral incentives rather than upon an indiscriminate use of corporal punishment.[77]

It might be concluded that the monitorial system met and accomplished a definite need in New York, as elsewhere, but that the Public School Society clung to it far longer than needed, when it should have explored other viable means of instruction.

The Educational Views of DeWitt Clinton

Among the supporters of the Lancasterian system, perhaps the most influential and loyal was DeWitt Clinton of New York. Clinton served in the United States Senate in 1802 and, in 1803, became mayor of New York City. During the period from 1817 to 1828, except for two short intervals, he was governor of the state of New York. Fitzpatrick, a careful scholar of Clinton and his writings, wrote in 1969, "That a lay person should, in the early nineteenth century, have held educational views of such insight and such breadth, is truly remarkable."[78]

Clinton viewed education as the salvation of mankind, "as the means through which society will set about consciously to improve itself, as the absolutely indispensable foundation to democracy."[79] He believed that all classes of society should be educated, and that vocational education should be included as well as the academic subjects. Many types of educational institutions should be utilized, the formal as well as the informal; that is, the historical, literary, or philosophical societies as well as elementary schools, academies, and colleges. A message to the legislature in 1825 exemplified his fundamental thesis.

A republican government is certainly most congenial with the nature, most propitious to the welfare and most conducive to the dignity of our species. Man becomes degraded in proportion as he loses the right of self-government. Every effort ought, therefore, to be made to fortify our free institutions; and the great bulwark of security is to be found in education; the culture of the heart and the head; the diffusion of knowledge, piety and morality. A virtuous and enlightened man can never submit to degradation; and a virtuous and enlightened people will never breathe in an atmosphere of slavery. *Upon education we must therefore rely for the purity, the preservation and the perpetuation of republican government.*[80]

It was Clinton's belief that government should encourage education, and his messages frequently referred to the importance of knowledgeable and educated citizens. Clinton saw the Lancasterian method as a viable one to carry out this task. His support of the system was apparent at the founding of the Free School Society in New York City, and in an address he gave at the opening of a new free school in 1809, he spoke highly of the Lancasterian method. In his address, he told the history of Lancaster and of the establishment of his system in England; he also related the history of the founding of the Free School Society. Clinton made public his high esteem for Lancaster and the monitorial method.

When I perceive that many boys in our school have been taught to read and write in two months, who did not before know the Alphabet, and that even one has accomplished it in three weeks—when I view all the bearings and tendencies of this system—when I contemplate the habits of order which it forms, the spirit of emulation which it excites—the rapid improvement which it produces—the purity of morals which it inculcates—when I behold the extraordinary union of celerity in instruction, and economy of expense—and when I perceive one great assembly of a thousand children, under the eye of a single teacher, marching with unexampled rapidity, and with perfect discipline, to the goal of knowledge, I confess that I recognize in Lancaster, the benefactor of the human race.[81]

Clinton added that "the trustees of this institution, after due deliberation, did not hesitate to adopt the system of Lancaster."[82] In this famous address, Clinton also referred to the increasing number of schools to which the system had spread in such a short time. After requesting pardon for such detail in his presentation, he further said of Lancaster:

His tree of knowledge is indeed transplanted to a more fertile soil, and a more congenial clime. It has flourished with uncommon vigor and beauty—its luxuriant and wide-spreading branches afford shelter to all who require it—its ambrosial fragrance fills the land—and its head reaches the heavens![83]

As governor, Clinton strongly supported the system and Lancaster as well. In 1818, he recommended the Lancasterian methods to the legislature, but "they were frosty to their charms and paid them no heed. Eight years later, in 1826, Clinton tried again, counseling the legislature 'to make provision for a seminary for the education of teachers in the monitorial system.' He tried again the year following, and again the year after that, but to no avail."[84]

In spite of Lancaster's lack of judgment in many of his actions, Clinton remained his loyal friend. Lancaster often wrote to Clinton and showed appreciation for the help and friendship shown to him. The public was no doubt much influenced and impressed by the friendship, a factor that Lancaster utilized. Clinton probably was not blind to Lancaster's faults, as may be indicated by a letter of recommendation for a Lancasterian teacher, Baker, in which he said, "But like many of the students of Lancaster, he resembles that great apostle of education, in excess of vanity and in defect of literature."[85] However, Fitzpatrick concluded that Clinton never lost faith in his belief in the superiority of the Lancasterian method, and his support of it was genuine and thorough.[86]

John Griscom and the New York High School

A prominent New Yorker, John Griscom toured Europe in 1818–1819, "visiting the schools, colleges, and charitable institutions of Great Britain, Holland, France, Switzerland, and Italy."[87] Griscom has been described as "a plain Friend and one of the most prominent educators of his day,"[88] "scientist, and eminent teacher of chemistry and natural philosphy,"[89] and McCadden called him an educator, an intellectual, and a scientist whose views on current scientific topics were often solicited.[90]

The results of this investigative trip were published in 1819 and in 1823 in a two-volume work entitled *A Year in Europe*. "The two volumes of this report contain an extensive description of the various types of monitorial, infant, and industrial schools, as well as the numerous social, agricultural, and industrial reforms, which were then in progress through Europe."[91] Eggertsen quoted the prominent journal, *North American Review*, which evaluated Griscom's book.

Professor Griscom seems to have gone to Europe in order to be able more effectually to do good, after this return home. His book, therefore, is simply a useful book, rendered very interesting by its relation to the present state of our own country. . . . It is chiefly filled with accounts of what he himself saw; the manufactories, mines, prisons, hospitals, public schools, and other similar establishments, which he visited; and consists, therefore, in a great measure, of what may be called the statistics of the benevolent and useful institutions, by which misery and guilt are diminished, and knowledge and power diffused in Europe. It is a book, which, in all respects, does credit to its author, as a member of the Society of Friends, and can, therefore, hardly fail of being interesting and useful to the public.[92]

While in Scotland, Griscom had visited the monitorial high school in Edinburgh conducted by James Pillans. (See chapter 4.) He wrote about the school in *A Year in Europe,* and was enthusiastic about the use of the monitorial system on the secondary level.

The very flourishing condition of the High School of Edinburgh, in which about 900 boys are taught by four masters and a rector, afforded, to my mind, a very satisfactory demonstration, not only of the practicability, but the excellence of the monitorial system, when applied to any or all of the exercises of a superior grammar school.[93]

Griscom wrote about the erroneous conclusions many had drawn about the efficacy of the monitorial system for higher education, and he related Pillans's example in his defense of the system's application beyond the elementary level. He said, "Many persons seem to have drawn the illogical conclusion, that it is not adapted to higher seminaries, or to the instruction of boys in the more elevated parts of learning," and then added, "Great merit is obviously due to the rector Pillans for bringing this method of teaching so perfectly to bear upon the higher parts of education, and showing its adaptation to subjects which have generally been thought beyond its reach."[94]

Griscom determined to establish a high school in New York patterned after the Edinburgh High School. On Mar 1, 1825, the New York High School opened, and soon it had an enrollment of approximately six hundred boys.[95] "It consisted of the introductory, junior, and senior departments, the last of which afforded instruction in secondary school subjects. In all the system of mutal instruction was employed."[*][96] One year late, a Female High School opened.[97] Cubberley speculated that American secondary schools were from that time on called high schools, after the Edinburgh High School.[98]

Fitzpatrick noted the friendship of Griscom and Clinton, pointing out that "it was Clinton who supplied him with the introductions to the prominent people in Europe whom he met. Under these circum-

---

*The Rennselaer School at Troy, New York, had opened approximately two months earlier. It was conducted along monitorial lines and emphasized vocational training. However, it never achieved the fame of the New York High School, which was probably more distinguished because of Griscom, its founder. For more information on the Rennselaer School, see Anderson, 1918.

stances it is a safe inference that Clinton was consulted in the planning and organization of the High School Society."[99]

In Griscom's famous address on the monitorial system, he stated his firm beliefs about the usefulness of the method. He said that "*Qui docet, discit*" (He who teaches, learns) is probably as true a maxim in its application to young people, as ever was uttered."[100] He added that "in the present stage of the progress of this system, the only question which can admit of controversy, is the advantage of its application to the higher branches of knowledge."[101]

Rost indicated that the monitorial system was used with discretion. As the teachers grew more experienced in using the monitorial system, they realized the need for reverting to lectures and recitation in certain courses. Griscom himself indicated certain caution in his address of 1825. He said, "But it would be entertaining a very erroneous and unjust opinion of the monitorial system, to suppose, that any one scholar or any one branch of learning is to be consigned *exclusively* to the agency of *monitors*. The time and attentions of the master in each department are devoted to his school."[102]

The New York High School, however, was considered eminently successful in its day. The *Southern Review* praised it by saying, "The High School of New York stands first in the list of the attempts to introduce the new system into the United States, as universally applicable to the various pursuits of the scholar, and is established on a scale commensurate with many other enlightened enterprises of that enterprising metropolis."[103] The school was widely influential, and many major cities adopted its pattern and plan.*[104] "For two decades the monitoral remained the prevailing method in secondary education."[105]

Rost pointed out that Lancaster had little influence on the development of these high schools. "Ironically, the institutions that developed on this level in Rochester, Buffalo, Geneseo, and Boston all stemmed from the Boys High School in New York, which in turn was modelled after the Edinburgh High School in Scotland."[106] He

---

* It is not the purpose of this book to list all the monitorial high schools that were established. Rost has included a description of the majority of these, and Anderson also described those in prominent cities.

added, "Only to the degree that Pillans became aware of monitorial methods by seeing its success in the common schools of Great Britain can one link Lancaster with the institutions in New York and Massachusetts.[107]

The New York High School continued until about 1831, when it was sold by the trustees to the Society of Mechanics and Tradesmen.[108]

THE MONITORIAL SYSTEM IN PENNSYLVANIA

The Lancasterian Schools of Philadelphia

Before the turn of the century, Pennsylvania had not made great studies in the area of education. Public money had been spent on secondary schools and colleges, but education for the poor was largely not available. McCadden wrote the following:

In spite of the existence of some excellent private or charity schools under religious or other auspices, the great majority of Pennsylvania residents were illiterate, and her future citizens were growing up equally devoid of the rudiments of learning. It was not until the early 1800's that a determined assault upon this situation began to make itself felt, first in Philadelphia, then throughout the entire State.[109]

Philadelphia led in the efforts to establish education for all, and the rest of the state eventually followed that example.

McCadden listed the reasons that gave impetus to educational advancement around the year 1800.

As with most movements that contemplate social betterment, the educational revival in Pennsylvania was the product of diverse insistent conditions and forces. There was the tradition of the Commonwealth's Quaker progenitors, which retained, as it does today, a vitality quite out of proportion to the numerical strength of the Society of Friends. There were economic developments which made the need for the education of the young, especially in the urban communities, more imperative and more glaring. There was the basic political requirement that the voters in a democracy be at least literate. There was the eventually vocalized demand of the poor themselves in certain localities that their offspring have the advantages which education alone could bestow. There were the abundant organizations and numerous individuals—journalists, teachers, philanthropists, and men in public life—who had resolved not to rest until the diffusion of learning was universally recognized as an obligation of the community. All of these, working by various means to the same end, finally succeeded in raising permanently the educational and cultural standard of Pennsylvania.[110]

Early educational movements in Philadelphia were brought about through the efforts of Quakers. They adopted the monitorial system because of the "economy, orderliness, and flexibility, and the experimental character of the Lancasterian system."[111] A report prepared by the Committee on Public Schools to the Pennsylvania Society for the Promotion of Public Economy recommended that the monitorial system be adopted in Philadelphia schools "because it was cheap and uniform, because it had worked in England and spread to the Continent, and because it gave the children 'habits of attention, order, and obedience.' "[112] The monitorial method was prescribed by the School Law of 1818. Section 10 of the law read: "The principles of Lancaster's system of education, in its most improved state, shall be adopted and pursued in all public schools within the district."[113] The matter of expense remained a crucial factor. Even as late as 1831, the annual report of the Controllers of the Public Schools for the first district of Philadelphia stated that for a student attending a school where mutual instruction was used, the cost was $4 a year, while in other schools, it was $12.[114]

The School Law of 1818 had prescribed education for poor children in Philadelphia. "This legislative sanction was later extended to most of Pennsylvania. Lancasterian schools soon sprang up in Harrisburg, Pittsburgh, Erie, Greencastle, Columbia, Milton, Pottsville, Newcastle, and, appropriately, in Lancaster."[115] McCadden pointed out that the system began to spread in the third decade of the century.[116] Kaestle stated, "By the 1840's monitorial instruction had waned, but the system as a whole had played a pivotal role in popularizing free nondenominational schooling, and in disseminating the program of urban school reformers to smaller towns."[117] The Lancasterian movement was successful in that it helped in the founding of a state system of schools that was available to all social

classes. "The Lancasterian System helped this movement by showing the possibility and the desirability of educating large numbers
of children at the public expense."[118]

Several philanthropic organizations were foremost in establishing
monitorial education in Philadelphia. In 1805, Lancaster had sent
copies of his *Improvements* to individuals in America, one of whom
was Thomas Scattergood.[119] Scattergood formed an association of
Quakers who called themselves the Philadelphia Association of
Friends for the Instruction of Poor Children. It was incorporated in
1807.[120] (Ellis showed the incorporation date as 1808.) Those who
formed the society were concerned "for the poor children of the
city, who were growing up in idleness and without education."[121]

The first school opened in January 1808 and was known as the
Adelphi School. Clinton, in his famous address of 1809, mentioned
that a deputation from Philadelphia had visited New York and had
been favorably impressed. He spoke of the "number of the more
enterprising and benevolent citizens, composed of members
belonging to the Society of Friends," who had founded the Adelphi
School, and stated that the school had two hundred children under
one teacher, and was "eminently prosperous."[122] McCadden stated
that "it is supposed to have been the first school in Pennsylvania,
and one of the first in the United States, to introduce the monitorial
system."[123] Other schools were established by the society and continued to operate until the School Law of 1818 went into effect,
"which provided adequately for the instruction of the poor. Then it
was judged best by the association that its schools should be suspended."[124]

In 1809, Clinton also mentioned the Aimwell School, which
originated in 1796 "by three Quaker women who at first taught the
girls themselves at the home of one of the foundresses. In 1799, they
found it necessary to hire a teacher. In 1807, their institution
became the Aimwell School."[125] The constitution of this society had
specified that the instruction was free to poor female children who
were not members of the Society of Friends.[126]

There is a record in the 1808 minutes of the society, which stated:
"The new method of education published by Joseph Lancaster,
which has been successfully practiced in his and several other seminaries, has claimed the attention of the Society."[127] The minutes
went on to say that a similar plan might be introduced into the

Aimwell School, and five women were appointed to consider the matter and bring their report to a future meeting. The system was adopted later that year.

In 1810, the Philadelphia Society for the Establishment and Support of Charity Schools adopted the Lancasterian system of instruction. The society had actually been established in 1799.

In the winter of 1799, a few young men, in the habit of meeting together on evenings for the purpose of social conversation, started the idea that they might employ their time very beneficially, by teaching gratuitously children of the poor, who had no means of obtaining it, the rudiments of an English education.[128]

The young men associated themselves under the title of the Philadelphia Society for the Free Instruction of Indigent Boys. A night school opened, and the members of the society alternated in teaching, "thus keeping their expenses down to a minimum."[129] By 1801, it was necessary to open a day school because of the extent of the work. A constitution was adopted, and the name was changed to the Philadelphia Society for the Establishment and Support of Charity Schools.[130] The society was aided by a bequest from a wealthy Philadelphia merchant, Christopher Ludwick.[131] This society "established other schools on the same plan later and was influential in obtaining the monitorial school law for Philadelphia in 1818."[132]

The society enthusiastically supported and utilized the Lancasterian system. A manual explaining the Lancasterian method of education had been published in 1809 by a printer in Philadelphia,[133] but the society came out with its own publication in 1817. An announcement to the public told of the forthcoming book and said, "The Lancastrian System, as detailed in the above Manual, presents the best mode yet discovered of spreading the benefits of Education, either in the hands of individual Tutors or School Societies."[134] The manual told the history of the establishment of the society and its accomplishments. It also urged the adoption of tax-supported monitorial schools for the entire state, and concluded the introductory section by saying, "The Lancasterian System seems to be a branch of that wonderful Providence, which is destined to usher in the millenial day. It is calculated to teach nations in the shortest period, and prepare them for the reception of truth."[135] The advertisement for the manual stressed that the views expressed in the manual were not to be confined to charity education. The copy read:

Every citizen is interested; because the effects of the general introduction of this System will be the same as the creation or gift of a vast capital to be expanded in Education: Its economy brings it within reach of the poor man's means; and to parents in moderate circumstances it will prove a saving of money, as well as a saving of time to their children. Nor are the most wealthy above the benefits which will flow from the general introduction of this System; its morality and the peculiar and happy fitness of all its details, to the capacities and feelings of children, no less than its economy, entitle it to the approbation and support of everyone who is interested in the welfare of the rising generation.[136]

The School Law of 1818 did not cause the society to abandon its school; rather, it changed its emphasis. "Conceding that the public schools were well caring for the elementary education of the poor, it became a question whether the funds . . . could not be more usefully applied by imparting instruction in the higher branches of learning."[137] Ellis stated that this attitude caused the discontinuance of the monitorial system. However, the schools continued to function for some time. "So well managed were the schools run by the Philadelphia Society for the Establishment and Support of Charity Schools that they continued in active existence long after a citywide system of public instruction had been established."[138]

In addition to the societies that established schools, private monitorial schools also existed. Philadelphia became the scene of an "acrimonious newspaper debate . . . in 1817" over the authenticity of the Lancasterian system.[139] James Edward had established a Lancasterian School in Philadelphia in 1816, when Edward Baker arrived and announced the opening of a school, the Real Lancasterian School. Baker had, in 1816, published a manual to explain the functions of a Lancasterian school to a visitor. He said in the introduction, "The following Pages contain a slight sketch of the Lancasterian System of Education, sufficient to enable persons who have read it attentively to understand something of the operations of any real Lancasterian School they may visit."[140] Also in the introduction, he stated that he had certificates from Clinton and Griscom, and had been employed "for some months past by the Trustees of the Free School Society of New-York, for the purpose of introducing the best mode of teaching on the Lancasterian plan."[141] This latter statement was included as a recommendation from Clinton. Public lectures followed, and newspaper advertisements were placed by both parties. Ellis summed up the controversy:

It was but two or three weeks until [James] Edward and [Edward] Baker were in a public controversy as to which had the genuine Lancasterian method, and the result was a partisan line-up. It is rather interesting to note the sublime indifference of these teachers of pay schools to the earlier Lancasterian Charity Schools of Philadelphia, which must have been established while they were both little more than monitors across the water. One might think, to read their statements, especially those of Edward, that Lancasterian darkness had reigned until their advent.[142]

The controversy apparently had little effect on the monitorial system as utilized in Philadelphia.

Lancaster arrived in Philadelphia in August 1818. Rost said, "His reception . . . was conducted with a degree of caution and prudence."[143] It is likely that Lancaster's reputation had preceded him from England since Quakers in both countries remained in contact. Nevertheless, Rost stated, "the prestige of having the originator of the system outweighed his unstable reputation and he was immediately employed to superintend the Model School for Boys, in spite of the fact that a contract of employment had already been extended to a Philadelphia teacher, Edward Baker, to conduct the Model School."[144] Lancaster was to organize the school, which would serve as a training center for Lancasterian teachers, and he was to make certain the school was conducted according to the exact principles of his system.[145] In December, the school opened; in February 1819, a similar school for girls also began operation. Lancaster supervised these schools for only a brief time. Rost stated:

The confusion and disharmony that had marked his relationship with the trustees of the British and Foreign School Society was again apparent in his new position. According to McCadden, his demands for an advance of salary, for an additional salary, in equal amounts for setting up the Girl's Model School, and for a greater amount of respect and cooperation from the visiting committee, all contributed towards the strained relationships that existed.[146]

Lancaster's tenure as superintendent lasted only until May 1819. Rost said that Lancaster had overestimated his possible influence and his past record, and had "acted irresponsibly and capriciously, exhibiting a vanity and conceit that did not wear well with the sober propriety of the Quakers in Philadelphia who were largely in control of the educational activities of that city, especially among the poor."[147]

Criticism of the monitorial schools in Philadelphia began as early as 1820, with a report from a visiting committee that had examined the Lancasterian Model School. The report pointed out that the committee had found improvements but added, "We privately spoke to the Teacher to endeavor to get his Monitors to perform their duties with greater care and attention."[148] In 1826, a special committee appointed by the board of the Philadelphia district said that the Lancasterian schools were "susceptible for great improvement."[149] The report recommended a plan of engaging monitors who would be older than the majority of the students and who would be permanent. In the current system, the report said, the teacher often found himself with more rather than less work because of the "pretended assistance of these boyish adjuncts."[150]

On June 13, 1836, an act was passed which "became the real basis of the system of public instruction throughout Pennsylvania," and the Lancasterian method was no longer mandatory.[151] After this point, the use of the system declined increasingly. "The Lancasterian Schools gradually gave way to schools with smaller classes and less rigid organization."[152]

Roberts Vaux and His Influence

In Lancaster's *Epitome*, he mentioned the name of Roberts Vaux, who treated him kindly during his stay in America.[153] McCadden said of Vaux:

There is. . . one individual who stands out for his pioneering, his long and active participation, and his purposeful and effective engineering in the uphill contest to make Pennsylvania education-conscious. That man is the Philadelphia Quaker and philanthropist, Roberts Vaux.[154]

Vaux had early begun his activities in behalf of education.* He was one of the earliest members of the Philadelphia Association of Friends for the Instruction of Poor Children, and for three years, he was director and secretary of the board. He had also joined the Philadelphia Society for the Establishment and Support of Charity Schools. Through these organizations, he had become acquainted with the monitorial methods. In addition, he had carried on a correspondence with foreign advocates of the system, particularly with Benjamin Shaw, a member of the Committee of the British and Foreign School Society.

In 1817, Vaux served on a committee that studied the conditions of the poor in Philadelphia. It was found, among other factors, that "fewer than one-third of the children of the indigent were being educated."[155] The committee recommended that a society be organized to administer funds collected for the poor. An organization was formed, which came to be known as the Pennsylvania Society for the Promotion of Public Economy. Robert Ralston was elected president. In addition to the nine committees that were formed for the administration of the society's work, the Committee on Public Schools was organized, with Vaux as chairman. It was from the work of this committee that the School Law of 1818 grew. Although the final bill did not reflect the exact recommendations of the committee, many aspects were the same. Pennsylvania was divided into districts, of which Philadelphia was the first. Schools were to be set up, controllers were to superintend them, and a model school was to be established for training teachers. The Lancasterian system was to be utilized in the schools.

Vaux was elected as the first president of the Board of Controllers of the First School District of Pennsylvania and was reelected annually until he resigned at the end of 1831. It was Vaux's Board of Controllers that hired Lancaster to establish the model schools, and no doubt Vaux was frequently caught in the friction that developed.

Vaux persisted in his use and advocacy of the Lancasterian plan. Although he may have seen the benefit of its organization and economy, it is more likely that it represented an improvement over what

---

*The majority of the information and further details on Roberts Vaux and his work are found in McCadden, 1969.

had taken place before. In addition, he saw that it had possibilities for "inexpensive mass education which it opened up at a time when the taxpayers were not accustomed and not willing to vote large sums for educational purposes."[156] He was not, however, fanatical in his devotion to the method; he saw it simply as a practical method when none better was available for the time.

As to Vaux's relationship with Lancaster, McCadden summed it up as follows:

> It is to the credit of Vaux's devotion to the Philadelphia schools and to Lancaster and his system that during all this conflict he managed to keep on good terms with the famous schoolmaster and also with his own school board. . . . It is also to the credit of Vaux's steadfastness as a friend, if not of his good judgment, that he carried on for the sixteen-odd years following Lancaster's departure from the service of the Philadelphia schools a most one-sided relationship with this man, in which all the giving was on the part of Vaux and all the receiving and begging on the part of Lancaster.[157]

Benjamin Shaw, the Promoter

Among the English philanthropists who were anxious to spread the Lancasterian system to foreign parts was Benjamin Shaw. He was "probably most influential in furthering the cause in the United States."[158] Shaw was also active in the monitorial movement both in England and in France.

In 1816 and in 1817, Shaw visited the United States. He expressed his disappointment at not finding any school that followed the plan perfectly, and criticized both the schools of New York and Philadelphia. Eggertsen said that the only school that met with Shaw's approval in Philadelphia was the one conducted by James Edward.[159] Ironically, Baker also claimed Shaw's backing, and Ellis quoted Shaw as saying that Baker was "the only Teacher I have met with in America certificated by the British and Foreign School Committee of which I am a member."[160]

Shaw not only gave advice to schools already in existence but also wrote newpaper articles and pamphlets. He had communicated with Vaux on several occasions and, in 1817, addressed a pamphlet to him and the Pennsylvania Society for the Promotion of Public Economy. The purpose of the report, *Brief Exposition of the Princi-*

ples and Details of the Lancasterian System of Education, was to give a sketch of the Lancasterian system, not necessarily because the committee needed the information, but because a majority of the Pennsylvania population was not familiar with the system. Shaw, in this pamphlet, also cited examples of where the system had been adopted successfully in other countries. He said, "This system, by its simplicity and facility in teaching, promises to extend over the whole earth."[161] He further said, "The order of the school, the organization of the classes, the obedience inculcated, the influence imperceptibly operating on the mind, to induce order and regularity, give to this mode of teaching an advantage over all others."[162]

When the School Law of 1818 was passed, Shaw wrote to the controllers of the Philadelphia schools, advising them how best to proceed with the establishment of the Lancasterian system of education. He continued corresponding with Vaux, not only advising and exhorting him, but informing him of the progress of the system in other countries.[163]

MONITORIAL EFFORTS IN BALTIMORE

Private teachers introduced the system in Baltimore. As early as 1812, Robert Ould, who had been a monitor under Lancaster and who had started a Lancasterian school at Georgetown, reported that he had trained a teacher for Baltimore. A newspaper report in 1813 stated that there were two monitorial schools in Baltimore at that time. From then on, notices of schools opening on the Lancasterian system were periodically published until Baltimore organized a public monitorial school system in 1828.[164]

Eggersten traced the development of the use of monitorialism in Baltimore through the annual reports of the commissioners of public schools. In 1830, the monitorial system was praised because it was cheap enough to allow persons to pay for the education of their children. The third annual report claimed that the commissioners' confidence in the monitorial system was "unimpaired," and in the 1836 report, the commissioners mentioned the efficacy of the system by comparing it to labor-saving machinery used in industry. By the tenth report, the commissioners admitted that public enthusiasm for the methods of the monitorial system, particularly the limited instruction it allowed, had declined, and that the use of the system had been greatly modified.[165]

Lancaster came to Baltimore in 1820 and established a Lancasterian Institute.[166] He changed his approach somewhat, however. Instead of conducting it in a similar manner to the Borough Road School or the Philadelphia Model Schools, where only reading, writing, arithmetic and some needlework for girls were taught, he added more subjects from the academy or high-school level. In this school, he was aided by two former pupils—Richard M. Jones and John E. Lovell. The Lancasterian Institute continued until 1824, when Lancaster departed for South America.[167]

Another noted Baltimore school was the McKim School, the oldest free school in Baltimore, founded by Quakers in 1821.[168] Quakers shared in the philanthropic spirit prevalent in the nineteenth century, and George Fox had early counseled his followers to care for the poor. John McKim was a member of the Society of Friends in Baltimore and had made plans for a school for the poor. These plans were carried out by his sons after his death, and in 1821, the school opened on the Lancasterian plan, which was "preferred to the former method of teaching particularly as a far greater number of Scholars could be educated at a less expense."[169]

The monitorial system was not as widespread in Maryland as it was in New York and Pennsylvania, and was largely confined to the Baltimore area.

THE USE OF THE SYSTEM IN MASSACHUSETTS

Bostonian Attitudes Toward the Monitorial System

The Lancasterian method never saw great success in Boston, and was sparingly used throughout New England. "In Salem and Boston he [Lancaster] was heartily disapproved of as a person, and when his system crept into some phases of their schools for economic reasons, they did not use his name with it but called it a System of Mutual Instruction."[170] Lancaster toured Massachusetts in 1819, and in Boston, he made the mistake of criticizing the school system, which he had not visited, and suggested the schools be improved by the use of his system, which would result in the dismissal of many teachers.[171]

A functional and well-established school system had long existed in Boston, and the schools were divided into classes, making the monitorial plan unnecessary. Butler stated that in spite of this, "the Lancastrian system might have made more headway against even the strong Bostonian pride, if the people of Boston had liked or trusted Joseph Lancaster as a person. None of the Massachusetts newspapers spoke well of him."[172] Butler made a study of education as it was reported in the New England newspapers in the early nineteenth century, and she concluded that "it was quite evident that Massachusetts did not trust him nor care for his system of education."[173]

Eggertsen summarized the situation in Boston as follows:

The people of Boston were never so enthusiastic about the Lancasterian idea as were the people of the other large cities of the time. No organized public or private educational institution there ever took upon itself as a major duty the fostering of Joseph Lancaster's idea, as organizations did in New York, Philadelphia, and Baltimore. The only attempts to reach the public with the concept were sporadic and generally unsuccessful, and were made by a few men like William B. Fowle who tried to convince the school committee to set up Lancasterian schools.[174]

Fowle himself stated in 1847 that "the plan was never generally adopted in any part of New England."[175]

William Bentley Fowle

William Bentley Fowle was born in Boston in 1795. After completing the Latin School, his early years were spent as apprentice to Caleb Bingham, the esteemed teacher in Massachusetts who owned a bookstore in Boston. His store was a center for Boston teachers, and education was continually discussed. Bingham did not believe in the prevalent method of education and was eclectic in advocating educational methods. Writings of educators were abundant in his bookstore, and Fowle became well read in educational methods.[176]

Fowle had become acquainted with the monitorial system, and he said, "It fell to my lot to make the first experiment on this plan in Boston."[177] He had been elected in 1821 to the Primary School Committee, which supervised almost all the schools that did not teach English grammar. The committee was concerned with the number of children who were too old for the primary schools but too ignorant for grammar schools. They worked to establish a school just for these children. Because of the lack of funds ($1,000 was granted by the town to experiment with such a school), it became evident that the monitorial system must be used.[178] Rost reported that "they were reluctant to advocate this plan because of the spirited opposition anticipated by the well-organized and vocal public-school teachers of Boston," whom Lancaster had already antagonized.[179]

The school opened in 1821, with a teacher who had come from Albany. After a few weeks, the teacher left, and Fowle assumed the responsibilities until a permanent teacher could be found. "The work of teaching, in which Mr. Fowle had temporarily engaged, he was thus led to continue quite against his intention; but he still regarded the booktrade as his permanent business."[180] Fowle continued to conduct this school for two years, using female monitors. When the school was examined at the close of the two years, its success was evident, and even the mayor of Boston declared it to be "second to no grammar school in the city."[181] The *American Journal of Education* listed a number of procedures, which they called improvements and innovations, that Fowle instituted in this school, including the admission of girls for the entire year instead of a portion of the year, no corporal punishment, teaching of English grammar and composition, children of all ages being instructed in one room, and every child engaged in useful activity at all times.[182]

The school was then disbanded, the children were declared competent to enter other schools, and Fowle resumed full-time work in his bookstore. However, he was soon asked to continue his work as an educator. He wrote in 1847, "A few days after my resignation, some members of the School Committee, with other gentlemen who had watched my experiment, proposed a school on the same plan for their own children."[183] Morrison called this a "promotion to a higher grade of work,"[184] and stated that the hundred citizens who raised money for this venture also furnished the school with sophisticated equipment virtually unknown and unused in the United States schools at this time.

This school was called the Female Monitorial School, and it opened in 1823 with about one hundred pupils. "The mutual instruction plan was used, modified to be sure, and adapted by the ingenuity of Mr. Fowle to all the higher branches."[185] Fowle, however, did not associate his educational methods with those of Lancaster. He said:

Lancaster came to this country, but he was out of his element here; and so little did he know of our wants, and of the expansive capabilities of his own system, that he spoke of New England as if it were old England, and denounced every deviation from his plan as a damning error. Lest, in my remarks upon the use I make of monitors, I should be suspected of using the plan as taught by Lancaster, it may be well for me to say, that, when he visited my school in Boston, he refused to acknowledge it as a legitimate branch of his system. I had retained the great principle of requiring pupils to teach as well as learn, but I had rejected all the machinery and tactics that he had used in teaching the uneducated and uncivilized masses of England.[186]

Rost pointed out that it was uncertain just how Fowle's system differed from Lancaster's. As far as the use of monitors, there was little difference. Rost added that "the lack of communication between these men may be attributed in great measure to the peculiar ability of Lancaster to antagonize those who could probably have done the most to further his system."[187] Fowle emphasized that monitors should be assistants, not substitutes for teachers.

The Female Monitorial School was greatly successful, and Rost wrote that "it was Fowle's extraordinary capabilities that made this institution so remarkable."[188] The school attracted a great deal of attention, and its success led to the establishment of a high school for girls by the Boston School Committee. It was taught on the monitorial plan. After about two years, other arrangements were made for the girls attending this school, and the Monitorial High School was discontinued.[189]

The Female Monitorial School continued, and in January 1826, the trustees reported, "Its success has equalled the most sanguine expectations," and they gave credit to the "able and indefatigable labors of Mr. W. B. Fowle the instructor, who has been obliged not only to pursue an untried path, but to do so with little aid from the experience or labors of others."[190] The trustees expressed the conviction that the system could be generally adopted, and that it should be adopted.

Fowle himself had given a report on the school to the trustees a month earlier, in December 1825. In it he detailed the method of instruction used in his school and thoroughly described the system. He said:

There is a different classification in every branch of study; and in classing the pupils in one branch, no regard is paid to their rank in another. Hence it not unfrequently happens that a monitor of reading teaches her monitor of arithmetic. . . In this way, every child has a fair chance to rise, if her genius leads to excellence in any thing.[191]

In this report, Fowle also answered some common objections. Some of these were that children were unqualified to teach others, that the master did not teach *all* the children himself, and that children were taught by rote. Fowle replied that children were not required to teach anything of which they were ignorant. He said:

The wisest and best of us go to church, and to lectures on all subjects, without suspecting that the teacher is only a monitor, who knows a little more than we do of the subject under consideration, but is perhaps our inferior in other respects. The art of teaching consists chiefly in adapting the explanation to the capacity of the learner. . . .Is it not a reasonable supposition, that the explanations of children to children, may be often better suited to their capacities, than the explanations of adults?[192]

In answer to the objection that the masters did not teach the children, Fowle stated:

He reviews them often enough to ascertain their improvement. . . . They are never out of his presence, and are always encouraged to ask his assistance when it is needed. . . . The master should bestow most of his attention upon the monitors; but no injustice is done to the lower classes; for they, in turn, will become monitors, and have so much of the master's exclusive care, that all former deficiencies will be amply made up.[193]

As to learning by rote, Fowle declared that he and his school could be guilty of this, not the monitorial system. It had simply been misapplied, if that objection could be sustained.

In 1826, William Russell, then editor of the *American Journal of Education*, prepared a manual of the mutual instruction system as utilized by Fowle. He intended it as a means of acquainting New England with the system, leading to its possible introduction in the schools of Massachusetts. Fowle called him "that most excellent of men and most judicious of teachers."[194] In an appendix to the volume, Russell listed some advantages of the system: (1) the system aided in the healthful growth of the student; (2) the moral influence resulting from the use of the system was superior; (3) the intellectual advantages were evident, such as the cultivation of understanding; and (4) the monitorial system prepared good teachers.

In 1828, the *American Journal of Education* reported that the monitorial system had been introduced in several private schools and in some of the public schools under the supervision of the School Committee. The results were "very satisfactory to many members of that Board."[195] A proposal was mentioned to introduce the monitorial system in all public schools of Boston. However, the article said that "much excitement of the public mind was produced by the arrangements proposed, which many deemed injurious in their tendency in regard to the school system of the city, and to the character of instruction in the schools individually." Much opposition had been voiced, and "many objections to it were urged with various ability in several of the newspapers."[196] The School Committee prudently dropped the attempts to introduce the system to all schools. The article also included a report that spoke favorably of mutual instruction.

In the following issue of the *American Journal of Education*, an article was reprinted from the *Boston Advertiser*, which criticized the report printed in the previous issue. It said, "We hope . . . that in no form whatever, will the introduction of the monitorial system into our private schools, be countenanced by the city authorities."[197] Following the reprint of the article, the *American Journal of Education* countered some of the objections found in that article. The discussion about the merits and disadvantages of the system of mutual instruction continued in the journals and newspapers.

In 1830, Lemuel Shattuck, who eventually taught in a Detroit Lancasterian school, was associated with the Concord schools. In a report that considered how Massachusetts schools could be improved, he stated that "the system of mutual instruction, though adopted several years since, in many populous towns, is comparatively unknown in the interior of New England."[198] He felt that the principles of the system were beneficial and perhaps should be gradually introduced in other New England schools. He said, "By this system a greater number of scholars are taught with equal ease, each scholar is more constantly employed, and the instruction is more practical."[199] He cited Fowle's school in Boston as an approved example.

The discussion continued, and in August 1830, Henry K. Oliver of Salem lectured in Boston to the American Institute of Instruction, an important national educational organization of that time. Oliver was "an educator, church musician, and hymn-tune composer" who had taught by the monitorial system in the 1820s.[200] He stated, "It has fallen to my lot, my respected friends, to address you, upon the advantages and defects of the monitorial system of instruction, and to endeavour to show how far it may be safely adopted into our schools."[201] He listed the advantages as follows: (1) more pupils could be taught within the same time and the same means; (2) there would be an economy of time; (3) every student would be constantly employed; (4) the enjoyment of school would be increased; and (5) the task of teaching would be easier for the teacher. As defects, Oliver noted: (1) the great amount of noise and confusion; (2) the difficulty of getting monitors who would be faithful and adequate; (3) the individual pupil would not receive proper attention; and (4) the superficial aspect of teaching.

Oliver then proposed the solution that what was "meritorious in the old" should be kept, and to "adopt what is good" from the new.[202] He added, "But we do not feel willing to say, 'Adopt the system of mutual instruction in full, since it is the very best that has been ever devised.' For we should then be saying what we cannot bring ourselves to believe."[203] He proposed that the teacher be given young assistants, which would, in essence, increase the number of teachers.

The School Committee proposed a plan similar to that espoused by Oliver. In 1831, it voted to conduct all Boston schools according to the mutual instruction plan. Fowle reported, "The School Committee, believing that some radical change in the city schools was necessary, voted, unanimously, I believe to introduce what they considered a monitorial plan into all the grammar schools."[204] Fowle objected to the manner in which the monitors were used since, under the new plan, young people who were no longer pupils were employed as assistants. In addition, older teachers, who opposed any type of monitorial plan, were the ones who would carry out the proposed changes. The plan was adopted, but "at the end of two years, it was declared a failure."[205] Bostonians pronounced the system of mutual instruction a failure, while Fowle maintained that the fault had been in the way the system was used, not because of a defect in the system itself. He said, "It has always been a source of regret to me that my friends, the Boston teachers, were so afraid of the system that I loved, because, knowing how arduous are their duties, I wish them to be furnished with the only means that, in my opinion, can afford them any substantial relief."[206]

The Female Monitorial School continued for seventeen years, but in 1840, Fowle resigned because of poor health. "This ended the attempt to reform the schools of Boston, by introducing the System of Mutual Instruction, usually called the Monitorial System."[207]

Fowle resumed his work as a bookseller in 1842, and in 1843, he became publisher of the *Common School Journal.* Horace Mann was editor of the journal, which had begun when the *American Annals of Education* ceased publication, and he edited it for ten years. In 1848, Fowle assumed the position of editor, and the journal was published until 1852. Fowle became editor when Mann was elected to the House of Representatives.[208]

During this time, Fowle continued to defend his beliefs about the monitorial plan. In 1848, he printed an answer to a report by William A. Walker, superintendent of schools for New York City, in which Walker had stated that monitorial instruction caused serious mental and moral evils. Fowle wrote:

I have never found a sensible person who did not acknowledge that "teaching" is one of the best methods of learning. I am unwilling to believe that what is so useful, can be productive of so much mental and moral evil as Mr. Walker supposes. I prefer to think that a good thing has been misused, and its influence misunderstood.[209]

Fowle also became increasingly active as a lecturer. The idea of teachers' institutes—having teachers gather together to discuss topics of interest to them relative to education—was begun in 1839 by Henry Barnard. "These institutes expanded rapidly in the later 1840s and 1850s."[210] Fowle called them temporary normal schools.[211]

Horace Mann, secretary of the Massachusetts Board of Education at the time, invited Fowle to lecture at these institutes. The *American Journal of Education* mentioned his great success in carrying out the institutes.[212] An interesting fact is that Mann, who was opposed to the monitorial system and who could see the system declining in popularity, employed Fowle, who lectured in defense of the system. Rost stated, "As Fowle was, in effect, working for Mann in these endeavors, it seems strange that Mann makes so little mention of it."[213] Mann wrote in his seventh annual report to the Massachusetts Board of Education expressing his dissatisfaction with the method. While it might be useful where many students must be taught at little expense, and although he had seen excellent monitorial teachers at the Borough Road School in Edinburgh and at Madras College in St. Andrews, Mann had nothing else to say that was favorable.[214]

Fowle wrote a number of books, but his most famous is a collection of his lectures entitled *The Teacher's Institute.* He said a great deal in defense of the monitorial system. He stated, "Another common objection against the use of children as assistants is, that their knowledge is imperfect, and of course their teaching must be of the same character. A judicious teacher would not set a child to teach what he did not know. . . ."[215] And yet, he said, "no child, but the very lowest, was so low that she could not teach something, and that something I always required her to teach if possible."[216] He also saw advantage in the system because, by teaching younger children, the older ones were constantly reviewing what they had learned. Another advantage of the system was that "by the judicious employment of monitors, and the proper selection and change of studies, the children can be all usefully employed, and employed all the time."[217] He felt that a well-conducted monitorial school served as a normal school as well, and said, "teaching is learning, and learning of the very best kind."[218]

SCHOOLS OF CONNECTICUT

Monitorial instruction was not widely used in New England; nevertheless, two schools in New Haven and Hartford, Connecticut, were notable. Butler traced the history of the New Haven monitorial school, conducted by John E. Lovell, a student of Lancaster.[219]

In May 1822, the New Haven School Committee printed two notices regarding the organization and opening time for the school. The notices stated that a Lancasterian school would be opened on May 27, and requested the help of parents in cooperating with the teacher, who would manage three hundred to four hundred boys of varying ages, capabilities, and dispositions. By August of that year, a report expressed great satisfaction with the progress of the pupils, and with the organization of the school itself. One writer stated:

Great praise is due to the enterprise and skill of the superintendent. Mr. Lovell seems to possess a thorough acquaintance with his business; combining an exact comprehension of the Lancastrian mode of instruction, and a thorough knowledge of the character and dispositions of children, adding to these a gentleness of manners, with a suitable degree of energy and decision, he cannot fail to give satisfaction.[220]

School Committee reports continued to praise the school and teacher, and in 1828, a new school building was occupied, where a girls' school was also conducted.

John Griscom also referred to the New Haven school, stating that "in New Haven, a place where enlightened views of education have long prevailed, a Lancasterian School has been for some time established."[221] He continued by quoting from the School Committee report, which highly praised the progress of the students. The report said:

In fact, until the Lancasterian School was established in New Haven, under Mr. Lovel [sic], we had no system at all, and every citizen will now bear witness to the very great improvement, not only in their studies, but in the manner and general conduct of the boys of New Haven even in the streets.[222]

Governor Wolcott of Connecticut addressed the legislature in 1825 and stated:

Happily the system of Monitorial or Lancasterian schools comes to our aid at a time, when, I trust, we are prepared to receive it. It has been sufficiently adopted in this country, to enable every well informed person to judge of its tendencies and principles. It is well known, that it has effected a highly beneficial change in the habits, character, and intelligence of the youth of New-Haven.[223]

He then proposed that schools based on the model in New Haven should be established in several parts of the state.

The school in New Haven was still operating by 1850, with Lovell as one of the teachers. While Lancaster's system and Lancaster himself were never in favor in Massachusetts, Connecticut newspapers informed the citizens of the school in New Haven, and it was a source of pride. "The Lancastrian School in New Haven was a favored child and contributed to the rise of a spirit of common school education for the state."[224]

According to Butler, Hartford also had a Lancasterian school, but it never received the attention the New Haven school did, nor was it under the continuous instruction of the same teacher for such a long period as Mr. Lovell provided in New Haven.[225]

Hartford, however, was the location of another famous school that utilized the Lancasterian system. In 1823, Catharine and Mary Beecher opened the Hartford Female Seminary, which offered instruction in a great many subjects, including grammar, geography, rhetoric, philosophy, chemistry, ancient and modern history, Latin, algebra, and geometry. The school became popular, and large numbers of students attended, which necessitated the use of brighter pupils in assisting the teacher. Harveson stated, "So we see cropping up here, as it did elsewhere, a phase of the Lancastrian plan, though it was apparently a spontaneous growth."[226]

In a report to the trustees of the seminary in 1829, Catharine Beecher suggested that "another defect in education is, that it has not been made a *definite object* with teachers *to prepare their pupils to instruct others*."[227] Beecher believed that knowledge cannot be acquired if it is not imparted to others. "That there is a best way of *teaching* as well as of doing everything else, cannot be disputed, and this can no more be learned by *intuition*, than can any of the mechanical arts."[228]

SPREAD OF THE SYSTEM

By the time Lancaster came to America in 1818, there were more than 150 monitorial schools in the United States. "They were located from Nantucket to Cincinnati, and from Detroit to New Orleans. There were Lancasterian schools for black children in New York and for Cherokee children in North Carolina. Private schools as well as charity schools adopted the system."[229]

Eggertsen stated that by 1820, "there were monitorial schools in over forty towns and cities of New Hampshire, Connecticut, New York, New Jersey, Pennsylvania, Maryland, District of Columbia, Virginia, Georgia, Mississippi, Tennessee, Kentucky and Ohio."[230] By 1840, schools had been established in such towns as Henrietta, New York, and Milton, Pennsylvania. "Once introduced into the United States, . . . the system quickly spread from Massachusetts to Georgia, and as far west as Cincinnati, Louisville, and Detroit."[231]

Typical of the reasons for the spread of the monitorial system are those stated in a report made to the citizens of Portsmouth.* The report by Ewing and Sargeant tried to urge the citizens to put the Lancasterian plan into execution.[232] It called the existing plan defective, stated that large numbers of poor received no benefit from it, and said that there was a lack of religious and moral improvement of children. The Lancasterian system, it said, "has long been tried and universally approved. It is unrivalled for its excellence and will remedy most of the evils of which we now complain."[233] The benefits were that every child was employed at every moment; learning took place with "astonishing rapidity";[234] it caused the artificial distinctions of society to be lessened by the mingling of rich and poor; and, finally, "another of the advantages of the Lancasterian system, is its cheapness. This we view as one of the last, and least of its excellencies."[235]

Good stated the following in summary:

In many cities the Lancasterian schools led directly to the establishment of public schools. Cincinnati, Louisville, and Detroit, in the far West of that time, and New Haven, Albany, and Baltimore, in the East, were only a

---

*The Portsmouth here mentioned is presumably in New Hampshire; no state was given in the report.

few of the scores of cities which welcomed the Lancasterian monitorial schools.[236]

MONITORIAL EFFORTS IN THE SOUTH

Of the southern states, Virginia showed the greatest interest, perhaps because Lancaster lectured there more extensively than in the other states. Another reason may be that in 1816, the governor of Virginia wrote to Jeremy Bentham, requesting his advice in establishing a system of public education. Bentham, in return, sent to Governor Nicholas the first part of his *Chrestomathia*. He also sent to the governors of all the states a circular that summarized what he called the new system of instruction, meaning the Bell and Lancaster system. The governors also received a copy of *Chrestomathia*. "What impression this endeavor of Bentham's had on official or public opinion is difficult to say. That some publicity and attention was given it is clear from two articles about the whole episode in the *Richmond Enquirer*."[237]

Numerous letters, of which a select few are mentioned here as examples, passed between Lancaster and his supporters, and they attest to the widespread interest in monitorialism in Virginia. In February 1819, James Stevenson requested information on how to receive instruction on the Lancasterian system of education.[238] Joseph C. Cabell, who assisted Thomas Jefferson in the efforts to establish a public-school system for Virginia, wrote to Lancaster in July 1819. He gently criticized the use of the system in the South because of the scattered population but requested information relative to its possible adaptation to the rural areas.[239] John H. Hall from Harper's Ferry corresponded with Lancaster about the schools there that used the monitorial system, and he requested advice. Lancaster was invited to visit there and inspect the schools.[240]

In 1816, a cornerstone was laid in Richmond for a Lancasterian school, and the speaker at the ceremony stated that "the time would come when such men as Franklin, Jenner, Fulton, and Lancaster would receive more acclaim than famous warriors of history, and of all these men, Lancaster would get the most credit."[241] Lancaster was worthy of this praise "because he had removed painful obstructions to learning and had invented a mode of instruction attractive to the youthful mind."[242] By 1840, Lancasterian schools had been established in Petersburg, Winchester, Fredericksburg, Lexington, Richmond, and Norfolk.

There is evidence from the Raleigh, North Carolina newspapers that the Lancasterian system was used in various schools of that city. In 1814, the *Raleigh Register* had the following item:

We congratulate our fellow-citizens on the prospect of establishing in the Preparatory School of our Academy, the highly approved mode of teaching children the first rudiments of Learning, invented by the celebrated Joseph Lancaster of London, by which one man can superintend the instruction of any number of scholars from 50 to 1000.[243]

The *Raleigh Star* reported in 1815 that "Mr. Lancaster's celebrated mode of teaching the elements of the English language will go into operation in the Preparatory Department of Raleigh Academy on Monday next."[244] Later that year, the newspaper stated that the advantage of using the Lancasterian system was that many more children could be instructed for the same price, and that children whose parents could not pay the expenses would be admitted free. The poor would retain their anonymity since only the trustee to whom the parent would apply for this privilege and the treasurer would know which children were attending without expense.[245]

Also in 1815, the *Raleigh Star* reported that "the trustees cannot pass over the Lancaster school without expressing their particular approbation of the manner in which it has been conducted during the short period it has been in operation."[246]

Lancaster had favorably impressed many notable individuals in North Carolina. Archibald D. Murphy, called the father of public schools in North Carolina, reported to the General Assembly in 1832 and recommended that the monitorial system be introduced into the proposed primary schools as well as the academies and the university. This proposal was not adopted by the General Assembly. The president of the University of North Carolina was also favorable to Lancaster and his methods.

In other parts of the South, Lancasterian schools were established in Nashville, Tennessee, 1813; Lexington and Louisville, Kentucky, 1817; Natchez, Mississippi, 1817; Savannah, Georgia, 1819; Augusta, Georgia, 1821; Frankfort, Kentucky, 1821; and Macon, Georgia, 1832.[247]

In the 1894–1895 report of the United States Commissioner of Education, Morrison considered the question of "What is there left in the monitorial or mutual system for the schools of the South?"[248] If the schools of the South were provided with modern buildings and equipment and had first-class teachers, Morrison felt that the system was not needed. However, "if . . . there exists to-day in the South a large number of children who, for lack of these provisions, are not being educated, and if for these children monitorial masters could be obtained, then there is certainly something in the monitorial system for the children of the South."[249]

LANCASTER IN CANADA

The monitorial movement in England did not escape notice in Canada. As early as 1809, a Rev. Mr. Strachan stated that "there is little or nothing in either of their [Lancaster and Bell] plans, which most Schoolmasters did not know."[250] However, he allowed that in large charity schools, the Lancaster plan may do well.

In 1810, the *Quebec Gazette* noted the successful efforts of a New York Lancasterian school and suggested that similar attempts should be made in that province.[251] Captain Walter Bromley promoted the Lancasterian plan in Nova Scotia, and founded there the Royal Acadian Society and the Royal Acadian School for the poor. His activities were described in the 1814 annual report of the British and Foreign School Society.[252] Also in 1814, Rev. Thaddeus Osgood opened a monitorial school in Quebec. Probably because of this school, the legislature in 1815 commented upon "the cheapness and efficacy of the Lancasterian method of teaching."[253] Osgood's school closed two years later, but soon other national schools were established in both Quebec and Montreal.

In Montreal, monitorial efforts were reported as early as 1813. By 1822, a British and Canadian School Society had been founded in Montreal, and a Borough Road teacher, Thomas Hutchings, was the first schoolmaster.[254]

Lancaster arrived in Montreal in 1829, wishing to establish a school there. He first requested from the committee of the Lancasterian School "the loan of eight ignorant boys of about six or seven years of age, who could spell words of two letters."[255] Lancaster reported that "they were soon qualified to teach each other, and in the space of five weeks were examined by their teacher."[256] The teacher was apparently greatly astonished by the progress of these pupils.

After the experiment, Lancaster began a school in 1830. He called this his second experiment and said, "In a short time another examination was held, and a more delighted auditory of friends and relations never assembled at any school."[257] His school was aided by grants from the legislature from 1830 to 1832.

Apparently, Lancaster planned to stay in Montreal for some time, but his plans were cut short in 1832. At the elections for the House of Assembly, Lancaster voted for a Mr. Bagg, who happened to be the father of one of his pupils. By doing this, he "knew he would incur the enmity of those in whose hands lay the power to withhold his legislative grant, and when, in the following session, the grant was not renewed he attributed the deprivation to his having exercised the liberty 'that any British subject can exercise.' "[258] Neither Spragge, who wrote an authoritative article on Lancaster's stay in Montreal, nor Lancaster himself in his own writings, mentions why the vote cast for Mr. Bagg became such a problem.

Lancaster felt he could not keep his school open with only paying pupils and without the stipend from the legislature, and he returned to the United States in 1833. Spragge commented as follows:

It can hardly be suggested that Lancaster's residence in Montreal had any special significance. When he reached the province the monitorial system of teaching was already in operation and highly thought of; when he left he had apparently accomplished nothing by which education in the province was influenced.[259]

By the late 1830s, the monitorial system had fallen into disfavor and largely into disuse in Canada.

CRITICISM AND EVALUATION OF THE SYSTEM IN NORTH AMERICA

It was probably inevitable that such a popular educational concept as monitorial instruction would receive extensive coverage in contemporary newspapers and journals. In 1818, *The Academician* printed an article about "the new school," stating that "a new era in education has commenced, and it is spreading its beneficial influence with unparralleled [sic] success."[260] It also said that "a method has been devised, and after various improvements, seems now to be brought very near to perfection—by which the blessings of education may be extended to persons of all ranks in society."[261] The article mentioned the "considerable attention" the method had received because of "certain hostile demonstrations on the part of biggoted [sic] and persecuting classes of society" but stated that it was increasing in popularity and it was hoped that the system would spread over "the whole inhabited globe." The article then described the system and pointed out "the leading principles."[262]

Criticism came early, and from as far west as Detroit. The *Detroit Gazette* printed an article in 1821 that stated that "teachers experienced in the *good old system* are much more valuable to the community than those who teach the specious and novel systems which have of late been palmed upon the world."[263] The article criticized the fact that a "juvenile monitor" was responsible for the moral development, behavior, and intellectual training of his peers.

By this ill-concerted plan a double loss is incurred: the monitors sustain a loss, because in place of prematurely teaching others, they should be studying to improve themselves. . . . The pupils under each monitor sustain a loss also, in consequence of the *want* of an *experienced teacher's immediate instruction*.[264]

In late 1827, the *American Journal of Education* printed a commentary on the progress of education during that year. On mutual or monitorial instruction, the article stated the opinion that "it seemed, and it still seems to us to be, when rightly understood, a very efficient instrument in promoting improvement."[265] The article appeared to take a sensible view of the method, saying, "It is an aid chiefly connected with the mechanical part of instruction—not, as has sometimes been supposed, a remedy for every evil, and a guaranty for every benefit." It went on to say that "the best instruction, it must never be forgotten, is that which one teacher gives to one pupil: nothing can be so effectual—nothing so well adapted to personal circumstances and character."[266] However, it recommended the use of monitorial instruction when a large number of pupils were to be taught in public schools. It concluded that "the great point for every teacher is to acquire a perfect knowledge of his business for himself, and to use the monitorial and every other system only as aids to his personal endeavors."[267]

Early in 1828, the *American Journal of Education* again printed a commentary on education, and included several statements about mutual instruction. It wrote that the system had been tried in several schools but had been less than satisfactory in the development of discipline and mental achievements. The article concluded that "perhaps, the failure has arisen from the error of applying the system to schools where there was too large a proportion of very young scholars—unfit, therefore, to govern themselves by any system of rewards and punishments."[268]

Also in 1828, the *American Journal of Education* published an extensive article with the purpose of discussing "the merits of the system of mutual instruction."[269] The article listed the advantages as: (1) economy of time; (2) constant employment of students; (3) rapid progress in schooling; (4) preparation of future teachers; and (5) economy in the expenditure of money. After a discussion of these points, the article went on to deal with the "*disadvantages* alleged against the system of mutual instruction." First, the incompetency of the monitors was discussed, and the article said that "the system of mutual instruction as such admits of no arrangement by which a scholar is to become a monitor till he is well qualified for the office. If in any school an exception to this rule exists, the blame ought to be with the master and not with the system he professes to adopt."[270] Second, the objection of the system only being applicable to the mechanical part of instruction was considered.

This is true chiefly of the higher branches of study, however, and has very little concern with the business of common schools; and, after all, monitorial teaching does a great deal, if it relieves the teacher of the burden of the more mechanical parts of instruction and recitation, and leaves him free to render his services where they are most needed—in the more intellectual departments of his business.[271]

Another complaint against the system was that monitors, because of their immaturity, could not have the authority needed in teaching. The article suggested that this could be remedied by a restriction of the monitor's power and by care in selecting monitors who were older and more mature.

Concerning the objection that monitorial instruction was detrimental to order, the article said that "neither the sacredness of the employment, nor the instruction of the scholars, is found to be in the least diminished by the buzz of earnest voices in the exercises of the various classes."[272]

Finally, the objection that mutual instruction was superficial was discussed. The article said, "Mutual instruction does nothing to hinder solitary application and profound thought, when the mind is able for them."[273]

In conclusion, the article said that the method of monitorial instruction, "like most others, is good or bad as it is applied, and that in the hands of one teacher it may effect much improvement, while in those of another it proves abortive and injurious."[274] The writer of the article expressed the wish that monitorial instruction be adopted in common and primary schools, and felt it would greatly improve instruction.

The Southern Review printed an article in 1828 that reviewed a number of publications on monitorialism. The article concluded that "it has undergone a most severe scrutiny in our own country, and that its preference is justified by the most ample and satisfactory proof which any reasonable mind can require for the purpose of rational conviction."[275] Furthermore, the article stated that "it would thus appear to be established almost beyond the power of denial, that the agency of mutual instruction is exceedingly favourable to the development of the mental faculties," and it also would facilitate the operation of a school.[276]

The *American Annals of Education* printed a commentary in 1831 on a book by John Wood, Esq., *Account of the Edinburgh Sessional School.* Wood had said that the system of monitorial instruction was not the very best, and the article agreed, stating that "hence we would be cautious in recommending to universal adoption, a system which is so often rendered mechanical—a mere machine for saving labour to the teacher and money to the parents—by the indolence, or error, of those who employ it."[277] But, the article stated emphatically, there was a lack of good and experienced teachers. Consequently, the method of mutual instruction "promises, at least, a *partial remedy of existing evils;* and that, until

competent teachers and assistants can be furnished, it is highly
desirable to endeavor to supply the deficiency by means of
monitors, suitably trained."[278]

In 1832, the *American Annals of Education* printed a presentation
by Walter R. Johnson to the American Lyceum that considered monitorial instruction and the extent to which it would be advisable and
practical to use the system in the common schools. Johnson
summed up his statements as follows:

In conclusion I would say, let the monitorial system be admitted so far as to
give the adult teacher all the aid which it is capable of affording, but not to
diminish the amount of his own instructions. It should, in no instance, be
employed as a *substitute* for the talents and information which ought to be
possessed by the master, much less to supply his deficiencies in dignity or
authority. . . . Let it be employed to invigorate effort, but not merely to give
an air of activity, which, after all, may be little more than useless bustle
and formality.

Neither the teacher, the patriot, nor the philanthropist, would wish for the
adoption of monitorial instruction solely for the purpose of giving a seem-
ing education to the *poor,* which, in reality, only serves to degrade their
condition, augment their dependence, and enable the rich to begin thus
early to prescribe their future destiny, and mar, rather than brighten, their
prospects in life; a proceeding utterly inconsistent with the sentiments of
freemen, and opposed to the earliest practice of our pilgrim father.[279]

Strong negative criticism appeared in two articles in the *Western Academician and Journal of Education and Science* in 1837. J.
W. Picket, editor of the journal, wrote about contemporary educational theories, and stated that the mutual or monitorial method
excluded "the exercise of reason and judgment" and substituted
"mere routine." He said, "So far, indeed, are we from believing
that Lancaster's plan is an improvement in education, we hesitate
not to assert that it has materially retarded and injured its solid
interests."[280]

Another article in the same journal considered Lancaster and
Pestalozzi, curiously lumping them together in condemnation of
their methods, as interpreted by the writer of the article. The
article questioned the mechanical drill, "which seems to be both
the body and soul of those methods."[281] Mechanical drill, the arti-

cle said, "can no more effect the purposes of rational education, than conceited ignorance can successfully put in motion the wonderful machinery of the human understanding."[282] It also wondered whether the new methods "are adequate to deep and extensive knowledge"[283] since no one schooled by that method had risen to literary eminence. It accused the systems of being designed to supply "absolute want of information, in cases where wailing orphans, or other objects of compassion, are cut off by their hard condition, from the extensive cultivation of science and elegant literature."[284]

The article lauded the efforts of the philanthropists who were supplying at a "trifling expense" an education for the innumerable poor, but it condemned the extension of "what has been termed the machinery of their systems, to the most complicated and elevated branches of science and language, as if mind could be measured by the square and line, and drilled into moral and literary excellence by the rattle of a whistle."* Above all, the article condemned the mechanical aspect of the system. "The 'mutual system,' or the new mode, compounded of Lancaster's and Pestalozzi's or, in other words, that recently invented way by which children may *teach* children, will be found on examination, wholly mechanical."[286]

In addition to opinions printed in newspapers and journals, persons active and prominent in education also voiced their beliefs about monitorial instruction. Clinton DeWitt, governor of New York, was an early advocate and earnest supporter of the system. However, in 1818, he received a letter from an Albany schoolmaster who wrote:

I have with care examined its operation, and beg leave with humble confidence to express my opinion,—that with respect to that part of the system which properly designates it Lancasterian, there is nothing in it calculated to facilitate the improvement of the pupil: and the experience of a few years, I am persuaded will reduce that system to its original and proper sphere—the instruction of those who cannot otherwise obtain instruction.[287]

---

*This is apparently in reference to Lancaster's use of a whistle to call pupils to order.[285]

The schoolmaster also expressed regret that since the brightest were frequently chosen to be monitors, their own studies were hindered.

On the other hand, a student who attended a Detroit Lancasterian school at about the same time, in 1818, wrote the following in his reminiscences:

That school was of more importance to me than all the others I ever attended for study, as it allowed the pupils to advance according to their industry and application to their studies, and were not held back by duller scholars, a fault I greatly fear often the case under our present school system.[288]

John Griscom, in his famous 1825 speech about monitorial instruction, expressed the positive opinion that "the monitorial scheme of instruction ... is held at the present moment in higher estimation than at any preceding period, and is making its way to a far more extensive adoption and influential practice."[289] This may have been the prevalent opinion in the twenties, but toward the latter part of the 1830s, considerable dissatisfaction with monitorial instruction had surfaced. Eggersten stated:

From 1825 to about 1845, the educational value of the system was under constant attack. This does not mean that it had no defense during these years, for strong supporters were advocating its use even in the late 1840's. It does mean that monitorialism did not continue after 1825 to receive friendly criticism only.[290]

It is interesting to note the comment of a European traveler, Grund, who wrote the following:

With regard to the plan of instruction, considerable improvements have been made within the last ten years. The mechanical Lancastrian system has everywhere been improved or superseded by the inductive method of Pestalozzi; which, as it is calculated to draw out the *thinking* faculties, is naturally better adapted for the instruction of republicans.[291]

Horace Mann, secretary to the Massachusetts Board of Education, wrote his most influential report in 1844. In this seventh report to the board, he described education as it took place in several European countries, and took particular note of the methods utilized. He was not favorably impressed by the use of monitorial instruction in those countries, nor did he advocate its use in America. He wrote:

At least nine-tenths of all the monitorial schools I have seen would suggest to me the idea that the name "monitorial" had been given them by way of admonishing the world to avoid their adoption. One must see the difference between the hampering, blinding, misleading instruction given by an inexperienced child, and the developing, transforming, and almost creative power of an accomplished teacher;—one must rise to some comprehension of the vast import and significance of the phase "to educate,"—before he can regard with a sufficiently energetic contempt that boast of Dr. Bell, "Give me twenty-four pupils today, and I will give you back twenty-four teachers to-morrow."[292]

David Perkins Page wrote a book, *Theory and Practice of Teaching*, that became an extremely popular text for teachers in the mid-nineteenth century. He warned teachers against the use of monitorial instruction: "Rely not too much upon simultaneous recitation."[293] He continued his advice:

This has become quite too fashionable of late. It had its origin in the large schools established some years since, known as Lancasterian schools, and perhaps was well enough adapted to schools kept upon that plan in large cities. But when this mode of reciting is adopted in our district and country schools, where the circumstances of large numbers and extreme backwardness are wanting, it is entirely uncalled for, and like other city fashions transferred to the country, is *really out of place.*[294]

Page felt that monitorial instruction destroyed the independence of the student, and because the student relied on others, he learned only superficially. Page did say, "It may *sometimes* be useful. A few questions thus answered may serve to give animation to a class when their interest begins to flag; but that which may serve as a *stimulant* must not be relied on for *nutrition.*"[295]

By the end of the century, monitorial instruction received little notice or was soundly condemned in most cases. Rice wrote in 1893, "While the aim of the old education is mainly to give the child a certain amount of information, the aim of the new education is to lead the child to observe, to reason, and to acquire manual dexterity as well as to memorize facts."[296] Rice also said:

But why do the mechanical schools still exist in an enlightened age and in a country so progressive as ours? It is frequently claimed, in support of the mechanical system, that the old education is more practical than the new. This assertion, however, is made in ignorance of facts. Indeed, facts prove that more is accomplished in a given period by scientific than by mechanical teaching. And further, that system of education that leads a child to observe and to think, as well as to give him manual dexterity while memorizing facts, is certainly more practical than the education whose aim is limited to leading the pupils to memorize facts.[297]

Apparently, the monitorial system was still used in the late nineteenth century, but this must have been minimal as no reference to actual schools or persons using it was found. Rice indicated that some schools did use monitorial instruction because he said, "The real causes for the existence of the mechanical schools at the present stage of civilization are no other than corruption and selfishness on the part of school officials, and unjustifiable ignorance, as well as criminal negligence, on the part of parents."[298]

The twentieth-century critics have, perhaps, a better perspective of the use of monitorial instruction, and their condemnation of the system is tempered with a view of its advantages as well. In 1915, Graves wrote that the Lancasterian schools were an improvement over previous methods, even though, eventually, they were judged to be "mechanical, inelastic, and without psychological foundation."[299] The monitorial schools had "met a great educational emergency in the United States,"[300] and the provisions that were made for the establishment of these schools later paved the way for increased spending and taxation for public schools.

Knight wrote in 1929 that the Lancasterian schools were weak because of the "formality of the routine work, the superficiality of much of the instruction, the rigid and mechanical discipline, memorization, and the absence of the psychological aspects of education." However, when Lancaster's schools were compared to the old schools, they "wore the color of effectiveness."[301] Knight pointed out two benefits from the monitorial movement.

It is probable also that the monitorial method provoked discussion on questions of education and promoted the idea of schools at public expense. Moreover, it served to improve the technique of classroom management and to draw attention to the necessity of special preparation for teachers.[302]

Cubberley noted, as the important consideration in favor of Lancasterian schools, the fact that they accustomed people to schools and to contributing to the support of schools. Cubberley stated that at the turn of the century, "it would not have been possible to have secured public support for any general state system of education." He also added the following:

The Lancasterian schools thus materially hastened the adoption of the free school system in all the Northern States by gradually accustoming people to bearing the necessary taxation which free schools entail. They also made the common school common and much talked of, and awakened thought and provoked discussion on the question of public education.[303]

Writing in 1947, Brubacher confirmed the view stated by Cubberley. He felt that the chief contribution made by monitorial schools was "to win the public to the support of schools, for it appeared at first glance as if public education would be quite inexpensive."[304] Once this had been accomplished, the use of the system diminished rapidly because, as Brubacher stated, "the public was soon persuaded that, if it was going to support education, it might as well have the best."[305]

Good, also writing in 1947, said, "The Lancasterian schools convinced many doubters that the cost of universal education would not need to be prohibitive and they accustomed many parents to pay something at least for the education of their children."[306]

In 1973, Kaestle made essentially the same evaluation. "It was through the establishment of nondenominational monitorial schools that people became accustomed to publicly funded elementary education; gradually they decided they could afford something better."[307]

In view of the previous statements, it is interesting to note that in 1903, when writing about the progress of education in the nineteenth century, Klemm and Hughes offered the following evaluation:

It is difficult to select the greatest among the many educational developments of the century, but the establishment of free national schools must be regarded as one of the most important steps in the progress of the race.

It extended the privileges of education to the children of all classes, and therefore did more than any other act or agency could have done to do away with the myriad evils of conventional classification of the human family on the basis of rank or fortune. It was the most widely effective step in the overthrow of the vicious class system and in the promotion of the great principle of universal community among men.[308]

In summary, while the monitorial method "constituted a practical and minimal approach to making information and skills of proven value available to many pupils by mechanical means,"[309] the adoption of the monitorial system eventually paved the way for a universal public-school system in the United States.

DECLINE OF THE SYSTEM

"The Lancasterian 'era' was almost finished when Lancaster died. As with all social panaceas, disillusionment followed upon the failure of the system to realize its exaggerated claims."[310] Cubberley stated that the monitorial system was most popular from about 1815 to 1830, while after 1830, its defects became more noted.[311] Kaestle declared that the peak of the monitorial movement was in the 1820s, when "it seemed a panacea for every educational problem."[312] By 1840, the use of the system on a large scale had generally been abandoned.[313]

Several reasons for the demise of the system have been presented. Eggertsen stated that professional educators began to doubt the value of the system by around 1830, and they began to criticize it.[314] In addition, the emphasis on teacher training, which the Lancasterian system advocated, gradually led to a professionalization of that training and an abandonment of monitors.[315]

Another cause for the downfall of the monitorial system was the extension of suffrage. As the idea grew that all citizens could serve in public office, or take part in the election of public officers, a concern for the lack of educated citizens increased. "Furthermore, as political power gradually began to slip from their hands, many upper-class people came to realize that popular education was actually to their advantage. If the people were going to rule, they ought at least to rule well."[316]

Still another reason came from the working class, for whom the system had originally been designed. "Indignant were the protests of workingmen against the pauper school and the element of charity in education. Labor demanded general and equal systems of education, not as charity but as the right of every child."[317] By 1835, the system had received a great deal of publicity, and it generated a strong desire for better schools, particularly among the poor. "The public rejected a method which, whatever its alleged pedagogical virtues, was designed explicitly for the poor."[318] Eggertsen pointed out that the lower economic classes "became accustomed to the sacrifices schools involved."[319]

"As public opinion became aroused on the subject of public education, as the material prosperity of the people increased and they recognized a need for schools and developed a willingness to provide for them by taxation, the Lancasterian system disappeared."[320]

NOTES

1. Edgar W. Knight, *Education in the United States* (Boston: Ginn and Co., 1929), p. 170.
2. Ibid., pp. 172–73.
3. Ibid., p. 174.
4. C. A. Eggertsen, "The Monitorial System of Instruction in the United States" (Doctoral diss., University of Minnesota, 1939), p. 46.
5. Frank Pierrepont Graves, *A Student's History of Education* (New York: The Macmillan Co., 1915), p. 242.
6. Edgar W. Knight, *Twenty Centuries of Education* (Boston: Ginn and Co., 1940), p. 269.
7. Graves, *A Student's History*, p. 242.
8. Carl F. Kaestle, ed. *Joseph Lancaster and the Monitorial School Movement: A Documentary History* (New York: Columbia University, Teachers College Press, 1973), pp. 34–35.
9. Graves, *A Student's History*, p. 243.
10. Eggertsen, "The Monitorial System," p. 88.
11. Ibid., p. 8
12. Paul Monroe, *Founding of the American Public School System*, vol. 1 (New York: The Macmillan Co., 1940), p. 363.
13. Eggertsen, "The Monitorial System," p. 45.
14. "Manual of the System of Monitorial or Mutual Instruction," *American Journal of Education* 1 (June 1826):335.
15. Monroe, *Founding of the American Public School System*, p. 363.
16. Frank Pierrepont Graves, *Great Educators of Three Centuries* (New York: The Macmillan Co., 1912), p. 243.

17. Ellwood P. Cubberley, *Public Education in the United States* (Boston: Houghton Mifflin Co., 1934), p. 129.

18. Kaestel, *Joseph Lancaster*, p. 36.

19. Ibid., p. 38.

20. Lewis F. Anderson, "The System of Manual Instruction and the Beginnings of High School," *School and Society* 8 (November 1918): 573−74.

21. E. O. Vaille, "The Lancastrian System. A Chapter in the Evolution of Common-school Education," *Education* 1 (January 1881): 274.

22. David Salmon, *Joseph Lancaster* (London: Longmans, Green, and Co., 1904), p. 59.

23. Ibid.

24. Ibid.

25. Joseph J. McCadden, "Joseph Lancaster in America," *The Social Studies* 28 (February 1937): 74.

26. John Franklin Reigart, *The Lancasterian System of Instruction in the Schools of New York City* (New York: Teachers College, Columbia University, 1916), p. 19.

27. McCadden, "Joseph Lancaster in America," p. 74.

28. "Joseph Lancaster," *American Journal of Education* 10 (June 1861): 261.

29. McCadden, "Joseph Lancaster in America," p. 73.

30. Kaestle, *Joseph Lancaster*, p. 41.

31. Reigart, *The Lancasterian System*, p. 18.

32. Joseph Lancaster, *Letters on National Subjects* (Washington City: Jacob Gideon, 1820).

33. Joseph Lancaster, *The Lancasterian System of Education* (Baltimore: Wm. Ogden Niles, Printer, 1821), p. 5.

34. McCadden, "Joseph Lancaster in America," p. 75.

35. Ibid., p. 76.

36. Kaestle, *Joseph Lancaster*, p. 42.

37. Henry Dunn, *Sketches* (London: Houlston and Stoneman, 1848), p. 21.

38. Kaestle, *Joseph Lancaster*, p. 41.

39. Salmon, *Joseph Lancaster*, p. 65.

40. Cubberley, *Public Education*, p. 134.

41. Reigart, *The Lancasterian System*, p. 15.

42. Cubberley, *Public Education*, p. 123.

43. Eggertsen, "The Monitorial System," p. 50.

44. Thomas Boese, *Public Education in the City of New York* (New York: Harper and Brothers, 1869), p. 26.

45. Ibid.

46. Reigart, *The Lancasterian System*, p. 17.

47. Archie Emerson Palmer, *The New York Public School* (New York: The Macmillan Co., 1905), p. 25.

48. Ibid., p. 4.

49. Reigart, *The Lancasterian System*, p. 17.

50. William Oland Bourne, *History of the Public School Society of the City of New York* (New York: Wm. Wood and Co., 1870), p. 609.

51. Reigart, *The Lancasterian System*, p. 13.

52. Ibid., p. 94.
53. DeWitt Clinton, "Free Schools," *The Life and Writings of DeWitt Clinton*, comp. W. W. Campbell (New York: Baker and Scribner, 1849), pp. 318–19.
54. Palmer, *The New York Public School*, p. 27.
55. Ibid., p. 42.
56. Boese, *Public Education*, p. 34.
57. Palmer, *The New York Public School*, p. 42.
58. *Manual of the Lancasterian System* (New York: Samuel Wood and Sons, Printers, 1820), preface.
59. Reigart, *The Lancasterian System*, p. 18.
60. Bourne, *History of the Public School Society*, p. 600.
61. Palmer, *The New York Public School*, p. 112.
62. Knight, *Education in the United States*, p. 162.
63. Cubberley, *Public Education*, pp. 125–26.
64. Eggertsen, "The Monitorial System," pp. 87 and 431.
65. A. C. Flagg, "Improvement of Common Schools," *American Journal of Education* 2 (April 1827): 198.
66. Ibid.
67. Ibid., p. 199.
68. Cubberley, *Public Education*, p. 137.
69. Ibid., p. 138.
70. Ibid.
71. Ibid., p. 124.
72. "Mutual Instruction in Common Schools," *American Annals of Education* 6 (October 1836): 437.
73. Ibid., p. 435.
74. Knight, *Education in the United States*, pp. 161–62.
75. Reigart, *The Lancasterian System*, p. 3.
76. Ibid., p. 95.
77. Ibid., p. 99.
78. Edward A. Fitzpatrick, *The Educational Views and Influence of DeWitt Clinton* (New York: Arno Press and *The New York Times*, 1969), p. 47.
79. Ibid.
80. Ibid., p. 48.
81. Clinton, "Free Schools," pp. 318–19.
82. Ibid., p. 320.
83. Ibid., p. 325. This address is also found in Calhoun, 1969.
84. Adolph E. Meyer, *An Educational History of the Western World* (New York: McGraw-Hill, 1965), p. 405.
85. Eggertsen, "The Monitorial System," p. 250.
86. Fitzpatrick, *The Educational Views*.
87. Cubberley, *Public Education*, p. 354.
88. H. H. Brinton, *Quaker Education in Theory and Practice* (Wallingford, Pa.: Pendle Hill, 1940), p. 40.
89. Ray Charles Rost, "The Influence of Joseph Lancaster and the Monitorial System on Selected Educational Institutions," (Doctoral diss., Rutgers University, 1968), p. 96.

90. Joseph J. McCadden, *Education in Pennsylvania, 1801–1835* (New York: Arno Press and *The New York Times*, 1969).

91. Monroe, *Founding of the American Public School System*, p. 236.

92. Eggertsen, "The Monitorial System," p. 98.

93. Edgar W. Knight, ed. *Reports on European Education* (New York: McGraw-Hill Book Co., Inc., 1930), p. 86.

94. Ibid., p. 94.

95. Rost, "The Influence of Joseph Lancaster," p. 96.

96. Anderson, "The System of Mutual Instruction," p. 575.

97. Rost, "The Influence of Joseph Lancaster," p. 96.

98. Cubberley, *Public Education*, p. 355.

99. Fitzpatrick, *The Educational Views*, pp. 118–19.

100. John Griscom, *Monitorial Instruction. An Address, Pronounced at the Opening of the New York High School* (New York: Mahlon Day, 1825), p. 37.

101. Ibid., p. 36.

102. Ibid., pp. 38–39.

103. "Review of Seven Contemporary Publications on Monitorialism," *Southern Review* 1 (May 1828): 495.

104. Anderson, "The System of Mutual Instruction," pp. 574–75.

105. Graves, *A Student's History*, p. 242.

106. Rost, "The Influence of Joseph Lancaster, p. 99.

107. Ibid.

108. Knight, *Twenty Centuries of Education*.

109. McCadden, *Education in Pennsylvania*, p. 3.

110. Ibid., p. 4.

111. Ibid., p. 38.

112. Ibid., p. 37.

113. Ibid., p. 190.

114. "Mutual or Monitorial Instruction," part 2, *American Annals of Education* 1 (April 1831): 177.

115. Kaestle, *Joseph Lancaster*, p. 37.

116. McCadden, *Education in Pennsylvania*, p. 6.

117. Kaestle, *Joseph Lancaster*, p. 37.

118. McCadden, *Education in Pennsylvania*, p. 91.

119. Charles Calvert Ellis, *Lancasterian Schools in Philadelphia* (Philadelphia: University of Pennsylvania, 1907), p. 5.

120. Eggertsen, "The Monitorial System," p. 52.

121. Ellis, *Lancasterian Schools*, p. 5.

122. Clinton, "Free Schools," p. 324.

123. McCadden, *Education in Pennsylvania*, p. 8.

124. Ellis, *Lancasterian Schools*, p. 8.

125. McCadden, *Education in Pennsylvania*, p. 9.

126. Ellis, *Lancasterian Schools*, p. 9.

127. Ibid.

128. *Manual of the System of Teaching Reading, Writing, Arithmetic, and Needlework*, 1st American ed. (Philadelphia: Benjamin Warner, 1817), p. v.

129. McCadden, *Education in Pennsylvania*, p. 7.
130. Ellis, *Lancasterian Schools*, p. 13.
131. McCadden, *Education in Pennsylvania*, p. 7.
132. Eggertsen, "The Monitorial System," p. 53.
133. *A Sketch of the Improved Method of Education* (Philadelphia: Kimber and Conrad, 1809).
134. Edgar W. Knight and Clifton L. Hall, *Readings in American Educational History* (New York: Appleton-Century-Crofts, Inc., 1951), p. 136.
135. *Manual of the System*, p. xii.
136. Knight and Hall, *Readings*, p. 136.
137. Ellis, *Lancasterian Schools*, p. 20.
138. McCadden, *Education in Pennsylvania*, p. 8.
139. Eggertsen, "The Monitorial System," p. 53.
140. Edward Baker, *A Brief Sketch of the Lancasterian System* (Troy, N.Y.: F. Adancourt, 1816), p. 3.
141. Ibid., p. 4.
142. Ellis, *Lancasterian Schools*, p. 29.
143. Rost, "The Influence of Joseph Lancaster," p. 173.
144. Ibid., pp. 173–74.
145. McCadden, *Education in Pennsylvania*, p. 37.
146. Rost, "The Influence of Joseph Lancaster," p. 175.
147. Ibid., p. 176.
148. Ellis, *Lancasterian Schools*, p. 57.
149. Ellwood P. Cubberley, *Readings in Public Education in the United States* (Boston: Houghton Mifflin Co., 1934), p. 141.
150. Ibid., p. 142.
151. McCadden, *Education in Pennsylvania*, p. 226.
152. Ibid., p. 91.
153. Joseph Lancaster, *Epitome of Some of the Chief Events and Transactions in the Life of Joseph Lancaster* (New Haven: Baldwin and Peck, 1833).
154. McCadden, *Education in Pennsylvania*, p. 4.
155. Ibid., p. 181.
156. Ibid., p. 232.
157. Ibid., p. 152.
158. Eggertsen, "The Monitorial System," p. 98.
159. Ibid., p. 99.
160. Ellis, *Lancasterian Schools*, p. 28.
161. Benjamin Shaw, *Brief Exposition of the Principles and Details of the Lancasterian System of Education* (Pennsylvania, 1817), p. 15.
162. Ibid., pp. 16–17.
163. McCadden, *Education in Pennsylvania*, p. 151.
164. Eggertsen, "The Monitorial System," pp. 55, 56.
165. Ibid., p. 156.
166. Lancaster, *The Lancasterian System of Education*, p. 5.
167. Eggertsen, "The Monitorial System."
168. Brinton, *Quaker Education*, p. 75.

169. William C. Dunlap, *Quaker Education in Baltimore and Virginia* (Philadelphia, 1936), p. 360.
170. Vera M. Butler, *Education as Revealed by New England Newspapers Prior to 1850* (New York: Arno Press and *The New York Times*, 1969), p. 328.
171. "William Bentley Fowle," *American Journal of Education* 10 (June 1861): 599.
172. Butler, *Education as Revealed*, p. 333.
173. Ibid., p. 335.
174. Eggertsen, "The Monitorial System," P. 161.
175. William B. Fowle, *The Teacher's Institute*, 2d ed. (Boston: William B. Fowle, 1847), p. 189.
176. "William Bentley Fowle," p. 597.
177. Fowle, *The Teacher's Institute*, p. 190.
178. "William Bentley Fowle," p. 598.
179. Rost, "The Influence of Joseph Lancaster," p. 139.
180. "William Bentley Fowle," p. 599.
181. Fowle, *The Teacher's Institute*, p. 191.
182. "William Bentley Fowle," pp. 600−602.
183. Fowle, *The Teacher's Institute*, p. 191.
184. G. B. Morrison, "The Bell and Lancaster System: What There Is in It for the Schools of the South," *Report of the United States Commissioner of Education, 1894−1895*, 2:1157.
185. "William Bentley Fowle," p. 604.
186. Fowle, *The Teacher's Institute*, p. 188.
187. Rost, "The Influence of Joseph Lancaster," p. 145.
188. Ibid., p. 133.
189. "William Bentley Fowle," p. 602.
190. J. Savage et al., "Boston Monitorial School," *American Journal of Education* 1 (January 1826): 31.
191. William B. Fowle, "Boston Monitorial School," *American Journal of Education* 1 (January 1826): 41.
192. William B. Fowle, "Boston Monitorial School," *American Journal of Education* 1 (February 1826): 74.
193. Ibid., pp. 76−77.
194. Fowle, *The Teacher's Institute*, p. 208.
195. "Monitorial Instruction," *American Journal of Education* 3 (January 1828): 245.
196. Ibid., p. 246.
197. Ibid., p. 313.
198. Lemuel Shattuck, "Improvements in Our Common Schools," *American Journal of Education* 1 (October-November 1830): 459.
199. Ibid., p. 460.
200. Gordon E. Fouts, "Music Instruction in Early Nineteenth-century American Monitorial Schools," *Journal of Research in Music Education* 22 (Summer 1974): 117.
201. Henry K. Oliver, *Lecture on the Advantages and Defects of the Monitorial System* (Boston: Hilliard, Gray, Little, and Wilkins, 1831), p. 4.

202. Ibid., pp. 21–22.
203. Ibid., p. 24.
204. Fowle, *The Teacher's Institute*, p. 192.
205. Ibid., p. 193.
206. Ibid.
207. "William Bentley Fowle," p. 608.
208. Rost, "The Influence of Joseph Lancaster," pp. 141–42.
209. William B. Fowle, "The Monitorial Plan," *Common School Journal* (September 1848): 91.
210. Rost, "The Influence of Joseph Lancaster," p. 189.
211. Fowle, *The Teacher's Institute*.
212. "William Bentley Fowle," p. 609.
213. Rost, "The Influence of Joseph Lancaster," p. 143.
214. Horace Mann, *Annual Reports on Education* (Boston: Horace B. Fuller, 1868), pp. 278–79.
215. Fowle, *The Teacher's Institute*, p. 198.
216. Ibid., p. 201.
217. Ibid., p. 203.
218. Ibid., p. 205.
219. Butler, *Education as Revealed*, p. 335.
220. Ibid., p. 337.
221. Griscom, *Monitorial Instruction*, p. 22.
222. Ibid., p. 24.
223. Ibid., pp. 24–25.
224. Butler, *Education as Revealed*, p. 348.
225. Ibid.
226. Mae Elizabeth Harveson, *Catharine Esther Beecher, Pioneer Educator* (New York: Arno Press and *The New York Times*, 1969), p. 41.
227. Catharine E. Beecher, "Improvements in Education," *American Journal of Education* 1 (1830): 63.
228. Ibid.
229. Kaestle, *Joseph Lancaster*, p. 40.
230. Eggertsen, "The Monitorial System," p. 88.
231. Cubberley, *Public Education*, p. 129.
232. John Ewing and John Sargeant, *Report of the Committee* (Portsmouth: S. Whidden, 1818).
233. Ibid., p. 9.
234. Ibid.
235. Ibid., p. 11.
236. H. G. Good, *A History of Western Education* (New York: The Macmillan Co., 1947), p. 404.
237. Eggertsen, "The Monitorial System," p. 265.
238. Edgar W. Knight, *A Documentary History of Education in the South Before 1860*, vol. 5 (Chapel Hill: University of North Carolina Press, 1953), p. 323.
239. Joseph C. Cabell, *Letter to Joseph Lancaster* (Lancaster Collection of the American Antiquarian Society, Worcester, Mass., written from Virginia, 1819).

240. Knight, *A Documentary History*, p. 332.
241. Eggertsen, "The Monitorial System," p. 78.
242. Ibid., pp. 78–79.
243. Charles L. Coon, *North Carolina Schools and Academies, 1790–1840: A Documentary History* (Raleigh: Edwards and Broughton Printing Co., 1915), p. 441.
244. Edgar W. Knight, "An Early Educational Fad in the South," *High School Journal* 31 (March-April 1948): 55.
245. Coon, *North Carolina Schools and Academies*, pp. 443–44.
246. Ibid., p. 445.
247. Eggertsen, "The Monitorial System," pp. 87, 341.
248. Morrison, "The Bell and Lancaster System," pp. 1160.
249. Ibid.
250. G. W. Spragge, "Joseph Lancaster in Montreal," *The Canadian Historical Review* 22 (March 1941): 38.
251. Ibid.
252. Henry Bryan Binns, *A Century of Education* (London: J. M. Dent and Co., 1908).
253. Spragge, "Joseph Lancaster in Montreal," p. 38.
254. Binns, *A Century of Education*, pp. 108–9.
255. Joseph Lancaster, *Report of the Singular Results of J. Lancaster's New Discoveries in Education Made at Montreal* (Montreal: 1833 [?]), p. 1.
256. Lancaster, *Epitome*, p. 13.
257. Lancaster, *Report*, p. 2.
258. Spragge, "Joseph Lancaster in Montreal," p. 41.
259. Ibid.
260. "The New School, or Lancasterian System," *The Academician* 1 (1818): 68–69.
261. Ibid.
262. Ibid., p. 69.
263. "Newspaper Criticism of the Lancaster System in Detroit, from *Detroit Gazette*, Nov. 23, 1821, and Feb. 15, 1822," *Education in the United States: A Documentary History*, ed. S. Cohen (New York: Random House, 1974), p. 988.
264. Ibid., p. 989.
265. "Retrospect," *American Journal of Education* 2 (December 1827): 759.
266. Ibid.
267. Ibid., p. 760.
268. "Introduction," *American Journal of Education* 3 (January 1828): 3.
269. "Review, Monitorial Instruction," *American Journal of Education* 5 (May 1828): 283.
270. Ibid., pp. 292–93.
271. Ibid., pp. 293–94.
272. Ibid., p. 295.
273. Ibid.
274. Ibid.
275. "Review of Seven Contemporary Publications," p. 490.

276. Ibid., p. 499.
277. "Monitorial System," *American Annals of Education* 1 (April 1831): 136.
278. Ibid., p. 138.
279. Walter Johnson, "Monitorial Schools," *American Annals of Education* 2 (August 1832): 420.
280. J. W. Picket, "Educational Theories," *The Western Academician and Journal of Education and Science* 1 (April 1837): 60.
281. "Lancaster and Pestalozzi," *The Western Academician and Journal of Education and Science* 1 (July 1837): 272.
282. Ibid.
283. Ibid., p. 273.
284. Ibid., p. 274.
285. Ibid.
286. Ibid., p. 275.
287. J. G. Hutton, "Criticism and Decline of the System," *Joseph Lancaster and the Monitorial School Movement: A Documentary History*, ed. C. F. Kaestle (New York: Columbia University, Teachers College Press, 1973), p. 177.
288. B. O. Williams, "Reminiscence of the Lancasterian School in Detroit," *Joseph Lancaster and the Monitorial School Movement: A Documentary History*, ed. C. F. Kaestle (New York: Columbia University, Teachers College Press, 1973), p. 169.
289. Griscom, *Monitorial Instruction*, pp. 28–29.
290. Eggertsen, "The Monitorial System," p. 344.
291. Francis Grund, *The Americans in Their Moral, Social, and Political Relations* (London: Longmans, Green & Co., Inc., 1837), p. 217.
292. Mann, *Annual Reports*, p. 279.
293. David P. Page, *Theory and Practice of Teaching* (New York: A. S. Barnes and Co., 1857), p. 116.
294. Ibid.
295. Ibid., p. 117.
296. Joseph Mayer Rice, *The Public School System of the United States* (New York: The Century Co., 1893), p. 21.
297. Ibid., p. 24.
298. Ibid., p. 26.
299. Graves, *A Student's History of Education*, p. 243.
300. Ibid., p. 243.
301. Knight, *Education in the United States*, p. 166.
302. Ibid., p. 167.
303. Cubberley, *Public Education*, p. 136.
304. John S. Brubacher, *A History of the Problems of Education* (New York: McGraw-Hill Book Co., Inc., 1947), pp. 218–19.
305. Ibid., p. 219.
306. Good, *A History of Western Education*, p. 405.
307. Kaestle, *Joseph Lancaster*, p. 44.
308. Louis R. Klemm and James Laughlin Hughes, *Progress of Education in the Century: The Nineteenth Century Series* (London: W. and R. Chambers, Ltd., 1903), p. 3.

309. Charles J. Brauner, *American Educational Theory* (Englewood Cliffs, N.J.: Prentice Hall, 1964), p. 28.

310. Kaestle, *Joseph Lancaster*, p. 43.

311. Cubberley, *Public Education*, p. 137.

312. Kaestle, *Joseph Lancaster*, p. 40.

313. Cubberley, *Public Education*, p. 137.

314. Eggertsen, "The Monitorial System," pp. 7, 79.

315. Kaestle, *Joseph Lancaster*, p. 43.

316. R. Freeman Butts and Lawrence A. Cremin, *A History of Education in American Culture* (New York: Henry Holt and Co., 1953), p. 191.

317. Knight, *Education in the United States*, p. 180.

318. Kaestle, *Joseph Lancaster*, p. 44.

319. Eggertsen, "The Monitorial System," p. 7.

320. Knight and Hall, *Readings*, p. 134.

CHAPTER 7

Use of Peer Teaching in Latin America in the Nineteenth Century

INTRODUCTION

The early nineteenth century in Latin America was a time of wars of independence. Dissatisfaction with the Spanish colonial system culminated in insurrections against the mother country, which received impetus from the North American and French revolutions. The North American revolution caused a desire for independence, and the French revolutionary ideals brought about a demand for reform. In addition, "geographical influences, lack of communications, the administrative division of the colonies, and traditional Spanish separation and individualism aided in creating sentiment for independence."[1]

Between 1815 and 1821, all of Spain's South American colonies revolted against her and declared their independence. In 1822, Brazil gained independence from Portugal. During that period, educational conditions in South America were in a formative state. Cubberley gave the following evaluation:

For approximately half a century these States, isolated as they were and engaged in a long and difficult struggle to evolve stable forms of government, left such education as was provided to private individuals and societies and to the missionaries and teaching orders of the Roman Church.[2]

Common people began to have more of a voice in the government and, as a result, began to demand better education. Although the liberators and rulers of South American States recognized the need for better education as a means of improving the condition of the common people, they were unable to accomplish a great deal. "Times were troublous and, even after a republican form of government had been established, public instruction remained in a position of secondary importance."[3]

During that time, the Lancasterian movement was promoted in Latin America, and it flourished for a while in a number of countries.* The British and Foreign School Society, aware of the dearth of educational facilities and opportunities in Latin American countries, sent James Thomson as its representative. Thomson also represented the British and Foreign Bible Society, and his sense of dual responsibility is evident in his letters, compiled into a book and published in 1827.

Despite revolutions and wars in many of the South American countries, Thomson was successful in establishing many schools throughout the continent. The system was firmly rooted for a time in Peru and in Colombia by a decree from the ruling powers. Kaestle indicated the duration of the success of monitorial instruction. He said, "For a whole generation of South Americans, the education of the masses was virtually synonymous with the Lancasterian system."[4]

Lancaster also went to South America in 1824 upon the invitation of Simon Bolivar, the liberator. However, it should be remembered that several years before Lancaster had severed connections with the British and Foreign School Society, and his stay in South America had no influence on or relationship to the work of the society and Thomson.

JAMES THOMSON AND PROMOTION OF THE MONITORIAL SYSTEM IN SOUTH AMERICA

Thomson's progress throughout South America is recorded in *Letters on the Moral and Religious State of South America*, and his route

---

*While primary sources were available for this chapter, these were not as numerous as for other chapters. Consequently, while the information is believed to be accurate, additional sources possibly available in Latin America could perhaps provide a more complete report on peer teaching in that part of the world.

as well as his work can be followed through these letters. There appear to be few other sources about Thomson himself. Browning stated that Thomson was from Scotland, was presumably a Presbyterian, had received a Doctor of Medicine degree, and was granted the Doctor of Divinity degree in recognition of his work. Browning further said, "His own reticence concerning himself, and his complete disregard of personal danger or personal ambition, have thrown a veil over his life before he began the work which has made him worthy of a place in history."[5]

Thomson arrived in Buenos Aires, Argentina, in 1818. Here he received the cooperation of a government official, Bernardino Rivadavia, as well as the support of a friar, Camilo Henriquez, who was in exile from Chile. Probably through the influence of Rivadavia, the first Lancasterian School Society in Latin America was founded. Thomson wrote of Rivadavia:

> I must also mention, and very particularly, that the interest taken by the government, under the direction of Don Bernardino Rivadavia, greatly contributed to carry forward this noble object. The labours of the gentleman now mentioned, in instructing his countrymen in true political wisdom, by precept and by example, and his exertions in forwarding the cause of knowledge and general education, have mainly contributed to give Buenos Aires . . . the first rank among the new American states. His name will ever be associated with the happiest part of the revolution of that country; and he will long be looked upon as its best benefactor.[6]

Thomson was able to establish eight schools for boys in Buenos Aires, all conducted on the monitorial system. The system spread throughout several provinces, and Thomson himself visited the provinces of Mendoza and San Juan after he had taken up residence in Chile.[7] In a letter written in London in 1826 to the British and Foreign School Society, Thomson reported that, while the society established in Buenos Aires floundered for a while, it had been recently reorganized, and continued its "useful exertions."[8] According to reports Thomson received after he left Argentina, approximately one hundred schools existed in Buenos Aires by 1826. Thomson also reported that a girls' school had been established in Buenos Aires by the time he left there in 1821.

While still in residence in Buenos Aires, Thomson visited Montevideo, Uruguay. He said:

I had paid a visit to Monte Video, where I was kindly received by the first ecclestiastic of that place . . . a friend to education. This gentleman laid the subject of the establishment of schools on the British system before the magistrates, and, in consequence, I was authorized to send a master to them.[9]

According to Browning, the Government of Uruguay requested Thomson to direct the schools recently organized there.[10] However, the Chilean Government presented a more attractive and pressing need, and Thomson signed a contract for one year to establish schools and train monitors. He wrote upon leaving Buenos Aires:

I have thought it my duty to set out for Chile without loss of time. From my former letters you would learn that the Chilian [sic] government has requested me to go there to establish schools on the Lancasterian plan. I had promised to go as soon as the state of the schools here would permit. The Chilian [sic] government, through their minister here, continues to show the same interest as before in regard to this matter, and has now made an agreement with me.[11]

Thomson arrived in Chile in July 1821. He was given a warm reception, and facilities were immediately provided for his work. A large room was made available at the university, where he would prepare monitors who, in turn, would make it possible to open other schools. Influential people assisted with plans of printing and publishing books for the monitorial schools.[12] In time, Thomson founded three Lancasterian schools in Santiago, and from the principal school that trained monitors, individuals were sent out to other parts of Chile to establish monitorial schools.[13]

Thomson wrote that the country's leader, Bernardo O'Higgins, "manifested a sincere desire to extend education throughout the country over which he was placed, and was ready to listen to any improvements in the manner of communicating knowledge, which might be brought before him."[14] In January 1822, Thomson wrote to the British and Foreign School Society and included a clipping from the *Chile Gazette*. The clipping was a decree by O'Higgins, which said, in part:

The Lancasterian system of mutual instruction, now introduced in most parts of the civilized world, and to which many places already owe an improvement in their habits, has been established amongst us, and in such a manner as prognosticates its beneficial effects. The propagation of this system holds out the surest means of extirpating those principles formed amongst us during the time of darkness. The government has resolved zealously to protect this establishment, and, as the best way of fulfilling its intention, has resolved to unite with it in this object those persons who have the same sentiments on the subject, and who, at the same time, possess that activity, zeal, and energy, which this important matter demands.[15]

O'Higgins continued to explain the establishment of a society, a branch of the British and Foreign School Society, and stated the objective of the society:

to extend, in every direction throughout Chile, the benefits of education; to promote the instruction of all classes, but especially of the poor; to seize all the advantages which this new system of education offers; and to point out those means by which it may be best adapted to the circumstances and necessities of the country."[16]

Thomson's contract was for only one year, and General Jose de San Martin had invited him to go to Peru. Anthony Eaton was sent to take Thomson's place in Chile, but Eaton soon became ill and had to return to England. In 1826, Thomson wrote, "In consequence of this misfortune, the cause in Chile began to decline, and I believe, at the present moment, the schools formerly established are in a very low state, if not given up altogether."[17]

According to Browning, the clergy became aroused and opposed the Lancasterian movement, which contributed to the lack of success of monitorial instruction in Chile. Eleven years later, the commission in charge of public instruction reported that proper teachers had not been available and, consequently, the work of monitors was not successful. The Lancasterian movement was abolished, although in 1840, four Lancasterian schools were again established as Sunday schools for the instruction of army personnel and other adults. However, because no attempt was made to train monitors or assistant teachers, the system failed once more.[18]

Thomson arrived in Peru in June 1822 and was welcomed by General San Martin. "San Martin expressed his great pleasure in welcoming him to Peru and pledged his support in furthering plans for the establishing of the Lancasterian schools throughout the country."[19] Very soon after, San Martin issued a decree establishing Lancasterianism as the plan to be adopted for the education of Peru, and Thomson was to establish a central school. Six months after the decree was issued, any public schools that were not taught on mutual instruction methods would be closed.[20]

Thomson wrote in May 1823:

We have, at length, got our school fairly begun, and under very favourable auspices . . . . The Congress and Government here are decidedly in favour of education. Their object is not merely the education of the few, but the education of the many, namely, of every individual in Peru.[21]

Later, Thomson said that progress in Peru was hindered by war. "Twice was Lima take possession of by the Spanish armies during my residence there."[22]

Political unrest continued; Bolivar became head of a new government and, by 1824, was able to drive out the remaining Spaniards from Peru. After Thomson had left Peru, he wrote in England about Bolivar and his attitudes toward education. Thomson said that Bolivar intended to benefit South America, "not by his military exertions only, but also by the gentler, more effectual means of early instruction."[23] Bolivar issued a decree that established the Lancasterian method throughout Peru, and he also sent two young men from each province to study in London.

Thomson left Peru in 1824. He had "succeeded in establishing a good work in Lima, in spite of the political difficulties of the time."[24] He wrote that the reason for his leaving was "the impossibility of moving forwards in our work under the pressure of existing circumstances."[25] He had been able to establish a model school with more than two hundred students, and a branch school already had eighty students in attendance. Bolivar's decree did not have much effect, and "the schools entirely disappeared in the changing conditions of the times."[26]

Thomson journeyed to Colombia and, on his way, was requested to establish schools both in Trujillo and in Guayaquil, but he continued to the larger cities of Quito and Bogotá. By this time, Browning reported, "his interest was now largely centered in the work of the British and Foreign Bible Society."[27]

Thomson wrote from Quito:

The state of elementary education is, at present, very low, but its prospects are more encouraging. Perhaps you are aware that the Colombian Government is taking active measures to extend education over all their share of South America. . . . It is the wish of the government to put a model school in the capital of each department, and from these schools to send out masters to all the towns and villages the department contains.[28]

On his journey from Quito to Bogotá, Thomson discovered three monitorial schools, one for girls and two for boys, established in other provinces of Colombia. In Bogotá, Thomson found that a school on the Lancasterian method had already been established by a friar who had learned of the system while in exile from Colombia during the revolution.

In a number of his letters, Thomson referred to his additional duty as representative for the British and Foreign Bible Society. For example, he wrote, "In Lima, the New Testament entire . . . was used as our principal school-book. In this precious volume the children in the higher classes read, and were questioned as to its contents."[29] In another letter he said, "Thus, you see, the Lord's work goes forward, even in this remote corner. . . . America, North and South, is the field for your operations. Lo! the poor Indian, begging from you the 'bread of life.' "[30] In late 1824, he wrote from Lima, "My principal business upon my journey will be the circulation of the Scriptures in the different places I may visit."[31]

Amunategui y Solar wrote a book in 1895 that was, to a great extent, a translation of Thomson's letters. In this book, he accused Thomson of using his promotion of the monitorial system as a cover for his real intentions of introducing the Bible to South American countries. Amunategui y Solar said that the leading men of the South American nations would have been shocked if they had realized that the schoolmaster was actually a missionary—and a Protestant at that—in disguise!

Thomson's last years were spent exclusively in the service of the British and Foreign Bible Society. He left South America "under the mistaken conviction that he had sown seed which would blossom into a bounteous harvest,"[32] presumably, in both his fields of endeavor. However, in time the church forces intervened and had great influence in the decline of the monitorial system in South America.[33] Also, there was "at that time a dearth of suitable material from which to develop efficient monitors, due to the lack of previous instruction."[34] This fact, probably more than any other, caused the Lancasterian system to fail in South America. Browning said several times that in this part of the world, "the system did not take deep root."[35]

LANCASTER IN SOUTH AMERICA

In 1821, Lancaster had been invited to go to Caracas (then a part of Great Colombia), but he spurned the invitation at that time. It had come to him through the British and Foreign School Society, and he felt that it was an attempt by the committee to see him "go to his grave seeing it open before him."[36] In 1824, however, Lancaster was "at Baltimore, when extremely sick, and recovering in a slow and languid manner, met with an officer, an aid of Bolivar's."[37] The officer learned of Lancaster's intention to go to the south of France and suggested that he come to Caracas instead. On March 16, 1825, Bolivar himself sent a letter of invitation, promising to advance him a sum of money, $20,000, to be used "in advancing the education of the children of Caracas."[38]

McCadden wrote of the South American venture, "It began gloriously and ended wretchedly."[39] The root of the problem appeared to be the money promised to Lancaster by Bolivar. The details are not clear, although Lancaster explained his side of the conflict in his *Epitome*. As McCadden stated, Lancaster "heaped vituperation on the head of Bolivar."[40] Lancaster and his wife left Caracas in 1827, and Lancaster wrote in the *Epitome:*

The Sum of the whole matter is, that Joseph Lancaster stated, in November 1828, 1. That he had returned from Colombia poor; 2. That he had been unjustly deprived of what he had earned; 3. That the famous bill of exhange *given* him by Bolivar, and given him with the promise that he might dispose of it as he pleased, had continued dishonored and unpaid![41]

Lancaster did establish an institute in Caracas, as is evidenced by a letter he wrote to DeWitt Clinton in 1826 telling about his success in Caracas.[42] However, his influence and efforts do not appear to have accomplished anything beyond that. Browning summed up Lancaster's South American experience as follows:

Joseph Lancaster, himself, . . . dwelt for a time in Caracas and promoted in that city and vicinity his methods of instruction. But, so far as the writer knows, there is no record of the results of his work. It is possible that his failing health and the increasing peculiarities of his disposition did not permit a thorough generalization of the system.[43]

MONITORIAL EFFORTS IN MEXICO

The first Lancasterian school opened in Mexico City in 1822 and was named La Escuela del Sol. Apparently, a chargé d'affaires from Mexico had learned the principles of the system in London and had returned to Mexico, where he had been active in the establishment of schools on that basis. This government official, Rocafuerte, addressed the British and Foreign School Society in 1826 and reported on the progress of monitorial instruction in Mexico. Rocafuerte said that soon after the opening of the first school, "the government granted to the Lancasterian Association of Mexico the large and beautiful convent of Bethlehem, and a second school was formed there."[44] Rocafuerte also stated:

This vast plan of human improvement is the great object of your noble institution, an institution which truly deserves the gratitude of the world and the most cordial support of all who are influenced by the love of their country and the principles of Christianity.[45]

An additional record of the establishment of La Escuela del Sol is available in a booklet containing the address presented at the opening of the school by the Lancasterian Association of Mexico. The speaker was the president and founder of the association, Manuel Codorniu y Ferreras. His address mentioned that the teacher's name was José María Alcantara. Codornui y Ferreras said that it gave him great satisfaction to announce that great progress had been seen in the students of La Escuela del Sol, and he was convinced that this system of teaching was founded in order to propagate wisdom and dispel ignorance.[46]

According to biographical records of the great Latin American landscapist, José María Velasco of Mexico, he attended a school founded by the Lancasterian Company in 1822, "based on a system of 'mutual instruction' conceived by an Englishman named Joseph

Lancaster."[47] Since Velasco's parents moved to Mexico City when he was young, presumably, he attended one of the schools established there, perhaps La Escuela del Sol, which was founded in 1822.

NOTES

1. W. L. Langer, *An Encyclopedia of World History* (Boston: Houghton Mifflin Co., 1948), p. 799.
2. Ellwood P. Cubberley, *The History of Education* (Boston: Houghton Mifflin Co., 1920), p. 717.
3. W. E. Browning, "Joseph Lancaster, James Thomson, and the Lancasterian System of Mutual Instruction," *The Hispanic American Historical Review* 4 (February 1921): p. 52.
4. Carl F. Kaestle, ed. *Joseph Lancaster and the Monitorial School Movement: A Documentary History* (New York: Columbia University, Teachers College Press, 1973), p. 34.
5. Browning, "Joseph Lancaster," p. 63.
6. James Thomson, *Letters on the Moral and Religious State of South America* (London: James Nisbet, 1827), p. 268.
7. Browning, "Joseph Lancaster," p. 69.
8. Thomson, *Letters*, p. 266.
9. Ibid., pp. 269–70.
10. Browning, "Joseph Lancaster," pp. 72-73.
11. Thomson, *Letters*, p. 5.
12. W. E. Browning, "The Lancasterian School System in England and the Americas," *Educational Foundations* 29 (April 1918): 469.
13. Browning, "Joseph Lancaster", pp. 75-81.
14. Thomson, *Letters*, p. 277.
15. Ibid., pp. 26–27.
16. Ibid., p. 28.
17. Ibid., p. 278.
18. Browning, "Joseph Lancaster," pp. 75-81.
19. Ibid., p. 81.
20. Ibid., pp. 81–89.
21. Thomson, *Letters*, pp. 80–81.
22. Ibid., p. 281.
23. Ibid., p. 284.
24. Browning, "Joseph Lancaster," p. 88.
25. James Thomson, "The Lancasterian Enthusiasm in South America," *Joseph Lancaster and the Monitorial School Movement: A Documentary History*, ed. C. F. Kaestel (New York: Columbia University, Teachers College Press, 1973), p. 145.
26. Browning, "The Lancasterian School System," p. 472.
27. Browning, "Joseph Lancaster," p. 89.
28. Thomson, *Letters*, pp. 220–21.

29. Ibid., p. 282.
30. Ibid., p. 104.
31. Ibid., p. 160.
32. Browning, "Joseph Lancaster," p. 65.
33. Kaestle, *Joseph Lancaster*, p. 34.
34. Browning, "Joseph Lancaster," p. 60.
35. Ibid., p. 61.
36. David Salmon, *Joseph Lancaster* (London: Longman, Green, and Co., 1904), p. 60.
37. Joseph Lancaster, *Epitome of Some of the Chief Events and Transactions in the Life of Joseph Lancaster* (New Haven: Baldwin and Peck, 1933), p. 35.
38. Ibid.
39. Joseph J. McCadden, "Joseph Lancaster in America," *The Social Studies* 28 (February 1937): 85.
40. Ibid., p. 75.
41. Lancaster, *Epitome*, p. 39.
42. C. A. Eggertsen, "The Monitorial System of Instruction in the United States" (Doctoral diss., University of Minnesota, 1939), p. 43.
43. Browning, "The Lancasterian School System," p. 471.
44. Browning, "Joseph Lancaster," p. 96.
45. Ibid., p. 97.
46. Manuel Codorniu y Ferreras, *Discurso Inaugural Que en la Albertura de las Escuelas Mutuas de la Filantropia* (Mexico: Martin Rivera, 1823), p. 5.
47. James B. Lynch, Jr. "José María Velasco, Images of Early Genesis," *Americas* 31 (January 1979): 5.

CHAPTER 8

Twentieth-Century Developments in Theory and Practice of Peer Teaching in the United States

INTRODUCTION

From the latter part of the nineteenth century until the 1960s, there is scant mention of peer teaching in educational literature. No major figures or movements appeared during that time, and the technique of peer teaching, if used, received virtually no attention.

There is one exception, however. Numerous writers mention the use of peer teaching in one-room schools of rural America in the latter part of the nineteenth and in the early twentieth centuries. Lippitt and Lippitt wrote:

Teachers in one-room rural schools often called upon their older students to help teach the younger ones. They did so in the hope that the younger children would benefit from the extra attention and help they got from their tutors and that the older ones, proud to be cast as assistant teachers, would be motivated to improve their own school work. Sometimes the hopes were justified, and sometimes they were not. Like most classroom expedients, this one needed perfecting by careful evaluation and redesigning.[1]

Tyler stated, "In an earlier period, the one-room school depended heavily upon cross-age teaching since the teacher could not manage alone the educational experiences in all the elementary school subjects for several grade levels."[2] Thelen pointed out that the idea of students helping students was hardly new. "Friends have always done some homework together. . . . The 'little red school house,' in which six to twenty students of all ages studied in one room presided over by a single teacher, relied heavily on students learning from each other—if only by eavesdropping on each other's recitations."[3]

In 1917, Woofter published a handbook, *Teaching in Rural Schools,* in which he advocated using older pupils as teacher's assistants. He wrote:

Nearly always there will be some older pupils who can be quickly shown how to assist with the younger ones. These older pupils should be appointed for this work. It will be very helpful for them, and will permit the teacher to give more time to other things. After a teacher has taught a reading or number lesson to first or second grades, some older pupil, who has been called to watch the lesson, can carry on the drill by showing cards for sight work, and by pointing to figures to be combined for number practice. Older pupils can conduct spelling lessons and correct written spelling. This will make the older ones more thorough, and it will help to organize the school into a wholesome working community. Different ones may be assigned these duties in turn, thus not making it a burden.[4]

J. H. Martin, writing in 1972, could see much merit in the one-room school because of the peer interaction it afforded. "In the one-room school, older children managed younger children. . . . Children in the one-room school expected each other to lead, direct, help, carry, follow, and ask. Their relationships seemed natural to them. . . . "[5] He also said that the one-room school forced students into a situation where giving help to each other seemed natural, and the teacher approved of this help. He concluded:

We would urge the creation of institutions that would include adults and children as learning partners. The success of older children tutoring younger ones derives in part from the drive to live up to culture heroes' expectation. Additionally, there is a recurrent finding that should not surprise any teacher that the older "hero" learns as much or more than the one he has taught.[6]

Apparently, peer teaching as experienced in the one-room school did not receive attention in educational literature until the 1930s. The fact that the technique was widely used in schools of this kind is often mentioned; it seemed to be considered a valued tool, but not one that merited professional attention.

Horst wrote in 1931 and in 1933 about his experiments with student-tutors. He explained the program conducted at West High School in Akron, Ohio, a program that the editor of *Clearing House* called "an unusual procedure."[7] At West High School, students were chosen to give their peers help in various school subjects. Horst did not claim to have arrived at the favorable results through any scientific approach but maintained that experience showed this peer tutoring program to be a success.[8] In 1933, he wrote again about the program at West High School, stating that it was an effort "to develop a feeling of responsibility on the part of the more able students toward those less fortunate."[9] He stressed the futility of comparing these student-teachers with trained teachers, saying,

The good they may do is done in spite of a lack of the training and maturity of the regular teachers. Perhaps in some cases their immaturity will enable them to get all the more quickly the viewpoint of the one whom they are trying to help. Perhaps their limited knowledge of subject matter may make them more appreciative of his difficulties.[10]

In 1938, A. I. David wrote about a student-tutoring program at Collingwood High School in Cleveland, Ohio. She stated the theory and aim of the program: "Only those pupils are encouraged to be tutored who seek aid because of prolonged absence from school, tardy registration, or weakness in a specific large unit of work not readily grasped."[11] According to the evaluation of the peer teaching program, 77.4 percent of the pupils raised their grade or kept it from being lowered. David anticipated much research done in the 1960s and 70s when she said: "For the tutor, we have found that the benefit is even richer. In teaching he learns, as all of us in the teaching profession have learned. Many have availed themselves of this opportunity in preparation for scholarships. . . . "[12]

No further mention of peer teaching is apparent in educational-literature indeces until 1956. Wayne wrote about a program conducted at Fresno State College for future business teachers. He commented, "It is said that the best way to learn something is to teach it, and that may well be one of the major benefits to the tutoring students."[13] Wayne listed four groups that benefited from tutoring:

those doing the tutoring, those receiving it, the school, and the institution that eventually would hire the student-tutors as teachers. The benefits to tutees were readily apparent. "The tutored students receive valuable benefits from such a service. They are given a great deal of individual attention if they want it. . . . Often they begin to do much better in their class work and show signs of renewed interest and enthusiasm."[14]

By 1960, the principle of student teaching student became more widely used and researched. Since that time, literature on the theory, research, and practice of peer teaching has proliferated.

THEORY AND RATIONALE OF PEER TEACHING

According to Tyler, the failure to use peer teaching in its various forms is a major source of waste in schools.[15] He stated that situations where children learn from each other have been shown to contribute significantly to children's learning.

Taba also found much that was beneficial in peer interaction. She said, "Perhaps the greatest source for mobilizing unused potentialities for learning and for controlling the factors which block or retard learning is the efficient use of group relations in the classroom and the school."[16]

Reinforcers are necessary to an individual's self-esteem in a learning situation, Bloom wrote in 1976, and these reinforcers can be dispensed by others, including one's peers. In addition, feedback and corrective procedures are necessary for all learning. These, Bloom pointed out, can be accomplished by students helping each other.[17]

Reviewing some studies that were applicable to in-school tutoring by students, Ellson stated that the same basic theory underlies both classroom teaching and tutoring. He said, "These important groups of factors can be identified, each of which has implications for the nature of tutoring. They are (a) structural factors, . . . (b) affective factors, . . . and (c) learning or environmental factors."[18] Structural factors are assumed to be within the individual and therefore unchangeable. These factors may include genetic handicaps. Teaching involves either adapting to these structural factors by modifying them or teaching around the handicap in several ways. Affective and environmental factors are changeable and can be manipulated and adapted to meet the needs of the student.

In 1977, Thelen wrote about peer teaching: "I can think of no other innovation which has been so consistently perceived as successful."[19] He listed the following factors as bases for peer teaching. The tutor can develop his academic skills or knowledge as he uses these to teach others. It is also hoped that "he will form a better character (for example, attitudes), become better adjusted or more adequate as a person, discover new interests or commitments for his life."[20] In addition, peer tutoring can aid in meeting individual needs, which become highly complex in today's society. "Student tutoring seems to be a promising answer, especially if it were built into the school day on a regularly scheduled basis."[21] Peer tutoring can be a way of dealing with prejudice when one considers the various helping relationships that are possible. It can also enhance cooperation. "Students learning through *helping* each other is a very promising alternative to learning through *competing with* each other. And it also makes the acquisition of knowledge and skills valuable, not in the service of competition for grades but as the means for personally significant interaction with others."[22] Finally, Thelen felt that peer teaching can be a means of bringing change through new ideas and inspiration because it calls for a new kind of interaction and cooperation among all groups involved in a school.

Johnson and Johnson have compiled research and information about competition versus cooperation.[23,24] They stated, "The research clearly indicates that the most desirable goal structure for promoting achievement in problem solving tasks is a cooperative one."[25] Cooperation, as compared with competition, serves as a means of teaching respect for individual differences, teaches the ability to communicate effectively, helps in the cognitive development of the individual, develops empathy, and, particularly, eliminates failure and its accompanying feelings. They wrote:

The research strongly supports the proposition that cooperative goal structures encourage positive interpersonal relationships characterized by mutual liking, positive attitudes toward each other, mutual concern, friendliness, attentiveness, feelings of obligation to other students, and desire to win the respect of other students.[26]

In their book, *Learning Together and Alone,* Johnson and Johnson discussed cooperative goal structures. Several advantages can be seen by the use of goal structures, which aid in cooperation, and these can also be viewed as reasons for peer teaching:

1. Peer tutors are often effective in teaching children who do not respond well to adults.
2. Peer tutoring can develop a deep bond of friendship between the tutor and the person being helped, the result of which is very important for integrating slow learners into the group.
3. Peer tutoring takes pressure off the teacher by allowing her to teach a large group of students; at the same time, it allows the slow learners the individual attention they need.
4. The tutors benefit by learning to teach, a general skill that can be very useful in an adult society.
5. Peer tutoring happens spontaneously under cooperative conditions, so the teacher does not have to organize and manage it in a formal, continuing way.[27]

Johnson and Johnson concluded:

Until it is demonstrated empirically that the pervasive use of competition does not result in damage to the person's self-attitudes, the authors recommend that students be informed of what goal structure is to be used within instructional activities and participate in competitively structured situations only on a voluntary basis.[28]

Schmuck also described the advantages of cooperation as compared to competition. "Research has shown that classroom groups with supportive friendship patterns enhance academic learning,[29] while more interpersonally tense class environments in which peer groups rejections are strong and frequent get in the way of learning."[29] Schmuck felt that peers can make a difference in scholastic achievement, and peers can be utilized to aid in learning. For these reasons, the psychological aspects of peer interaction as they affect learning, particularly the positive factors as seen through peer teaching, must be considered by educators.

Elliott reviewed the advantages of using students in tutoring roles and stated, "Perhaps the most compelling reason for the use of students as tutors is to change the social-psychological climate of the school from individual competitiveness to concern for each other."[30]

Buckholdt and Wodarski summarized a series of studies in which they found that children from various socioeconomic classes, ranging in age from three to eleven, in classrooms of four to seven members, can cooperate in instructional situations. "Moreover, the studies indicate that when appropriate reinforcement is provided for cooperative behavior, helping behaviors as well as student performance can be increased." They concluded that "there is evidence to support the argument that individualistic, competitive systems serve to limit student academic performance and aspirations and to depress satisfaction with school."[31]

Peer teaching can be a means through which to achieve cooperation, and Buckholdt and Wodarski listed several advantages, which they had gleaned from reviewing research. Among them are the following:

1. Peer teaching can reduce anxiety caused by vast differences in age, status, and background between students and teachers. A peer tutor may possibly communicate more easily with a student, particularly a slow one.
2. More individualized instruction is possible.
3. The tutor may increase his own understanding as well as self-esteem and self-confidence.
4. Additional motivation for learning may come through peer teaching.
5. Peer tutors might be more patient with a slow learner.
6. Peer teaching reinforces previous learning, may reorganize knowledge more effectively and increase understanding.[32]

Gartner, Kohler, and Riessman wrote the first major volume on peer teaching in 1971. In the introduction, they stated:

It has long been obvious that children learn from their peers, but a more significant observation is that *children learn more from teaching other children*. From this a major educational strategy follows: namely, that every child must be given the opportunity to play the teaching role, because it is through playing this role that he may really learn how to learn.[33]

They further added that "in learning by teaching, the child who is teaching finds a meaningful use for the subject, . . . a utility for his knowledge."[34]

Other benefits are enumerated in this book by Gartner et al. Peer teaching makes individualization of instruction possible. "It can be attuned to the style and way of learning of the individual child as well as to the individual child acting as a teacher."[35] Gartner et al. also wrote about the positive effect that the helping act or situation has upon the helper. "Programs of children teaching may not only lead to direct cognitive effect but may also have emotional, social, and psychological impact that in turn may affect cognitive growth."[36] They noted some observable changes in the tutor: "a greater sense of responsibility, especially as it relates to another; a greater maturity, seriousness of purpose; a better understanding of individual differences."[37] By a child's being able to participate in roles other than just the subordinate, he may be better prepared to fit into today's complex society.

In a volume on peer teaching published in 1976 and edited by Allen, the first section deals with theoretical considerations underlying peer teaching. Allen quoted Bruner, who stated that students should have more responsibility for educating their peers. "I would strongly urge . . . that we use the system of student-assisted learning from the start in our schools."[38] Bruner saw difficulty in the long period of time during which a young person can only live one role, that of a student. Decision making is delayed in our society. Peer teaching could give a sense of purpose and participation so often lacking in children's lives.

In the first section of the book edited by Allen, various theories of peer teaching are offered. First, peer teaching can contribute to the socialization of children; second, teaching is a social activity, and through this activity, social skills can be developed. In addition, clarification of roles, often confusing to a child, is possible through the broadening of pupil-teacher activities.[39]

Lippitt listed various reasons for using cross-age teaching.[40] Among these were:

1. the need to individualize instruction,
2. the need for children to diversify their friendships,

3. the need to feel useful and influential, especially on the part of older children,
4. the possibility of motivating students,
5. a way of aiding students to fill in gaps in their learning,
6. an increase in communication and appreciation between various ages.

Melaragno pointed out the following as bases for peer tutoring.[41] Students can learn, but instruction must be effective in order for the individual learning needs to be met. Through peer teaching, instruction can be individualized, and new relationships can develop that will aid the progress of the student.

Melaragno also listed five conclusions relative to the effectiveness of peer teaching that can be viewed as reasons for its implementation.[42] First, many content areas may utilize peer teaching. Second, while peer teaching has usually yielded favorable results, the more structured the situation, the more successful the tutoring encounter. Third, both participants in a peer teaching relationship show cognitive gains. Fourth, positive affective changes are discernible. Fifth, a tutoring program can be established without great difficulty.

Various additional reasons and theories for the utilization of peer teaching can be found. Good and Brophy pointed out that young children can learn to trust and, consequently, ask for information from older students, whereas they may be intimidated by the authority figure of a teacher. Consequently, students learn the advantages of openly seeking information and help. In addition, the tutor may develop more interpersonal skills and a caring attitude for others. "Peer tutoring, then, has been advocated as a tool for helping both tutors and tutees to make progress in mastering subject matter as well as to increase interpersonal communication skills."[43]

Writing at a time when peer teaching was just beginning to receive renewed notice, Wright spoke of the two promises of mutual instruction as "its promise for helping children learn and its promise for relieving today's teacher shortage."[44] Wright cited research that indicated that students who had experienced a teaching role in the past were more likely to choose teaching as a career when faced with that decision. Whether or not a teacher shortage exists, the fact that peer teaching may help in the career choice of an individual particularly suited for teaching is something to consider.

The bulk of research has been conducted with the average student or with students who are socially or economically deprived. Lindsey and Watts pointed out that the very same reasons for using peer teaching are also valid for the exceptional student, and could be used as a complement for activities to meet individual education plans (IEP) prescribed by public law 94-142.[45]

Perhaps the most prevalent reasons for adopting peer teaching can be summarized by a statement by Wilson. "In the teaching process meaningful learning occurs as content is transformed into concepts and then related to learning activities."[46] In addition, Wilson stated that "everyone benefits. . . . The older students have an opportunity to be appreciated, influential and heeded, while the younger recipients have the benefit of increased attention and interest."[47] Although much remains to be proved and discovered relative to the rationale and theories that serve as bases for peer teaching, there is "mounting evidence that successful communicating of knowledge can, in addition to reinforcing and deepening learning, be a means of increasing the child's confidence and self-respect, and of reforming negative attitudes he may have toward school and teachers, making school and learning more acceptable and desirable."[48]

REVIEW OF RESEARCH ON PEER TEACHING

Since 1960, peer teaching has been the subject of research to an extent never before matched. The research has examined the efficacy of tutoring programs by peers, cross-age tutoring, same-age tutoring, benefits to tutors and tutees, specific uses of programs and their value, and other subjects of interest pertaining to peer teaching. In a review of research on the subject, Dillner stated, "The focus of the materials and skills has been on the tutee even when the major concern of the researcher was with the tutor."[49] In more recent years, the emphasis has been on the effect of tutoring on the tutor. It has been assumed that the tutee will benefit, and this assumption has also been backed by research.

It should be pointed out that there are contradictions in the research that has been conducted, and conclusions cannot always be drawn. Devin-Sheehan, Feldman, and Allen wrote, "Rather than identifying critical issues and problems based upon theoretical considerations, most studies to date have been designed only to determine if the particular tutoring situation employed is efficacious," and they concluded that "until research becomes more systematic it will be impossible to draw valid generalizations and conclusions."[50] However, in spite of the shortcomings of research, enough valid conclusions are available to guide the teacher who is considering using this method. This study is not intended to be a comprehensive review of all research on peer teaching; other works of that nature have already been attempted and will be listed in this section.

That children *can* teach and do so effectively was the subject of an article by Steinberg and Cazden. Both writers have been involved with peer teaching, in actual teaching and in doing research. They have found that " . . . children may display surprising competence in dealing with educational tasks outside of the teacher's span of direct control."[51]

In 1965, Weitzman conducted a study on the effects of tutoring on the performance and motivation of high-school students. Tutoring sessions took place outside of school hours, and participation was voluntary. The results showed that the tutored students showed greater improvement on reports, essays, homework exercises, and other assignments than did the control group. Other effects were that tutored students showed increased motivation, interest in the subject, and improvement in study habits.[52]

Mohan found that peer teaching could be used as a technique to aid the unmotivated.[53] In a tutoring program that lasted eight months, unmotivated students from grades seven and eight were asked to teach unmotivated children from grades two and three. The evaluation was made on statements made by the subjects, teachers, and the principal. The results, according to these evaluations, were successful. All except one tutee felt that the experience had been worthwhile.

Sharan evaluated and examined five methods of small-group learning, which included Aronson's Jigsaw Classroom, DeVries's Teams-Games-Tournaments, Slavin's Student Teams and Academic Divisions, and Johnsons' cooperative learning approach, and Sharan's Small-Group Teaching methods.[54] The first three are considered to be peer tutoring methods. Sharan reviewed the research on these methods and discussed their effectiveness in terms of academic achievement, attitudes, and ethnic relations. The lengthy review concludes that team-learning methods reflect higher academic achievement although the results are not visible in all groups. The studies also seem to indicate that cooperative methods such as peer tutoring increase the helping behaviors of the participants and bring about better perceptions of giving and receiving help. However, Sharan again points out that this result was not true for all the research studies, and he raises questions pointing to future research. Ethnic relations are improved as a result of team-learning efforts. While most studies seemed to confirm this, critical questions remain unanswered.

A study conducted by Trovato and Bucher involved the use of peer tutoring in a corrective reading program. The subjects, second- to fourth-graders, were assigned to three groups: peer tutoring only, peer tutoring with home-based reinforcement, and control. According to the researchers, "both reading and comprehension were significantly increased by peer tutoring, relative to the control group."[55]

Steiner reviewed research of peer tutoring that had been conducted in reading classes. Her conclusions were as follows:

Do peer tutoring programs in reading work? The answer must be a qualitative "yes." Under some circumstances, with some groups of students, to reach some specific goals, the effectiveness of peer tutoring cannot be denied. Although the precise factors which characterize the "successful" program have not, as yet, been confirmed such programs can clearly afford valuable opportunties for social and academic gain.[56]

Another article that reviewed literature on tutorial systems was written by Lewis in 1979. He concluded that some of the research indicated higher academic achievement for tutees, and other research supported the hypothesis that tutees do not show a difference in achievement after tutoring. He also pointed out contradictory results on the benefits to the tutor. Some studies showed that tutors benefit in academic achievement as a result of the tutoring experience, while other studies indicated no favorable results. Lewis stated: "When interpreting the above research, one needs to be careful about the types of tutoring treatments given, the duration of tutoring sessions, and the availability of control conditions for comparisons."[57]

Dillner reviewed studies that indicated that both tutors and tutees showed gains in reading, and that both capable and less capable students functioned well as tutors.[58] Perhaps, she surmised, the latter did better because of greater sympathy for the tutee. Another study indicated that tutors who were poor or average academically could function successfully as tutors. Other studies found that the tutorial experience was valuable for both tutors and tutees. In addition, teacher attitudes toward students changed when they saw that tutors could act in a constructive manner. Since self-confidence and self-concept are influenced by a teacher's behavior, this change is one beneficial result of tutoring. In another study that Dillner cited, the attitudes of tutoring participants were helped. The self-image of tutors improved because of the responsibility given to them. However, Dillner also quoted a study that indicated that behavior did not show marked improvement as a result of tutoring. Other studies showed that both tutored students and tutors gained in reading ability: the tutees gained four months or more; the tutors advanced a year in reading ability. In reviewing the research, Dillner found that the evidence is largely favorable toward the use of peer teaching.

Devin-Sheehan, Feldman, and Allen compiled a review of research in order to discuss available research on peer teaching, its implications and shortcomings, and to make suggestions. They wrote: "We can conclude from the evidence presented above that several different kinds of tutoring programs can effectively improve academic performance of tutees and, in some cases, that of tutors as well."[59]

An increasing amount of research has been done on the effect of tutoring on the tutor. Dillner stated, "Concern about the tutor seems to be an increasing trend. Though the majority of the tutoring programs still appear to focus on the effect upon the tutee, there tends to be more and more studies pointing out the positive effects upon the helper."[60] She cited studies that showed an obvious and favorable impact on tutors. Tutors experienced attitudinal changes, while tutees showed gains in achievement. Tutors showed positive identification with the teacher role. At times, the tutor could reach a child that a teacher could not, and as a result, tutors were able to change their own attitudes toward learning, and they experienced the satisfaction of helping others. Other studies indicated that tutors gained in reading scores, improved their language skills, showed improved interest in the subjects, attended school more regularly, and got better grades. Dillner concluded that "even the most precise of the studies have not been able consistently to isolate the factors that lead to the successful tutoring experiences for the tutors. In fact, in some cases, it seems the tutors were successful in spite of the conditions in which they tutored."[61]

Devin-Sheehan et al. wrote the following at the conclusion of their research review on the benefits of tutoring on the tutor:

Taken together, the literature on tutor characteristics suggests quite convincingly that a very broad range of students may benefit from acting as a tutor. Whether or not the tutee will improve more from being tutored by a particular type of tutor is an open question; the evidence is mixed. The crucial factor may be the relative level of competence between the tutor and tutee.[62]

In 1967, Cloward reported on a study that is widely quoted. The Mobilization for Youth was an antipoverty program whose objective was to provide tutoring for underachieving poor children and to make work available for tenth- and eleventh-grade students who were paid to be tutors. The tutors were also low-achieving students. Cloward found that high-school tutors benefited significantly, as did the tutees. Both groups made significant gains in reading skills.[63]

Hassinger and Via conducted a study in which high-school students were hired to work with fourth- through sixth-grade students for a six-week period.[64] Tutors came from low socioeconomic families and were retarded in reading or had low grades and poor attendance. The tutors showed an average of an eight-month gain in their reading scores. In addition, changes in attitudes and personal appearance were visible by the end of the second week of the experiment. The mean gain for the tutees during the six weeks was 4.6 months.

In 1970, Morgan and Toy did research in a rural school system, using tutors from grades eight to twelve and tutees from grades two to five. The tutors showed a thirteen-month achievement gain on the Wide Range Achievement Test over a four-month period. Morgan and Toy stated: "It is proposed here, in fact, that children *need* the opportunity to teach in order to learn effectively."[65]

Allen and Feldman performed an experiment with low-achieving fifth-grade children who taught third-graders. At the end of the two-week period, the low achiever's performance was significantly better in the tutoring condition than in the solitary studying condition. The results suggest that serving as a tutor may be a particularly useful method for enhancing the academic performance of low-achieving children.[66]

Fitz-Gibbon also conducted a study using low-achieving junior high-school students as tutors in mathematics for fourth-graders. Before each tutoring session, the tutors received coaching on the materials they were to present to the younger students. Test results showed significant gains in mathematics for the tutors.[67]

Dineen, Clark, and Risley studied the academic effect on tutors. They found that while the tutees' spelling improved, the tutors' spelling also improved an equivalent amount on the words used to tutor the other children. "These findings, that peer tutoring is profitable for the tutor as well as the tutee, provide a basis for recommending peer tutoring as one method of individualized education."[68]

Peer teaching may involve students of the same age or an older tutor helping a younger tutee, a situation that is called cross-age tutoring. In same-age peer teaching research, the results appear to be mixed. In 1977, Rosen, Powell, and Schubot experimented with using undergraduate classmates to discover whether there was greater and more positive desirability to be a tutor, or whether an equitable relationship could exist. They found that "changes in assigned role status, and in the extent to which the assignment is status congruent and therefore equitable to the present context, directly influence both individual performance and satisfaction." Their most important conclusion was "that it is more satisfying to move into the role of tutor than into that of tutee, especially if the role assignment becomes equitable."[69]

In 1978, Rosen, Powell, Schubot, and Rollins did a follow-up study that investigated the effects of status level, congruence of achievement, and satisfaction in a same-age tutoring situation. "As predicted, once tutors were made to exchange roles with their tutees, these former tutors exhibited a decline in perceived performance and satisfaction. By way of contrast, their former tutees, now tutors, showed an increase in these variables."[70]

Allen and Boraks developed a peer tutor training program in which children were taught teaching behaviors to be used in a same-age teaching situation. "Children of the same ages and similar ability levels are paired as tutoring teams. Because children learn to be a tutor and so alternate tutor and tutee roles for different lessons, the term 'Reciprocal Peer Tutoring' (RPT) was chosen as a label for the process."[71] The purpose of the study was to discover whether RPT could affect the reading achievement of elementary-school children who needed remedial reading. "The results of this study indicate that same-aged peers of similar ability levels were able to tutor one another in reading skills and benefit from the experience."[72]

Howell conducted a study to determine whether same-age peer tutors can deliver drill-type instruction, and whether they can identify errors if, perhaps, they themselves cannot give the right answer. They concluded that students can successfully monitor the responses of same-age peers, particularly if tutor and tutee are matched in performance ability. "The second study does indicate that the use of peers for the delivery of multiplication fact drills is an effective technique."[73]

A review of research on cross-age teaching was conducted by Paolitto.[74] She quoted Rasmussen, who had reviewed sixteen cross-age teaching programs. Of the sixteen, ten showed beneficial results such as in morale building for the tutor.

Johnson and Bailey found that in a cross-age tutoring program, where fifth-grade students tutored kindergarten children in basic arithmetic skills, the fifth-graders served effectively as teachers. Results showed that the experimental group made far greater gains than did the control group. Johnson and Bailey wrote: "At a time when many school systems are training paraprofessionals and aides to assist teachers in various classroom duties, cross-age tutoring offers an opportunity to utilize untapped resources already in the schools to assist in the teaching process."[75]

Medway and Lowe researched the reasons for success in cross-age tutoring programs. Both tutors and tutees, they found, felt that success in learning by tutoring depended on effort rather than on ability. The students credited positive results with efforts expended by the tutors but attributed negative results to themselves.[76]

A review of research on cross-age tutoring was conducted by Mavrogenes and Galen in which they discussed research dealing with both cognitive gains and affective gains. They concluded that numerous studies show gains in the cognitive areas, but less evidence is available for affective gains. Mavrogenes and Galen also discussed how a cross-age teaching program could effectively be implemented.[77]

In reviewing research on cross-age teaching, Devin-Sheehan et al. stated the following: "In light of these . . . studies, it appears that a greater age difference between tutor and tutee results in somewhat better tutee performance."[78]

Dillner found that research results favored cross-age tutoring. The age difference made it possible for younger children to be helped without an unfavorable comparison with the tutor's more advanced skills. In addition, a tutor may communicate more effectively with the younger child because of their similiar language patterns. The older child may present a more realistic level of achievement and may lack the inhibiting effects of the teacher as an authority figure.[79]

The training of tutors does not seem to have any discernible effect on tutoring results. Devin-Sheehan et al. stated, "Taken together, available research does not indicate unequivocally that any one particular method of training is superior to any other. Indeed, there are surprisingly little data showing that training of tutors, per se, has a beneficial effect on tutoring."[80]

Holliday and Edwards showed that peer teaching may be applied to specific circumstances to achieve favorable results. In a program geared to a predominantly black student body, the teachers used peer teaching because "the program was consistent with the extended family structure of black culture."[81] The program was intended to reinforce cultural strengths in an effort to improve the learning experiences. The tutees showed improvement in reading comprehension ranging from fifteen to twenty-three months, indicating an average of sixteen months. Vocabulary growth reflected a range of fourteen to thirty-six months, with an average of twenty-three months gain.

Tutoring is also increasing in use for exceptional children. Lazerson reported that after a five-week experiment with peer tutoring, children who were aggressive and withdrawn had achieved higher self-concepts and better behavioral patterns.[82] These children also became more interested in school and in learning.

Additional research reviews can be found in *Children as Teachers*.[83] The second section of this book reports on research in peer teaching, and there is an additional chapter in the closing section that also reviews research. Other research reviews that are worthwhile perusing in detail are those by Dillner,[84] Devin-Sheehan et al.,[85] and Stainback, Stainback, and Lichtward.[86]

Dillner summarized as follows:

The implication for the classroom teacher who is looking for a workbook exercise to teach some skill, such as the use of the dictionary, is to look instead for a teacher of younger students who wants to teach her students the same skill. Both groups would benefit, but it would appear that the tutor would benefit more than he has in the past—and not at the expense of the tutee.[87]

NOTES

1. Peggy Lippitt and Ronald Lippitt, "Cross-age Helpers," *NEA Journal* 57 (March 1968): 24.
2. Ralph W. Tyler, "Wasting Time and Resources in Schools and Colleges," *Viewpoints* 51 (March 1975): 69.
3. Herbert A. Thelen, "Tutoring by Students," *The School Review* 77 (September–December 1969): 229.
4. Thomas Jackson Woofter, *Teaching in Rural Schools* (Boston: Houghton Mifflin Co., 1917), pp. 52, 54.
5. John Henry Martin, "The Grade School Came from Prussia," *Educational Horizons* 51 (Fall 1972): 31.
6. Ibid., p. 32.
7. H. M. Horst, "History of Student Tutoring at West High School, Akron, Ohio," *Clearing House* 6 (December 1931): 245.
8. Ibid., pp. 245-49.
9. H. M. Horst, "An Experiment with Student Tutors," *The Journal of the National Educational Association* 22 (November 1933): 206.
10. Ibid.
11. Aranka Irene David, "Student Tutoring: A Success at Collinwood High School," *Clearing House* 12 (January 1938): 288.
12. Ibid., p. 289.

13. William C. Wayne, "Tutoring Service: A Project for Future Busines ers," *The Journal of Business Education* 31 (April 1956): 330.
14. Ibid.
15. Tyler, "Wasting Time and Resources," p. 69.
16. Hilda Taba, *Curriculum Development: Theory and Practice* (New York: Harcourt, Brace and World, Inc., 1969), p. 160.
17. Benjamin S. Bloom, *Human Characteristics and School Learning* (New York: McGraw-Hill Book Company, 1976), p. 120.
18. Douglas G. Ellson, "Tutoring," *The Psychology of Teaching Methods*, ed. N. L. Cage (Chicago: National Society for the Study of Education, 1976), p. 143.
19. Thelen, "Tutoring by Students," p. 230.
20. Ibid., p. 229.
21. Ibid., pp. 236–37.
22. Ibid., p. 238.
23. David W. Johnson and Roger T. Johnson, "Instructional Goal Structure: Cooperative, Competitive, or Individualistic," *Review of Educational Research* 44 (Spring 1974).
24. David W. Johnson and Roger T. Johnson, *Learning Together and Alone* (Englewood Clifs, N. J.: Prentice-Hall, 1975).
25. Johnson and Johnson, "Instructional Goal Structure," p. 221.
26. Ibid., p. 228.
27. Johnson and Johnson, *Learning Together and Alone*, p. 37.
28. Johnson and Johnson, "Instructional Goal Structure," p. 234.
29. Richard A. Schmuck, "Peer Groups as Settings for Learning," *Theory into Practice* 16 (October 1977): 273.
30. Arthur Elliot, "Student Tutoring Benefits Everyone," *Phi Delta Kappan* 54 (April 1973): 538.
31. David R. Buckholdt and John S. Wodarski, "The Effects of Different Reinforcement Systems on Cooperative Behaviors Exhibited by Children in Classroom Contexts," *Journal of Research and Development in Education* 12 (Fall 1978): 64.
32. Ibid., pp. 50–51.
33. Alan Gartner, Mary Conway Kohler, and Frank Riessman, *Children Teach Children: Learning by Teaching* (New York: Harper and Row, 1971), p. 1.
34. Ibid., p. 60.
35. Ibid., p. 8
36. Ibid., p. 63.
37. Ibid., pp. 67–68.
38. Vernon L. Allen, ed., *Children as Teachers: Theory and Research on Tutoring* (New York: Academic Press, 1976), p. 1.
39. Ibid.
40. Peggy Lippitt, *Students Teach Students* (Bloomington, Ind.: Phi Delta Kappa Educational Foundation, 1975).
41. Ralph J. Melarango, *Tutoring with Students* (Englewood Cliffs, N.J.: Educational Technology Publications, 1976).
42. Ralph J. Melaragno, "Pupil Tutoring: Directions for the Future," *The Elementary School Journal* 77 (May 1977): 385.

43. T. L. Good and J. E. Brophy, *Looking in Classrooms* (New York: Harper and Row, 1978), p. 313.

44. Benjamin Wright, "Should Children Teach?" *The Elementary School Journal* 60 (April 1960): 357.

45. Jimmy D. Lindsey and Elaine H. Watts, "Cross-age (Exceptionality) Peer Tutoring Programs: Have You Tried One?" *Clearing House* 52 (April 1979): 366–67.

46. Marian L. Wilson, "Students Learn Through Cross-age Teaching," *American Secondary Education* 7 (June 1977): 35.

47. Ibid.

48. Janet Callender, Antonette Port, and Gerald Dykstra, "Peer-tutoring: A Rationale," *Educational Perspectives* 12 (March 1973): 9.

49. Martha Dillner, *Tutoring by Students: Who Benefits?* (Gainesville, Fla.: Florida Educational Research and Development Council, 1971), p. 27.

50. Linda Devin-Sheehan, Robert S. Feldman, and Vernon L. Allen, "Research on Children Tutoring: A Critical Review," *Review of Education Research* 46 (Summer 1976): 377.

51. Zina D. Steinberg and Courtney B. Cazden, "Children as Teachers—of Peers and Ourselves," *Theory into Practice* 18 (October 1979): 263.

52. David L. Weitzman, "Effect of Tutoring on Performance and Motivation Ratings in Secondary School Students," *California Journal Of Educational Research* 16 (May 1965): 108–15.

53. Madan Mohan, "Peer Tutoring as a Technique for Teaching the Unmotivated," *Child Study Journal* 1 (Summer 1971): 217–25.

54. See Robert E. Slavin, "Effects of Student Teams and Peer Tutoring on Academic Achievement and Time On-Task, *The Journal of Experimental Education* 48 (Summer 1980): 252–57; Shlomo Sharan, "Cooperative Learning in Small Groups: Recent Methods and Effects on Achivement, Attitudes, and Ethnic Relations," *Review of Educational Research* 50 (Summer 1980): 241–71.

55. Joseph Trovato and Bradley Bucher, "Peer Tutoring with or Without Home-based Reinforcement, for Reading Remediation," *Journal of Applied Behavioral Analysis* 13 (Spring 1980): 129.

56. Karen Steiner, "Peer Tutoring in the Reading Class," *Journal of Reading* 21 (December 1977): 268.

57. James M. Lewis, "Analysis of the Tutoring Variable in Individualized Instruction," *Educational Technology* 19 (March 1979): 42.

58. Dillner, *Tutoring by Students*.

59. Devin-Sheehan, et al., "Research on Children Tutoring," p. 363.

60. Dillner, *Tutoring by Students*, p. 7.

61. Ibid., pp. 26–27.

62. Devin-Sheehan et al., "Research on Children Tutoring," p. 368.

63. Robert D. Cloward, "Studies in Tutoring," *The Journal of Experimental Education* 36 (Fall 1967): 14–25.

64. Jack Hassinger and Murray Via, "How Much Does a Tutor Learn Through Teaching Reading?" *Journal of Secondary Education* 44 (January 1969): 42–44.

65. Robert F. Morgan and Thomas B. Toy, "Learning by Teaching: A Student-to-student Compensatory Tutoring Program in a Rural School System and Its Relevance to the Educational Cooperative," *The Psychological Record* 20 (Spring 1970): 167.

66. Vernon L. Allen and Robert S. Feldman, "Learning Through Tutoring: Low-achieving Children as Tutors," *Journal of Experimental Education* 42 (Fall 1973): 1–5.

67. Carol Taylor Fitz-Gibbon, *Improving Practices in Inner-city Schools: Two Contributions* (Washington, D.C.: American Educational Research Association, 1975, ERIC Document Reproduction Service No. Ed 107 746).

68. John P. Dineen, Hewitt B. Clark, and Todd R. Risley, "Peer Tutoring Among Elementary Students: Educational Benefits to the Tutor," *Journal of Applied Behavior Analysis* 10 (Summer 1977): 231.

69. Sidney Rosen, Evan R. Powell, and David B. Schubot, "Peer-tutoring Outcomes as Influenced by the Equity and Type of Role Assignment," *Journal of Educational Psychology* 69 (June 1977): p. 251.

70. Sidney Rosen et al., "Competence and Tutorial Role as Status Variables Affecting Peer-tutoring Outcomes in Public School Settings," *Journal of Educational Psychology* 70 (August 1978): 610.

71. Amy Roseman Allen and Nancy Boraks, "Peer Tutoring: Putting It to the Test," *The Reading Teacher* 32 (December 1978): 274.

72. Ibid., p. 277.

73. Kenneth W. Howell, "Using Peers in Drill-type Instruction," *Journal of Experimental Education* 46 (Spring 1978): 56.

74. Diana Pritchard Paolitto, "The Effect of Cross-age Tutoring on Adolescence: An Inquiry into Theoretical Assumptions," *Review of Educational Research* 46 (Spring 1976): 219.

75. Martha Johnson and Jon S. Bailey, "Cross-age Tutoring: Fifth Graders as Arithmetic Tutors for Kindergarten Children," *Journal of Applied Behavior Analysis* 7 (Summer 1974): 231.

76. Frederic J. Medway and Charles A. Lowe, "Causal Attribution for Performance by Cross-age Tutors and Tutees," American Educational Research Journal 3 (Fall 1980): 377–87.

77. Nancy A. Mavrogenes and Nancy D. Galen, "Cross-age Tutoring: Why and How," *Journal of Reading* 22 (January 1979): 344–53.

78. Devin-Sheehan et al., "Research on Children Tutoring," p. 371.

79. Dillner, *Tutoring by Students*.

80. Devin-Sheehan et al., "Research on Children Tutoring," p. 375.

81. Frances B. Holliday and Carole Edwards, "Building on Cultural Strengths: A Route to Academic Achievement," *Educational Leadership* 36 (December 1978): 210.

82. David B. Lazerson, " 'I Must be Good if I Can Teach!'—Peer Tutoring with Aggressive and Withdrawn Children," *Journal of Learning Disabilities* 13 (March 1980): 43–48.

83. Allen, *Children as Teachers*.

84. Dillner, *Tutoring by Students*.

85. Devin-Sheehan et al., "Research on Children Tutoring," pp. 355–85.

86. William C. Stainback, S. B. Stainback, and F. Lichtward, "The Research Evidence Regarding the Student-to-student Tutoring Approach to Individualized Instruction," *Educational Technology* 15 (February 1975): 54–56.

87. Dillner, *Tutoring by Students* p. 27.

Educational and social history seems to confirm, at least in part, the arresting statement in Ecclesiastes that "there is no new thing under the sun," or the German proverb "What is new is seldom true; what is true is seldom new." That changes come slowly and that many so-called "new" things in education may be old things in new guises add to the value of the historical and comparative approach to the study of education.*

*From Edgar W. Knight, *Twenty Centuries of Education* (Boston: Ginn and Co., 1940), p. 7.

Implementation Ideas

Teachers who intend to implement peer teaching in their classrooms may find the following materials helpful. These sources report on the practice of peer teaching.

Lippitt reported on cross-age tutoring programs that were developed as early as 1961.[1] Her *"Phi Delta Kappan Fastback"* described the origin of the cross-age tutoring program. Also included are useful suggestions for implementing a similar program. One chapter deals with the key elements of a program, another with possible pitfalls, and an additional chapter reviews other types of tutoring programs considered successful.

Lippitt and Lohman reported on pilot projects carried out by the Institute for Social Research at the University of Michigan.[2] They divided the process of educating children into two interrelated parts: the process of socialization; and the process of subject-matter learning. They listed the following five program aspects:

1. providing opportunities for cross-age interaction through collaboration between adults,
2. teacher-student collaboration,
3. Building a peer-group attitude that supported the value of helping younger students and being helped by older students,
4. training for the helper role,
5. providing "at-the-elbow" help.

In 1968, Lippitt and Lippitt gave an updated report on cross-age teaching programs.[3] They described elements of the programs, which included tutor training, and listed favorable results. Younger students made gains in achievement because of participation with a cross-age helper. Older students challenged the younger ones to work and aided them in achieving success. Older students also provided the younger ones with a listener and a companion. Students showed increased self-respect, self-confidence, and pride in their progress. Benefits for the older students included learning how to help someone else's learning experiences, developing social skills, and increased academic achievement.

Gartner, Kohler, and Riessman published one of the first books on the practice of peer teaching.[4] The second chapter reviews programs that have been used, which can be a valuable source for planning similar peer teaching programs. Chapter three outlines the mechanisms of peer teaching. Chapter four describes in detail the Youth Tutoring Youth Program,[5] and chapter five is a "how-to" manual.

Thiagarajan wrote of a program he had tested in his native Madras, India, and also in Indiana.[6] He described the basic things that a student does in his system: learning the contents of a unit, teaching the contents, and testing. He also diagramed the model and gave suggestions for implementing the program.

Durlak and Vassallo described other successful programs.[7,8] Durlak outlined the Elementary Student Aide Program in which ninth-graders who were maladjusted, who showed poor academic performance, and who complained of being bored were chosen to serve as tutors. The aides showed a considerable rise in their grades, and both they and their teachers viewed the program as having a beneficial impact. Vassallo described a program initiated by high-school National Honor Society members who wished to do something helpful. Results are apparent in several ways: grades improve for both tutors and tutees; students develop increased self-confidence; and cultural, social, and economic barriers are broken down. Both programs are useful as sources for initiating a high-school peer teaching program.

Dollar provided a rather detailed account of the Youth Tutoring Youth Program developed by the National Commission on Resources for Youth.[9] Dollar gave realistic examples of programs as they actually operate in school settings.

Jackson and Riessman described a children-teaching-children program now being used in a school district in Harlem.[10] The article told of the implementation and actual function of the program, and listed the objectives and goals.

Pellegrene and Dickerson wrote about the formation of a tutors' club at Glasgow High School in Newark, Delaware.[11] They conclude that everyone, including the tutors, benefits from the experience of tutoring.

Nelson reported on a program conducted by one school in Detroit, and his suggestions can serve as a guide in establishing peer teaching programs in large cities.[12] The project was called HIT (High Intensity Tutoring) and had been in practice for eight years. Nelson reported that it had assisted students in reaching grade-level achievement in reading and in mathematics.

Melaragno published a manual that discussed the Tutorial Community Program.[13] This is a detailed and outlined format useful for establishing peer teaching programs.

Hoffman's paper, presented to the Council for Exceptional Children, can serve as a brief introduction to information on peer teaching.[14] Hoffman briefly described Lippitt and Lohman's work, the Mobilization for Youth Program, the Youth Tutoring Youth Program, and others less well known. He also discussed programmed tutoring versus directed tutoring, and gave a brief survey of the research done on these programs and on others. While lacking details, this paper is good introductory material.

Allen edited a book about peer teaching that includes chapters on theoretical considerations and research as well as reviews of programs existing in schools at the time the book was compiled.[15] It can serve as a thorough manual on peer teaching.

Wilkes compiled an annotated bibliography in which she attempted to provide a comprehensive listing of pre-1975 sources, information, and research on all aspects of peer teaching.[16]

Good and Brophy included a section on peer teaching in their book *Looking in Classrooms*.[17] They established guidelines that could be used to establish peer tutoring.

1. Teacher should create mental set that we can all learn from each other.
2. Teacher should work out procedural details.

3. Skill in creative organization should be developed.

Wilson provided suggestions on how cross-age tutoring can be included in the curriculum, and listed possible goals for such programs.[18]

Lundell and Brown discussed peer tutoring as an efficient instructional model.[19] They explained how a program was developed in a large urban school system. They also discussed the rationale of peer tutoring and presented several alternative models.

The sources discussed above are not intended to be an exhaustive review of literature related to recent and current practice of peer teaching; rather they are listed as possible aids for the practitioner wishing to implement a peer teaching program.

NOTES

1. Peggy Lippitt, *Students Teach Students* (Bloomington, Ind.: Phi Delta Kappa Educational Foundation, 1975.)
2. Peggy Lippitt and John Lohman, "Cross-age Relationships—An Educational Resource," *Children* 12 (May–June 1965).
3. Peggy Lippitt and Ronald Lippitt, "Cross-age Helpers," *NEA Journal* 57 (March 1968).
4. Alan Gartner, Mary Conway Kohler, and Frank Riessman, *Children Teach Children: Learning by Teaching* (New York: Harper and Row, 1971).
5. Bruce Dollar, *Learning and Growing Through Tutoring* (New York: The National Commission on Resources for Youth, 1974).
6. Sivasailam Thiagarajan, "Madras System Revisited: A New Structure for Peer Tutoring," *Educational Technology* 13 (December 1973).
7. Joseph A. Durlak, "Ninth Graders as Student Aids: Making Use of the Helper Therapy Principle," *Psychology in the Schools* 10 (July 1973).
8. Wanda Vassallo, "Learning by Tutoring," *American Education* 9 (April 1973).
9. Dollar, *Learning and Growing Through Tutoring*.
10. Vivian Copeland Jackson and Frank Riessman, "A Children Teaching Children Program," *Theory into Practice* 16 (October 1977).
11. Tom Pellegrene, Jr., and Frances E. Dickerson, "Student Tutors Are Effective," *Journal of Reading* 20 (March 1977).
12. Jeffrey B. Nelson. "Big Hit in the Inner City," *American Education* 14 (December 1978).
13. Ralph J. Melaragno, *Tutoring with Students* (Englewood Cliffs, N.J.: Educational Technology Publications, 1976).
14. Charles Hoffman, *Peer Tutoring: Introduction and Historical Perspective* (Atlanta, Ga.: Council for Exceptional Children, 1977, ERIC Document Reproduction Service No. ED 140 593).

15. Vernon L. Allen, ed., *Children as Teachers: Theory and Research on Tutoring* (New York: Academic Press, 1976).

16. Roberta Wilkes, *Peer and Cross-age Tutoring and Related Topics: An Annotated Bibliography* (Madison, Wis.: Research and Development Center for Cognitive Learning, 1975, ERIC Document Reproduction Service No. ED 114 372).

17. T. L. Good and J. E. Brophy, *Looking in Classrooms* (New York: Harper and Row, 1978).

18. Marian L. Wilson, "Students Learn Through Cross-age Teaching," *American Secondary Education* 7 (June 1977).

19. Kerth T. Lundell and William E. Brown, "Peer Tutoring: An Economical Instructional Model," *Academic Therapy* 14 (January 1979).

BIBLIOGRAPHY

Abrahamson, J. N. "Mutual Instruction in Denmark." *American Journal of Education* 2 (November 1827):694–96.

Adamson, John William. *Pioneers of Modern Education, 1600–1700*. London: Cambridge University Press, 1905.

————. *A Short History of Education*. London: Cambridge University Press, 1919.

————. *English Education*. London: Cambridge University Press, 1930.

Allen, Amy Roseman, and Boraks, Nancy, "Peer Tutoring: Putting It to the Test." *The Reading Teacher* 32 (December 1978):274–78.

Allen, Vernon L., ed. *Children as Teachers: Theory and Research on Tutoring*. New York: Academic Press, 1976.

Allen, Vernon L., and Feldman, Robert S. "Learning Through Tutoring: Low-Achieving Children as Tutors." *The Journal of Experimental Education* 42 (Fall 1973):1–5.

Allen, William, "William Allen to the Russian Ambassador." *Joseph Lancaster and the Monitorial School Movement: A Documentary History*. Edited by C. F. Kaestle. New York: Columbia University, Teachers College Press, 1973.

Amunategui y Solar, Domingo. *El Sistema de Lancaster en Chile y en otros paises Sud-Americanos*. Santiago: Imprenta Cervantes, 1895.

Anderson, Lewis F. "The System of Mutual Instruction and the Beginnings of High School." *School and Society* 8 (November 1918):571–76.

"Andrew Bell and the Madras System of Mutual Instruction." *American Journal of Education* 10 (June 1861):467–91.

Andrews, Charles C. *The History of the New York African Free-schools from Their Establishment in 1787 to the Present Time*. New York: M. Day, 1830.

Armytage, W. H. G. *The French Influence on English Education*. London: Routledge and Kegan Paul, 1968.

————. *Four Hundred Years of English Education*. Cambridge, England: Cambridge University Press, 1970.

Arnett, L. D., and Smith, A. T. "Denmark, Education in." *A Cyclopedia of Education*. Edited by P. Monroe, vol. 2. New York: Macmillan, 1913.

Arnold, Matthew. *Popular Education in France.* London: Longmans, Green, Longmans, and Roberts, 1861.

Bache, Alex Dallas. *Report on Education in Europe.* Philadelphia: Lydia B. Bailey, 1839.

Baker, Edward. *A Brief Sketch of the Lancasterian System.* Troy, N.Y.: F. Adancourt, 1816.

Balfour, Graham. *The Educational Systems of Great Britain and Ireland.* Oxford: Clarendon Press, 1898.

Barnard, Henry. *National Education in Europe.* 2d ed. New York: Charles B. Norton, 1854.

———. *Organization and Instruction of Common Schools in Germany.* New York: F. C. Brownell, 1861.

———. *National Education: Systems, Institutions, and Statistics of Public Instruction in Different Countries.* 2 vols. New York: E. Steiger, 1872.

———. *Memoirs of Teachers and Educators.* New York: Arno Press and The New York Times, 1969.

Barnard, H. C. *The French Tradition in Education.* London: Cambridge University Press, 1922.

———. *A Short History of English Education from 1760–1944.* London: University of London Press, 1949.

Barnard, John. *Autobiography of the Rev. John Barnard.* Collections of the Massachusetts Historical Society, 3rd series, Vol. 5. Boston: John E. Eastburn, 1836.

Battersby, W. J. *De La Salle, a Pioneer of Modern Education.* London: Longmans, Green, 1949.

Beecher, Catharine E. "Improvements in Education." *American Journal of Education* 1 (1830):63–66.

"Bell and Lancaster's System of Education." *Quarterly Review* 6 (October 1811):264–304.

Bell, Andrew. *The Madras School.* London: T. Bensley, 1808.

———. *Instruction for Conducting a School.* London: John Murray, 1813.

———. *Mutual Tuition and Moral Discipline.* London: G. Roake, 1823.

Bentham, Jeremy. "Chrestomathia." *Works of Jeremy Bentham.* Edited by J. Bowring, vol. 8. New York: Russell and Russell, 1962.

Bernard, Thomas. *Education of the Poor.* London: W. Bulmer, 1809.

———. *The Barrington School.* London: W. Bulmer, 1812.

Binns, Henry Bryan. *A Century of Education.* London: J. M. Dent, 1908.

Bloom, Benjamin S. *Human Characteristics and School Learning.* New York: McGraw-Hill, 1976.

Boese, Thomas. *Public Education in the City of New York.* New York: Harper and Brothers, 1869.

Bogoslovsky, Christina. *The Educational Crisis in Sweden.* New York: Columbia University Press, 1932.

Bonner, Stanley. *Education in Ancient Rome.* London: Methuen, 1977.

Bourne, William Oland. *History of the Public School Society of the City of New York.* New York: Wm. Wood, 1870.

Brandon, Isaac. *Instruction: A Poem.* London: Richard Taylor, 1811.

Brauner, Charles J. *American Educational Theory*. Englewood Cliffs, N.J.: Prentice-Hall, 1964.

Brinsley, John. *Ludus Literarius*. London: Thomas Man, 1612.

———. *A Consolation of our Grammar Schooles*. New York: Scholar's Facsimiles and Reprints, 1943.

Brinton, H. H. *Quaker Education in Theory and Practice*. Wallingford, Pa.: Pendle Hill, 1940.

"British and Foreign School Society." *American Journal of Education* 10 (June 1861): 371–80.

Brother Constantius. "Christian Brothers." *A Cyclopedia of Education*. Edited by P. Monroe, Vol. 1 New York: Macmillan, 1913.

Browning, W. E. "The Lancasterian School System in England and the Americas." *Educational Foundations* 29 (April 1918):465–75.

———. "Joseph Lancaster, James Thomson, and the Lancasterian System of Mutual Instruction, with Special Reference to Hispanic America." *The Hispanic American Historical Review* 4 (February 1921):49–98.

Brubacher, John S. *A History of the Problems of Education*. New York: McGraw-Hill, 1947.

Brunskill, Francis R. "Bishop Barrington's Educational Experiment." *The London Quarterly and Holborn Review* 168 (January 1943):71–75.

Buckholdt, David R., and Wodarski, John S. "The Effects of Different Reinforcement Systems on Cooperative Behaviors Exhibited by Children in Classroom Contexts." *Journal of Research and Development in Education* 12 (Fall 1978): 50–68.

Burston, W. H. "The Utilitarians and the Monitorial System of Teaching, in Education and Philosophy." *The Yearbook of Education*. Edited by G. Z. F. Bereday and J. A. Lauwerys. New York: World Book, 1957.

Butler, H. E., trans. *The Institutio Oratorio of Quintilian*. Vol. 1. New York: G. P. Putnam's Sons, 1920.

Butler, Vera M. *Education as Revealed by New England Newspapers Prior to 1850*. New York: Arno Press and *The New York Times*, 1969.

Butts, R. Freeman, and Cremin, Lawrence A. *A History of Education in American Culture*. New York: Henry Holt, 1953.

Cabell, Joseph C. *Letter to Joseph Lancaster*. Lancaster Collection of the American Antiquarian Society, written in Virginia, 1819. Worcester, Mass.

Calhoun, Daniel, ed. *The Education of Americans: A Documentary History*. Boston: Houghton Mifflin, 1969.

Callender, Janet; Port, Antonette; and Dykstra, Gerald. "Peer-tutoring: A Rationale." *Educational Perspectives* 12 (March 1973):8–11.

Clinton, DeWitt. "Free Schools." *The Life and Writings of DeWitt Clinton*. Compiled by W. W. Campbell. New York: Baker and Scribner, 1849.

Cloward, Robert D. "Studies in Tutoring." *The Journal of Experimental Education* 36 (Fall 1967):14–25.

Codorniu y Ferreras, Manuel. *Discurso Inaugural Que en la Abertura de las Escuelas Mutuas de la Filantropia*. Mexico: Martin Rivera, 1823.

Cole, Luella. *A History of Education, Socrates to Montessori*. New York: Holt, Rinehart, and Winston, 1964.

Coon, Charles L. *North Carolina Schools and Academies, 1790–1840: A Documentary History*. Raleigh: Edwards and Broughton, 1915.

Cousin, Victor. *On the State of Education in Holland*. Translated by L. Horner. London: John Murray, 1838.

Cressy, David. *Education in Tudor and Stuart England*. New York: St. Martin's Press, 1974.

Cubberley, Ellwood P. *The History of Education*. Boston: Houghton Mifflin, 1920.

————. *Readings in the History of Education*. Boston: Houghton Mifflin, 1920.

————. *Public Education in the United States*. Boston: Houghton Mifflin, 1934.

————. *Readings in Public Education in the United States*. Boston: Houghton Mifflin, 1934.

Curtis, S. J. and Boultwood, M. E. A. *An Introductory History of English Education Since 1800*. London: University Tutorial Press, 1962.

Darton, F. J. Harvey. "Bell and the Dragon." *Fortnightly Review* 85 (May 1909): 896–909.

David, Aranka Irene. "Student Tutoring: A Success at Collinwood High School." *Clearing House* 12 (January 1938):288–89.

Dempsey, M. *John Baptist de la Salle: His Life and His Institute*. Milwaukee: Bruce Publishing, 1940.

Devin-Sheehan, Linda; Feldman, Robert S.; and Allen, Vernon L. "Research on Children Tutoring: A Critical Review." *Review of Educational Research* 46 (Summer 1976):355–85.

Dillner, Martha. *Tutoring by Students: Who Benefits?* Gainesville, Fla.: Florida Educational Research and Development Council, Spring–Summer 1971.

Dineen, John P.; Clark, Hewitt B.,; and Risley, Todd R. "Peer Tutoring Among Elementary Students: Educational Benefits to the Tutor." *Journal of Applied Behavior Analysis* 10 (Summer 1977):231–38.

Dobb, A. E. *Education and Social Movements, 1700–1850*. London: Longmans, Green, 1919.

Dollar, Bruce. *Learning and Growing Through Tutoring*. New York: The National Commission on Resources for Youth, 1974.

Dunlap, William C. *Quaker Education in Baltimore and Virginia*. Philadelphia, 1936.

Dunn, Henry. *Sketches*. London: Houlston and Stoneman, 1848.

Durlak, Joseph A. "Ninth Graders as Student Aides: Making Use of the Helper Therapy Principle." *Psychology in the Schools* 10 (July 1973):334–39.

"Education of the Poor." *Edinburgh Review* 19 (November 1811):1–41.

Eggertsen, C. A. "The Monitorial System of Instruction in the United States." Doctoral dissertation, University of Minnesota, 1939.

Elliot, Arthur. "Student Tutoring Benefits Everyone." *Phi Delta Kappan* 54 (April 1973):535–38.

Ellis, Charles Calvert. *Lancasterian Schools in Philadelphia*. Philadelphia: University of Pennsylvania, 1907.

Ellson, Douglas G. "Tutoring." *The Psychology of Teaching Methods*. Edited by N. L. Cage. Chicago: National Society for the Study of Education, 1976.

Evans, Keith. *The Development and Structure of the English Educational System*. London: University of London Press, 1975.

Ewing, John, and Sargeant, John. *Report of the Committee Appointed at a Meeting of the Several School Committees, and other Citizens of Portsmouth, to Consider the Expediency of Introducing the Lancastrian System of Education.* Portsmouth (no state given): S. Whidden, 1818.

Fanti, Aristide. "Italy, Education in." *A Cyclopedia of Education.* Edited by P. Monroe, vol. 3. New York: Macmillan, 1913.

Farrell, Allan P. *The Jesuit Code of Liberal Education: Development and Scope of the Ratio Studiorum.* Milwaukee: Bruce Publishing, 1938.

Farrington, Frederic E. "Maintenon (Mme. de), Francoise d'Aubigne, Marquise de Maintenon." *A Cyclopedia of Education.* Edited by P. Monroe, vol. 4. New York: Macmillan, 1913.

————. "Rollin, Charles." *A Cyclopedia of Education.* Edited by P. Monroe, vol. 7. New York: Macmillan, 1913.

Fitz-Gibbon, Carol Taylor. *Improving Practices in Inner-city Schools: Two Contributions.* Washington, D.C.: American Educational Research Association, 1975. (ERIC Document Reproduction Service No. ED 107 746.)

Fitzpatrick, Edward A. *The Educational Views and Influence of DeWitt Clinton.* New York: Arno Press and The New York Times, 1969.

Flagg, A. C. "Improvement of Common Schools." *American Journal of Education* 2 (April 1827): 193–205.

Fontainerie, F. de la, trans. *The Conduct of the Schools of Jean-Baptiste de la Salle.* New York: McGraw-Hill, 1935.

Fouts, Gordon E. "Music Instruction in Early Nineteenth-century American Monitorial Schools." *Journal of Research in Music Education* 22 (Summer 1974): 112–19.

Fowle, William B. "Boston Monitorial School." *American Journal of Education* 1 (January 1826): 32–42.

————. "Boston Monitorial School." *American Journal of Education* 1 (February 1826): 72–80.

————. *The Teacher's Institute.* 2d ed. Boston: William B. Fowle, 1847.

————. "The Monitoral Plan." *Common School Journal* (September 1848): 98–91 [sic].

Gartner, Alan; Kohler, Mary Conway; and Riessman, Frank. *Children Teach Children: Learning by Teaching.* New York: Harper and Row, 1971.

Gill, John. *Systems of Education.* Boston: D. C. Heath, 1889.

Good, H. G. *A History of Western Education.* New York: Macmillan, 1947.

————. *A History of American Education.* New York: Macmillan, 1956.

Good, T. L., and Brophy, J. E. *Looking in Classrooms,* New York: Harper and Row, 1978.

Gosden, P. H. J. H., comp. *How They Were Taught: An Anthology of Contemporary Accounts of Learning and Teaching in England, 1800–1850.* New York: Barnes and Noble, 1969.

Graves, Frank Pierrepont. *A History of Education.* New York: Macmillan, 1910.

————. *Great Educators of Three Centuries.* New York: Macmillan, 1912.

————. *A Student's History of Education.* New York: Macmillan, 1915.

Griscom, John. *A Year in Europe, Comprising a Journal of Observations in England, Scotland, Ireland, France, Switzerland, the North of Italy, and Holland, in 1818 and 1819.* 2 vols. New York: Collins, 1823.

————. *Monitorial Instruction. An Address, Pronounced at the Opening of the New York High School.* New York: Mahlon Day, 1825.

Grund, Francis J. *The Americans in Their Moral, Social and Political Relations*. London: Longmans, Green, 1837.

Guimps, Roger de. *Pestalozzi, His Life and Work*. New York: D. Appleton, 1897.

Hager, Phil E. "Nineteenth Century Experiments with Monitorial Teaching." *Phi Delta Kappan* 40 (January 1959):164–66.

Harveson, Mae Elizabeth. *Catharine Esther Beecher, Pioneer Educator*. New York: Arno Press and *The New York Times*, 1969.

Hassinger, Jack and Via, Murray. "How Much Does a Tutor Learn Through Teaching Reading?" *Journal of Secondary Education* 44 (January 1969):42–44.

Hine, Grace M. *The Lancastrian School for Girls, Chichester, 1812–1962*. Chichester City Council, 1962.

Hoffman, Charles. *Peer Tutoring: Introduction and Historical Perspective*. Atlanta, Ga.: Council for Exceptional Children, 1977. (ERIC Document Reproduction Service No. ED 140 593.)

Holliday, Frances B. and Edwards, Carole. "Building on Cultural Strengths: A Route to Academic Achievement." *Educational Leadership* 36 (December 1978):207–10.

Hoole, Charles. *A New Discovery of the Old Art of Teaching Schools; in Four Small Treatises*. Liverpool: The University Press, 1913.

Horner, Leonard. "Preliminary Observations." Introduction to *On the State of Education in Holland*, by Victor Cousin. London: John Murray, 1838.

Horst, H. M. "History of Student Tutoring at West High School, Akron, Ohio." *Clearing House* 6 (December 1931):245–49.

———. "An Experiment with Student Tutors." *The Journal of the National Education Association* 22 (November 1933):206.

Howell, Kenneth W. "Using Peers in Drill-type Instruction." *Journal of Experimental Education* 46 (Spring 1978):52–56.

Hurt, John. *Education in Evolution: Church, State, Society and Popular Education, 1800–1870*. London: Rupert Hart-Davis, 1971.

Hutton, J. G. "Criticism and Decline of the System." *Joseph Lancaster and the Monitorial School Movement: A Documentary History*. Edited by C. F. Kaestle. New York: Columbia University, Teachers College Press, 1973.

"Introduction." *American Journal of Education* 3 (January 1828):1–8.

Jackson, Vivian Copeland and Riessman, Frank. "A Children Teaching Children Program." *Theory into Practice*, 16 (October 1977):280–84.

Jarman, T. L. *Landmarks in the History of Education*. New York: Philosophical Library, 1952.

"The Jesuits and Their Schools." *American Journal of Education* 5 (June 1858):213–28.

Johnson, David W., and Johnson, Roger T. "Instructional Goal Structure: Cooperative, Competitive, or Individualistic." *Review of Educational Research* 44 (Spring 1974):213–40.

———. *Learning Together and Alone*. Englewood Cliffs, N.J.: Prentice-Hall, 1975.

Johnson, Martha, and Bailey, Jon S. "Cross-age Tutoring: Fifth Graders as Arithmetic Tutors for Kindergarten Children." *Journal of Applied Behavior Analysis* 7 (Summer 1974):223–32.

Johnson, Walter. "Monitorial Schools." *American Annals of Education* 2 (August 1832):413–20.

Johnson, William H. E. *Russia's Educational Heritage*. Pittsburgh: Carnegie Press, 1950.

"Joseph Fox." *American Journal of Education* 10 (June 1861):363–65.

"Joseph Lancaster." *American Journal of Education* 10 (June 1861):355–62.

Kaestle, Carl F., ed. *Joseph Lancaster and the Monitorial School Movement: A Documentary History*. New York: Columbia University, Teachers College Press, 1973.

Karaczan, F. F. *Der Wechselseitige unterricht nach der Bell-Lancasterschen Methode*. Kaschau, Germany: Otto Wigand, Buchhandler, 1819.

Keatinge, M. W. *The Great Didactic of John Amos Comenius*, part 1. London: A. and C. Black, 1921.

———. *The Great Didactic of John Amos Comenius*, part 2. London: A. and C. Black, 1923.

Kennedy, George, *Quintilian*. New York: Twayne Publishers, 1969.

Klemm, L. R. "An Interview Between Pestalozzi and Dr. Bell." *Education* 7 (April 1887):559–64.

Klemm, Louis R., and Hughes, James Laughlin. *Progress of Education in the Century: The Nineteenth Century Series*. London: W. and R. Chambers, 1903.

Knight, Edgar W. *Education in the United States*. Boston: Ginn, 1929.

———. *Reports on European Education by John Griscom, Victor Cousin, Calvin E. Stowe*. New York: McGraw-Hill, 1930.

———. *Twenty Centuries of Education*. Boston: Ginn, 1940.

———. "An Early Educational Fad in the South." *High School Journal* 31 (March–April 1948): 54–60.

———. *A Documentary History of Education in the South Before 1860*. Vol. 5. Chapel Hill: University of North Carolina Press, 1953.

Knight, Edgar W. and Hall, Clifton L. *Readings in American Educational History*. New York: Appleton-Century-Crofts, 1951.

Krüsi, Hermann, *Pestalozzi: His Life, Work and Influence*. Cincinnati: Wilson, Hinkle, 1875.

Laborde, Alexandre de. *Plan d'Education*. Londres: Berthoud et Wheatley, 1815.

"Lancaster and Pestalozzi." *The Western Academician and Journal of Education and Science* 1 (July 1837):272–76.

Lancaster, Joseph. *Manual Folio*, Box 4. Lancaster Collection of The American Antiquarian Society, Worcester, Mass.

———. *The British System of Education*. Georgetown, Washington, D.C.: Joseph Milligan, 1812.

———. *Letters on National Subjects*. Washington City: Jacob Gideon, 1820.

———. *The Lancasterian System of Education*. Baltimore: Wm. Ogden Niles, 1821.

———. *Epitome of Some of the Chief Events and Transactions in the Life of Joseph Lancaster*. New Haven: Baldwin and Peck, 1833.

———. *Report of the Singular Results of J. Lancaster's New Discoveries in Education Made at Montreal, from the Commencement in 1829 to Complete Development of Systematic Principle in 1833*. Montreal: 1833 (?).

———. *Improvements in Education as it Respects in Industrous Classes of the Community*. 3d ed. Clifton: Augustus M. Kelley, 1973.

Langer, W. L. *An Encyclopedia of World History*. Boston: Houghton Mifflin, 1948.

"LaSalle, St. John Baptist de." *A Cyclopedia of Education*. Edited by P. Monroe, vol. 3. New York: Macmillan, 1913.

Laurie, S. S. *John Amos Comenius, Bishop of the Moravians: His Life and Educational Works*. Syracuse, N.Y.: C. W. Bardeen, 1892.

Lazerson, David B. " 'I Must Be Good if I can Teach!'—Peer Tutoring with Aggressive and Withdrawn Children." *Journal of Learning Disabilities* 13 (March 1980):43−48.

Leitch, James. *Practical Educationists and Their Systems of Teaching*. Glasgow: James Maclehose, 1876.

Lewis, James M. "Analysis of the Tutoring Variable in Individualized Instruction." *Educational Technology* 19 (March 1979):41−44.

"Life and Educational System of John Sturm." *American Journal of Education* 4 (September 1857):167−82.

"Life and Educational System of John Sturm." *American Journal of Education* 4 (December 1857):400−15.

Lindsey, Jimmy D., and Watts, Elaine H. "Cross-age (Exceptionality) Peer Tutoring Programs: Have You Tried One?" *Clearing House* 52 (April 1979):366−67.

Lippitt, Peggy. *Students Teach Students*. Bloomington, Ind.: Phi Delta Kappa Educational Foundation, 1975.

Lippitt, Peggy, and Lippitt, Ronald. "Cross-age Helpers." *NEA Journal* 57 (March 1968):24−26.

Lippitt, Peggy, and Lohman, John E. "Cross-age Relationships—An Educational Resource." *Children* 12 (May−June 1965):113−17.

Lundell, Kerth T., and Brown, William E. "Peer Tutoring: An Economical Instructional Model." *Academic Therapy* 14 (January 1979):287−92.

Lynch, James B., Jr. "José María Velasco, Images of Early Genesis." *Americas* 31 (January 1979):5.

Male, George A. *Education in France*. Washington, D.C.: U.S. Department of Health, Education, and Welfare, 1963.

Mann Horace. *Annual Reports on Education*. Boston: Horace B. Fuller, 1868.

Manual of the Lancasterian System. New York: Samuel Wood and Sons, 1820.

"Manual of the System of Monitorial or Mutual Instruction." *American Journal of Education* 1 (June 1826):335−48.

Manual of the System of Teaching Reading, Writing, Arithmetic, and Needle-Work. 1st American ed. Philadelphia: Benjamin Warner, 1817.

Marsh, Herbert. A Vindication of Dr. Bell's System of Tuition. London: Law and Gilbert, 1811.

Martin, John Henry. "The Grade School Came from Prussia." *Educational Horizons* 51 (Fall 1972):28−33.

Mavrogenes Nancy A. and Galen, Nancy D. "Cross-age Tutoring: Why and How." *Journal of Reading* 22 (January 1979):344−53.

McCadden, Joseph J. "Joseph Lancaster in America." *The Social Studies* 28 (February 1937):73−77.

────. *Education in Pennsylvania, 1801−1835*. New York: Arno Press and *The New York Times*, 1969.

Medway, Frederic J., and Lowe, Charles A. "Causal Attribution for Performance by Cross-Age Tutors and Tutees." *American Educational Research Journal* 3 (Fall 1980): 377−87.

Meiklejohn, John Miller Dow. *An Old Educational Reformer, Dr. Andrew Bell*. Edinburgh and London: William Blackwood and Sons, 1881.

Melaragno, Ralph J. *Tutoring with Students*. Englewood Cliffs: N.J.: Educational Technology Publications, 1976.

————. "Pupil Tutoring: Directions for the Future." *The Elementary School Journal* 77 (May 1977): 384–87.

Meyer, Adolph E. *The Development of Education in the Twentieth Century*. 2d ed. New York: Prentice-Hall, 1949.

————. *An Educational History of the Western World*. New York: McGraw-Hill, 1965.

Midwinter, Eric. *Nineteenth Century Education*. New York: Harper and Row, 1970.

Mohan, Madan. "Peer Tutoring as a Technique for Teaching the Unmotivated." *Child Study Journal* 1 (Summer 1971):217–25.

"Monitorial Instruction." *American Journal of Education* 3 (January 1828):245–49; 313–17.

"Monitorial Schools." *American Annals of Education* 1 (April 1831):180.

"Monitorial Schools in Europe." *American Annals of Education* 1 (February 1831):84–85.

"Monitoral System." *American Annals of Education* 1 (April 1831):135–40.

"Monitorial System." *American Journal of Education* 10 (June 1861):461–66.

Monroe, Paul. *Founding of the American Public School System*. Vol. 1. New York: Macmillan, 1940.

Morgan, Robert F. and Toy, Thomas B. "Learning by Teaching: A Student-to-student Compensatory Tutoring Program in a Rural School System and Its Relevance to the Educational Cooperative." *The Psychological Record* 20 (Spring 1970):159–69.

Morrison, G. B. "The Bell and Lancaster System: What There Is in It for the Schools of the South." *Report of the United States Commissioner of Education*. Vol. 2. 1894–1895.

Musgrave, P. W. *Society and Education in England Since 1800*. London: Methuen, 1968.

"Mutual Instruction in Common Schools." *American Annals of Education* 6 (October 1836):433–41.

"Mutual Instruction in Denmark." *American Annals of Education* 1 (July 1831):332.

"Mutual or Monitorial Instruction." *American Annals of Education* 1 (April 1831):177.

"National Society." *American Journal of Education* 10 (June 1861):499–501.

Nelson, Jeffrey B. "Big Hit in the Inner City." *American Education* 14 (December 1978):23–27.

"The New School, or Lancasterian System." *The Academician* 1 (1818):68–70.

"Newspaper Criticism of the Lancaster System in Detroit, from *Detroit Gazette*, Nov. 23, 1821, and Feb. 15, 1822." *Education in the United States: A Documentary History*. Edited by S. Cohen. New York: Random House, 1974.

Oliver, Henry K. *Lecture on the Advantages and Defects of the Monitorial System*. Boston: Hilliard, Gray, Little and Wilkins, 1831.

Orme, Nicholas. *English Schools in the Middle Ages*. London: Methuen, 1973.

Packard, R. L., and Smith, A. T. "Spain, Education in." *A Cyclopedia of Education*. Edited by P. Monroe, vol. 5. New York: Macmillan, 1913.

Page, David. P. *Theory and Practice of Teaching*. New York: A. S. Barnes, 1857.

Palmer, Archie Emerson. *The New York Public School*. New York: Macmillan, 1905.

Paolitto, Diana Pritchard. "The Effect of Cross-age Tutoring on Adolescence: An Inquiry into Theoretical Assumptions." *Review of Educational Research* 46 (Spring 1976):215–37.

Pellegrene, Tom, Jr., and Dickerson, Frances E. "Student Tutors Are Effective." *Journal of Reading* 20 (March 1977):466–68.

Pestalozzi, Johann Heinrich. *How Gertrude Teaches Her Children*. Translated by L. E. Holland and F. C. Turner. London: George Allen and Unwin, 1915.

Picket, J. W. "Educational Theories," *The Western Academician and Journal of Education and Science* 1 (April 1837):57–62.

Plumptre, James. *The Way in Which We Should Go: A Sermon*. Cambridge, England: Francis Hodson, 1809.

Pollard, Hugh M. *Pioneers of Popular Education, 1760–1850*. Cambridge: Mass.: Harvard University Press, 1957.

Quick, Robert Herbert. *Essays on Educational Reformers*. New York: D. Appleton, 1896.

Reigart, John Franklin. *The Lancasterian System of Instruction in the Schools of New York City*. New York: Teachers College, Columbia University, 1916.

"Retrospect." *American Journal of Education* 2 (December 1827):754–69.

"Review, Monitorial Instruction." *American Journal of Education* 5 (May 1828):283–96.

"Review of Jeremy Bentham's Chrestomathia." *Westminister Review* 1 (January 1824):43–79.

"Review of Seven Contemporary Publications on Monitorialism." *Southern Review* 1 (May 1828):488–503.

Rice, Joseph Mayer. *The Public School System of the United States*. New York: Century, 1893.

Rollin, Charles. *The Method of Teaching and Studying the Belles Lettres*. London: W. Otridge and Son, 1810.

Rosen, Sidney; Powell, Evan R.; and Schubot, David B. "Peer-tutoring Outcomes as Influenced by the Equity and Type of Role Assignment." *Journal of Educational Psychology* 69 (June 1977):244–52.

Rosen, Sydney; Powell, Evan R.; Schubot, David B.; and Rollins, Patricia. "Competence and Tutorial Role as Status Variables Affecting Peer-tutoring Outcomes in Public School Settings." *Journal of Educational Psychology* 70 (August 1978):602–12.

Rost, Ray Charles. "The Influence of Joseph Lancaster and the Monitorial System on Selected Educational Institutions." Ph.D. dissertation, Rutgers University, 1968.

Russell, William. *Manual of Mutual Instruction, Consisting of Mr. Fowle's Directions*. Boston: Wait, Greene, 1826.

Sadler, Michael E. "Bentham, Jeremy." *A Cyclopedia of Education*. Edited by P. Monroe, vol. 1. New York: Macmillan, 1913.

Salmon, David. *Joseph Lancaster*. London: Longmans, Green, 1904.

"The Monitorial System in France." *Educational Review* 40 (June 1910):30–47.

_____. "Monitorial System." *A Cyclopedia of Education*. Edited by P. Monroe, vol. 4. New York: Macmillan, 1913.

_____. "Trimmer, Mrs. Sarah." *A Cyclopedia of Education*. Edited by P. Monroe, vol. 5. New York: Macmillan, 1913.

_____. *The Practical Parts of Lancaster's Improvements and Bell's Experiment*. London: Cambridge University Press, 1932.

Savage, J.; Phillips, Jonathan; Oliver, Francis J.; and Foster, John S. "Boston Monitorial School." *American Journal of Education* 1 (January 1826):29–31.

Schmuck, Richard A. "Peer Groups as Settings for Learning." *Theory into Practice* 16 (October 1977):272–79.

Seaborne, Malcolm. *The English School: Its Architecture and Organization, 1370–1870*. Toronto: University of Toronto Press, 1971.

Seeley, Levi. *The Common-school System of Germany and Its Lessons to America*. New York: E. L. Kellogg, 1896.

_____. *History of Education*. New York: American Book, 1899.

Selden, Judith. "Learning by the Numbers." *American Education* 11 (May 1975):25–27.

Shattuck, Lemuel. "Improvements in Our Common Schools." *American Journal of Education* 1 (October-November 1830):457–62.

Sharan, Shlomo, "Cooperative Learning in Small Groups: Recent Methods and Effects on Achievement, Attitudes, and Ethnic Relations." *Review of Educational Research* 50 (Summer 1980):241–71.

Shaw, Benjamin. *Brief Exposition of the Principles and Details of the Lancasterian System of Education*. Pennsylvania: (?) 1817.

Sherman, Robert R., and Kirschner, Joseph. *Understanding History of Education*. Cambridge, Mass.: Schenkman Publishing, 1976.

Silber, Kate. *Pestalozzi, The Man and His Work*. London: Routledge and Kegan Paul, 1960.

Silver, Pamela, and Silver, Harold. *The Education of the Poor: The History of a National School, 1824–1974*. London: Routledge and Kegan Paul, 1974.

Simon, Brian. *Studies in the History of Education, 1780–1870*. London: Lawrence and Wishart, 1960.

A Sketch of the Improved Method of Education. Philadelphia: Kimber and Conrad, 1809.

Slavin, Robert E. "Effects of Student Teams and Peer Tutoring on Academic Achievement and Time On-task." *The Journal of Experimental Education* 48 (Summer 1980):252–57.

Smith, Anna Tolman. "Russia." *A Cyclopedia of Education*. Edited by P. Monroe, vol. 5. New York: Macmillan, 1913.

Smith, Anna Tolman, and Hillegas, M. B. "Greece, Education in Modern." *A Cyclopedia of Education*. Edited by P. Monroe, vol. 5. New York: Macmillan, 1913.

Smith, Anna Tolman, and Plugge, C. H. "Netherlands, Education in." *A Cyclopedia of Education*. Edited by P. Monroe, vol. 4. New York: Macmillan, 1913.

Smith, Catherine Ruth, trans. *Quintilian on Education: Selections from the Institutes of Oratory*. New York: New York University, n.d.

Smith, Sydney. "Review of Sarah Trimmer's Comparative View." The *Edinburgh Review* 9 (1806):177–84.

Southey, Charles Cuthbert. *The Life of the Rev. Andrew Bell*. Vols. 2 and 3. London: J. Murray, 1844.

Southey, Robert. *The Life of the Rev. Andrew Bell*. Vol. 1 London: J. Murray, 1844.

Spragge, G. W. "Joseph Lancaster in Montreal." *The Canadian Historical Review* 22 (March 1941):35−41.

Stainback, William C.; Stainback, S. B.; and Lichtward, F. "The Research Evidence Regarding the Student-to-student Tutoring Approach to Individualized Instruction." *Educational Technology* 15 (February 1975):54−56.

Steinberg, Zina D., and Cazden, Courtney B. "Children as Teachers—of Peers and Ourselves." *Theory into Practice* 18 (October 1979):258−66.

Steiner, Karen. "Peer Tutoring in the Reading Class." *Journal of Reading* 21 (December 1977):266−69.

Stewart, W. A. Campbell. *Quakers and Education*. London: Epworth Press, 1953.

Stewart, W. A. C., and McCann, W. P. *The Educational Innovators, 1750−1880*. New York: St. Martin's Press, 1967.

Sutton, Robert B. "Historical Report from Madras." *School and Society* 92 (Summer 1964):321−23.

Taba, Hilda. *Curriculum Development: Theory and Practice*. New York: Harcourt, Brace and World, 1962.

Thelen, Herbert A. "Tutoring by Students." *The School Review* 77 (September−December 1969):229−43.

Thiagarajan, Sivasailam. "Madras System Revisited: A New Structure for Peer Tutoring." *Educational Technology* 13 (December 1973):10−13.

"A Thing That India Has Taught Europe." *The American Review of Reviews* 40 (July 1909):114−15.

Thomson, James. *Letters on the Moral and Religious State of South America, Written During a Residence of Nearly Seven Years in Buenos Aires, Chile, Peru, and Colombia*. London: James Nisbet, 1827.

─────. "The Lancasterian Enthusiasm in South America." *Joseph Lancaster and the Monitorial School Movement: A Documentary History*. Edited by C. F. Kaestle. New York: Columbia University, Teachers College Press, 1973.

Trimmer, Sarah. *A Comparative View of the New Plan of Education*. London: T. Bensley, 1805.

Trovato, Joseph, and Bucher, Bradley. "Peer Tutoring with or Without Home-based Reinforcement, for Reading Remediation." *Journal of Applied Behavioral Analysis* 13 (Spring 1980):129−41.

Tyler, Ralph W. "Wasting Time and Resources in Schools and Colleges." *Viewpoints* 51 (March 1975):59−73.

Vaille, E. O. "The Lancastrian System. A Chapter in the Evolution of Common-school Education." *Education* 1 (January 1881):265−75.

"Valentine Friedland Trotzendorf." *American Journal of Education* 5 (June 1858):107−13.

Vassallo, Wanda. "Learning by Tutoring." *American Education* 9 (April 1973):25−28.

Watson, John Selby, trans. *Quintilian's Institutes of Oratory*. London: G. Bell & Sons, 1913.

Wayne, William C. "Tutoring Service: A Project for Future Business Teachers." *The Journal of Business Education* 31 (April 1956):330.

Weitzman, David L. "Effect of Tutoring on Performance and Motivation Ratings in Secondary School Students." *California Journal of Educational Research* 16 (May 1965):108–15.

Wilkes, Roberta. *Peer and Cross-age Tutoring and Related Topics: An Annotated Bibliography.* Madison, Wis.: Research and Development Center for Cognitive Learning, 1975. (ERIC Document Reproduction Service No. ED 114 372.)

"William Allen." *American Journal of Education* 10 (June 1861): 365–70.

"William Bentley Fowle." *American Journal of Education* 10 (June 1861):597–610.

"William Corston." *American Journal of Education* 10 (June 1861):363.

Williams, B. O. "Reminiscence of the Lancasterian School in Detroit." *Joseph Lancaster and the Monitorial School Movement: A Documentary History.* Edited by C. F. Kaestle. New York: Columbia University; Teachers College Press, 1973.

Williams, Samuel G. *The History of Modern Education.* Syracuse, N.Y.: C. W. Bardeen, 1892.

Wilson, Marian L. "Students Learn Through Cross-age Teaching." *American Secondary Education* 7 (June 1977):35–37.

Wise, John. *The History of Education.* New York: Sheed and Ward, 1964.

Woofter, Thomas Jackson. *Teaching in Rural Schools.* Boston: Houghton Mifflin, 1917.

Wright, Benjamin. "Should Children Teach?" *The Elementary School Journal* 60 (April 1960):353–69.

Zacek, Judith Cohen. "The Lancastrian School Movement in Russia." *The Slavonic and East European Review* 45 (July 1967):343–67.

INDEX

About the Author

Lilya Wagner is an Assistant Professor of English at Union College in Lincoln, Nebraska. She is the author of several articles that have appeared in various journals and magazines; a book, *To Linger is to Die*; and a curriculum guide on study skills. Her previous experience includes high school English teaching as well as public relations work. She received her doctorate from the University of Florida.